Eternal Word and Changing Worlds

Theology, Anthropology, and Mission in Trialogue

HARVIE M. CONN

ETERNAL WORD AND CHANGING WORLDS:
THEOLOGY, ANTHROPOLOGY, AND MISSION IN TRIALOGUE

ACADEMIE BOOKS is an imprint of Zondervan Publishing House,
1415 Lake Drive, S.E., Grand Rapids, Michigan 49506.

Library of Congress Cataloging in Publication Data

Conn, Harvie M.
Eternal word and changing worlds.
Bibliography: p.
Includes indexes.
1. Missions—Theory. 2. Christianity and other religions. 3. Ethnology. 4. Religion. I. Title.
BV2063.C627 1984 266'.001 81-11878
ISBN 0-310-45321-6

Edited by Ed van der Maas
Designed by Louise Bauer

Printed in the United States of America

84 85 86 87 88 89 / 10 9 8 7 6 5 4 3 2 1

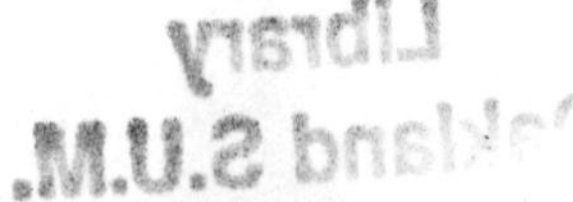

To my incomparable teachers—
David, Elizabeth, Peter,
Andrew, and Ruth

Contents

Preface 5

Part I: Shaped by the Past

1 Before the Beginnings *11*
Questions and Presuppositions
The Ferment of the Eighteenth Century
Enlightenment's Reappraisal of Paganism
Rationalist Studies of the Development of Religions and Cultures
The End of the Beginning

2 Consciousness One *47*
The Warfare Metaphor
Shared Concerns of Anthropology and Theology
Anthropology's Part in the Formation of Consciousness One
Evangelicalism's Response: Apprension
Shared Characteristics of Consciousness One

3 Consciousness Two *89*
The Revised Agenda
Anthropology's New Mood: Revision
Anthropological and Theological Concerns in Consciousness Two
Evangelical Theology's Response: Retrenchment
Shared Characteristics of Consciousness Two

Part II: Challenged by the Present

4 Converging Streams for a New Wave *129*
A New Situation
A New Partner: Missionary Anthropology
A New Agenda: Ethnology

5 Perilous Currents in the Tide 163
Overextension of Models
Syncretism
Provincialism

Part III: Reaching for the Future

6 Theology and Theologizing: A New Course 211
Winds of Change
The Missiological Call for New Directions in Theology
Criteria for Doing Theology

7 Theological Education: Looking for New Models 263
History of the Current Discussions
Western Concepts of Ministry
Biblical Focal Points of Renewal

8 Where Do We Go From Here? An Agenda for Consciousness Three 315
Paradigm and Worldview
Myth and Symbolism
Relativism

Bibliography 339
Indexes 359

Preface

Several things prompted me to initiate this study. In January 1978 I had the privilege of participating in a consultation on Gospel and Culture. Held at Willowbank, Bermuda, under the sponsorship of the Lausanne Committee for World Evangelization, it brought together theologians and practitioners, exegetes, linguists, and anthropologists. Out of it came for me a deep sense of excitement and stimulation as I learned from the experience and wisdom represented there. Out of it came also a sense of frustration, which was felt by others there as well: It seemed that frequently the theologians and the anthropologists were using the same words but speaking very different languages. We needed to hear one another better, to work harder at learning one another's verbal symbols.

Some time later I received an invitation from the School of World Mission, Fuller Theological Seminary, to give the 1980 Church Growth lectures. Their leadership in the area of anthropology as applied to world missions prompted me to turn to the topic that is the theme of this book. All of chapters 2 and 3 and parts of chapters 4 and 8 represent the substance of my lectures there. I was not disappointed in my choice; I benefited then, and do so even now, from the encouragement and support of their staff. I count as very precious to me personally and academically the friendship and help of people like Donald McGavran, Arthur Glasser, and Charles Kraft in particular. Theirs is a school from which I hope never to graduate. With great literary reluctance, I refer in this manuscript to Kraft and not, as I would wish, to Chuck.

With appreciation, I thank those who have been kind enough to read all or parts of the manuscript. They have given freely and helpfully of their time from extremely busy schedules to offer support and Christian disagreements. Many of the disagreements are likely to remain even after this book appears. But that testifies only to the obstinacy of the author and the wisdom of his commentators. Thank you, Miriam Adeney and Vern Poythress, Dick Gaffin, Lin Barney, Ed van der Maas, and Charles Craft. It is a marvel of the Spirit that He has gifted His church with people like yourselves.

I am grateful also for the reactions and beneficial criticisms of the students at Trinity Evangelical Divinity School who in the summer of 1983 used these materials in a course in the doctoral program in missiology. The addition of a summary at the beginning of each chapter was their suggestion.

Most of the material in chapter 7 on theological education and some portions of chapter 6 were culled from articles of mine that originally appeared in the *Westminster Theological Journal*. I am thankful to the editor, Dr. Moisés Silva, for permission to reproduce them in this form.

The Scripture and author indices were prepared by Mr. John Tung, my research associate at Westminster and a vary efficient brother in the Lord.

Harvie M. Conn

Part One

Shaped by the Past

Chapter One

Before the Beginnings

SUMMARY

The angry dialogue between cultural anthropology and theology must trace its tensions to the eighteenth century, the Age of Reason. There, in the Enlightenment mentality and its animosity toward biblical supernaturalism, man built ultimate presuppositions—those beliefs over which no other takes precedence. Scholars reexamined classical mythology in their pursuit of rationalistic explanations for religion and its origins. Behind the myths they discovered, not allegorical symbolism or deified heroes, but a primitive mentality that actually believed the accounts of the Olympian gods. Myths came to be seen as products of trickery, imagination, and the natural corruption of language.

Christianity was not exempt from these charges. And through deism, Christian theology accepted the Enlightenment view of the sufficiency of human reason as a way of evaluating "natural religion." By the end of the eighteenth century, deism as a Christian response to Enlightenment criticism had faded. But rationalism and its deploring of primitive life and mentality had emerged triumphant. It touched even the missionary movement. The objects of evangelism were seen as "primitives," "savages." Civilizing became a missionary goal parallel to that of evangelism.

From this mentality, cultural anthropology inherited its set of questions for the nineteenth century: What is the nature of "primitive religions"? Given man's basically rational, upward mobility, how will we explain the origin of myths? Given Enlightenment animosity toward the concept of a revealed religion, what is the functional role of mankind in the production of religion and culture? Out of these questions, rooted in a rationalistic worldview, came the agenda of the nineteenth century.

Chapter One

Before the Beginnings

World missions today faces a jungle of problems. African Independent churches exist as a form of institutional fatigue—groups tired of a Christianity for Africa that bears the label "Made in Wheaton." The 1970s heard strident calls for a moratorium on missionaries—outcries against, among other things, cultural chauvinism. Missionary ears are assaulted with new condemnations: not colonialism but capitalism, not WCC but CIA, not indigenization but culture rape. There is a new vocabulary to learn: Afericasia, "double wrestling" with the text, homogeneous units, praxis, contextualization. Traditional reading lists are being revised; alongside the names of Roland Allen, David Livingstone, and Robert Morrison appear those of Claude Lèvi-Strauss, Gustavo Gutiérrez, and John Mbiti.

Added to this clatter and jangle are the sounds and concerns of a new ally, cultural anthropology. Missionaries are urged to struggle with enculturation and acculturation, with things like the effects of kinship patterns on the progress of the gospel. Behind the amusing anecdotes about language mistakes the missionary shares with the home church lies the question of linguistics and the nature of understanding. What is the meaning of meaning? And how complicated does it become when meaning seeks to cross cultural boundaries?

"Applied missionary anthropology" has become a standard course now found in most preparatory programs. Many recognize its value. But there are concerns and suspicions. The behavioral sciences have not had the strong evangelical presence one can speak of in connection with philosophy or the natural sciences. Few educational institutions still serious about their Christian commitment have majors in cultural anthropology or linguistics. Ignorance breeds suspicion. Some remember the relativism of anthropological studies and wonder what the effect of those studies will be on their Christian faith. Others mistakenly connect anthropology with comparative religions, and the danger of total relativism seems even stronger: the nonexpert equates "comparative religion" with Darwinism and the evolutionary patterns of the nineteenth century.

Some of these concerns have legitimacy. The history of the interaction between cultural anthropology and theology will bear this out. At the same time, many of the concerns, particularly at this point in time, may be groundless—yet they persist. Why?

Part of the answer may come from the large number of still unanswered questions in these areas. What of the anthropological systems from which this "applied missionary" strategy is drawn? How much of these strategies can be used without borrowing also the theoretical structures from which they come? How can the missionary aim for cultural contextualization and avoid theological syncretism? How is the Bible to sit in judgment on the evangelist's often makeshift application of anthropological systems he or she does not fully understand? What is the place of anthropology and the behavioral sciences under the authority of Scripture? Where does functional authority really lie—in the behavioral sciences or in Scripture? Related to this problem, what is the relationship between cultural anthropology and theology? To most missionaries this last question especially is a new one.

Another possible answer also exists. It is what Alvin Toffler has called "future shock."[1] Like the parallel term "culture shock," it describes a state of disorientation, bewilderment, and frustration—not produced, however, by immersion in a strange culture but by immersion in a greatly accelerated rate of change, too much change in too short a time.

In this case, it may be "future shock" caused by the new shape of the dialogue between anthropology and theology as it relates to missions. These two disciplines have been talking to, or about, each other for a long time. And where we are now is in many respects the result of those discussions—discussions based on what Paul Hiebert calls a "love/hate relationship."[2] Out of this interaction has come something similar to Toffler's "waves of change, colliding and overlapping, causing conflict and tension around us."[3]

But if the discussions have been going on for quite some time, why "future shock"? Our present situation may represent the formation of a new wave of change. The breakers are still forming. It is the third wave of the exchange. And it may be so radically different from the past, with such an entirely different set of cues to react to, that our initial reaction is "theory dislocation."

One of the purposes of this book is to sketch the history of the dialogue. Dizziness can be minimized when one can orient oneself. What are the two waves that have preceded our current free-floating pace? How were they shaped? Where did they take us?

These two waves have not disappeared with time. They are still with us. They are more than eras or periods. They represent heart-worldviews of reality, warehouses of images through which we perceive God, the world, and humanity. Out of these

[1]Alvin Toffler, *Future Shock* (New York: Bantam, 1971), 4.

[2]Paul Hiebert, "Missions and Anthropology: A Love/Hate Relationship," *Missiology* 6 (April 1978): 165.

[3]Alvin Toffler, *The Third Wave* (New York: Morrow, 1980), 22.

worldviews come "images of man," paradigms shaped by the way we see things. They give out information signals, messages coded to conform to our system-analyses of reality. That is why I have called them Consciousness One and Consciousness Two. Through them we hope to trace the complicated relationships between evangelical theology and anthropology and their effect on world evangelization.

Out of that history I make my predictions for the future and suggest the flow of situations that may be shaping the new wave, Consciousness Three.

My preoccupation in the latter part of the book is largely with the theological partner in the new dialogue. As one whose educational background is largely in that area, I feel that that is proper. I am a rank amateur in the study of cultural anthropology. Besides, my purpose is not the writing of a text on that subject. Rather, my focus is on interrelationships as they best serve the missionary community—a missionary community that is still better acquainted with theology than with anthropology.

More narrowly, I address the Western, white evangelical community of professionals in this book. It is their questions I have tried hardest to listen to and their skepticism I have kept in mind. So my questions are in-house questions addressed to that community of listeners. What can evangelical theology learn from anthropology? What shape must a theologizing that operates out of a full respect for the integrity of Scripture take as it ventures out into the world of human cultures? Theological education in the West has been the major model for theologizing. What form should it, might it take in a multicultural world so as to best serve these new contexts?

I warn the reader that he or she will not find much reflection on current efforts in the Third World churches to reflect on and act in their own settings. Perhaps that is a mistake. On the other hand, I am wary for reasons the book will, I hope, make clear. These pages are the closest I feel a white Westerner can come to theologizing for another culture's set of problems while avoiding the ethnocentric paternalism I see at the root of so many missionary mistakes in the past.

QUESTIONS AND PRESUPPOSITIONS

R. G. Collingwood states,

> You cannot find out what a man means by simply studying his spoken or written statements. . . . In order to find out his meaning you must also know what the question was (a question in his own mind, and presumed by him to be in yours) to which the thing he has said or written was meant as an answer.[4]

In chapter two, we will begin to look at the answers. Our search now is for the questions. In that quest, we need to remember something similar to what Collingwood said: Questions not only come packaged and wrapped in words—they also come in nonverbal form, written implicitly between the lines, providing richer insights than we expected.

Perhaps "nonverbal" is a somewhat misleading term. What we mean are the deep-level-of-meaning questions, what theologians like Cornelius Van Til and others have called "presuppositions" and what social scientists might call "worldviews." We refer to those culturally oriented beliefs that take precedence over, and therefore serve as criteria for, other beliefs. An *ultimate* presupposition, to use the language of a colleague, John Frame, is a belief over which no other takes precedence.

As deep-level commitments, these presuppositions, assumed by a given culture during a given period, are more than simple mental road maps or intellectual decisions. They are rooted in basic commitments of the "heart." They become systems of interpretation of our world, "computerized" ways of putting it

[4]R. G. Collingwood, *An Autobiography* (London: Oxford University Press, 1939), 31.

together. They provide us with religious paradigms for "seeing" things, pre-answers that shape our questions.[5]

Evans-Pritchard illustrates this tiered, multidimensional way of looking at questions. Commenting on the earlier anthropological writers—people like Tylor, Frazer, Malinowski, and Durkheim—he notes that their writings on religion demonstrate an animosity toward the concept of revealed religion. If they could explain away what were then called "primitive religions" as intellectual aberrations or as merely social phenomena, they could discredit and explain away the higher religions as well.[6] He concludes that

> social anthropology has been the product of minds which, with very few exceptions, regarded all religion as outmoded superstition, suited no doubt to a pre-scientific age and historically justified, like classes in the eye of Marxists, for a given period, but now useless, and even without ethical value, and worse than useless because it stood in the way of a rational regeneration of mankind and social progress.[7]

On one level, all these men were simply looking for facts: How does one understand the nature of "primitive religions" and the cultures with which they are associated? What has mankind contributed to the form and content of his religion? How will we explain the origin of myths (a special interest of the early nineteenth century)?

But these very questions begin to reveal presuppositions behind them. We are forced to move deeper, to ask the unasked questions: Why do they speak of "primitive" religions? What is the distinguishing mark that differentiates "primitive" from "sophisticated"? Why the heavy emphasis on the functional role of mankind

[5]John M. Frame, "Doctrine of the Knowledge of God." Mimeographed lecture notes, Westminster Theological Seminary (1980), 31–32.

[6]E. E. Evans-Pritchard, *Theories of Primitive Religion* (London: Oxford University Press, 1965), 15.

[7]E. E. Evans-Pritchard, "Religion and the Anthropologists," *Practical Anthropology* 19 (1972): 205.

in the production of religion? In what way does this concept of "primitive" affect also their search for the origins of myth?

At this level we still deal with written words, with verbal responses. And the answers take us back repeatedly to the place of human reason in the theories of these authors. "Primitive" becomes "less rational". Myths find their origins in the twisted routes taken by a confused reason. "Prescientific" is "prelogical." The origins of nineteenth-century anthropology are found in the Enlightenment, more specifically in the eighteenth-century Age of Reason.

But there is still another level we must reach. How are we to explain the *religious* animosity of these early anthropology pioneers, so intent on their rational pursuit of understanding *religions?* We can explain them only if we recognize that their commitment to reason was a deeply religious commitment, a "presupposition" that was far more than simply, or even largely, mental. Why else does Evans-Pritchard suggest that these pioneers "were looking for a weapon which could be used with deadly effect against Christianity"? Why does one commentator speak of the diaries of Malinowski as displaying an animus toward missionaries that has overtones of an unresolved Oedipal problem. "Missionaries had fathered the work to which he was dedicating himself with typical missionary zeal—on the other side of the fence."[8]

To summarize, we are not suggesting that anthropologists function out of subterfuge, seeking to make their facts cohere with their "interpretational presuppositions." Scholars do seek to make their interpretations cohere with the "facts." At the same time, they determine what the facts are and which facts are important by reference to their "religious" systems of interpretation. And that, to quote John Frame,

> is as it should be. Determining what the facts are, and determining the best system of interpretative 'understand-

[8]Kenelm O. Burridge, "Introduction: Missionary Occasions," in *Mission, Church and Sect in Oceania,* ed. James A. Boutilier et al. (Ann Arbor: University of Michigan Press, 1978), 5.

> ings'—these are not two processes (with one of them utterly 'prior to' the other). Rather, they are the *same* process, seen from different perspectives. It is perfectly true to say that our knowledge (even of theology) must be 'based on' the facts. But it is equally true to say that our factual judgments must be 'based on' an adequate interpretation of our situation.[9]

Why do I bring all this up at this stage of the argument? Partly to lay the groundwork for questioning the massive influence of phenomenology as a tool in anthropology. I am thinking specifically of phenomenology's emphasis on the need for presuppositionlessness in the study of religions. I am calling into historical and theological judgment its demand for "bracketing" (suspending belief in the existence of) metatheoretical, personal religious judgments of other religions and cultures. This has not been possible at any time in the history of either theology or anthropology, either in the past or now. And I call into question on biblical grounds, underlined by Van Til, the assumption that there are "brute facts," realities totally devoid of any interpretation, human or divine. All facts have been interpreted by God; and since all things are what they are by virtue of God's eternal plan, we must say that "the interpretation of the facts precedes the facts."[10] Neither the behavioral sciences nor theology as a science are "neutral" when it comes to deep-level commitments. The Bible and reason and societal relationships can all function as "canon" in the search for truth.

I see this also as a helpful psychological reminder for the Christian missionary now struggling with the question of the usefulness of anthropology as a tool in world evangelization. His or her fears of "relativism" have some warrant when one remembers the presuppositional interpretations with which early anthropology in particular carried on its work (this is still true in

[9]John M. Frame, "Doctrine of the Knowledge of God," 51.

[10]Cornelius Van Til, *The Defense of the Faith* (Philadelphia: Presbyterian and Reformed, 1955), 132–37, 191–95.

modern anthropology, albeit less overtly so). The multiplication of facts about cultures and their religions seems a grave threat to our core values.

But this perspective is a naive sort of realism that needs correcting. Quoting a statement made by Ian Barbour in another connection, such a "naive realism" sees scientific theories as merely "accurate descriptions of the world as it is in itself. . . . Theoretical terms [are] said to denote real things of the same kind as physical objects in the perceived world."[11] Charles Kraft adds that it sees "virtually a one-to-one relationship between reality (whether physical or spiritual) and the concept of that reality held by the advocate of [the naive realism] position."[12] Seeing reality and concepts of reality as multitiered visions of life-in-its-totality can minimize the antagonistic posture. It does not overlook the religious commitments both missionary and anthropologist bring to their studies—but neither does it maximize them into a "conspiracy mentality."

This is by no means the only area where the polarization between missionary and anthropologist appears. Kraft lists ten poles of conflict, all of which are extremely helpful for understanding the tension.[13] He notes also, among his many "household hints" for dealing with the tensions, that contemporary anthropologists have largely turned against naive realism and toward what is called "critical realism." This perspective, like naive realism, "takes theories to be representative of the world." But unlike the naive realist, the proponent of critical realism "recognizes the importance of human imagination in the formation of theories. . . . [He or she] thus tries to acknowledge both the creativity of man's mind and the existence of patterns in events not created

[11]Ian Barbour, *Myths, Models and Paradigms* (New York: Harper and Row, 1974), 34ff.

[12]Charles H. Kraft, "Conservative Christians and Anthropologists: A Clash of Worldviews," *Journal of the American Scientific Affiliation* 32 (September, 1980): 145.

[13]Ibid., 141–42.

by man's mind. Descriptions of nature are human constructions but nature is such as to bear descriptions in some ways and not in others."[14]

Kraft's distinction here is reassuring for us. But it must be remembered that "critical realism" is a relatively recent turn for anthropologists. It most certainly was not present during the period we call Consciousness One. And further, critical realism still does not recognize the religious commitments that enter into its constructions and paradigms.[15] Human constructions, because they have their source in mankind made in the image of God, can never escape that ultimate faith-dimension in their paradigm. Even critical realists have very deep memory banks.

This last sentence leads me to the third reason for beginning this work as I do. A study of the eighteenth-century backgrounds of the dialogue between anthropology and theology is more than simply a historical prelude to beginnings. It is also a study of the religious foundations of that beginning. Using the terminology of current anthropology, we need to observe this period from both a synchronic and a diachronic perspective.

The synchronic approach, used in the study of language, is concerned with the structure and functioning of a given language at a given moment in history. It is in a sense one-dimensional, focusing on the immediate, on the structure of language as it exists now or as it existed at a point of time in the past. On the basis of a great deal of predictability, it analyzes two levels of language structure: the system for organizing sounds (phonetics) and the system for organizing meanings (grammar).

The diachronic approach does not limit itself to the predict-

[14]Barbour, *Myths*, 37, quoted by Kraft, "Conservative Christians and Anthropologists," 145.

[15]For a philosophical analysis of the religious motives behind the origin and development of modern science, consult Herman Dooyeweerd, *Roots of Western Culture: Pagan, Secular and Christian Options* (Toronto: Wedge, 1979), 148–56. An excellent historical study is R. Hooykaas, *Religion and the Rise of Modern Science* (Grand Rapids: Eerdmans, 1972).

able structure of language at a given time. Languages change throughout history. The diachronic approach moves through the levels of history in search of change. It seeks to understand language as a stack of transparent three-by-five cards. Through the transparent cards one sees the continuities and the divergencies, how the language symbols are reinforced by the past and shift in the present.

What does this mean when applied to our study of the origins of the dialogue? It indicates the need for a synchronic approach, the search for systems of predictability in the exchange between anthropology and theology. But it underlines also the need for diachronic study, a search for the future in the present and the present in the past. Lévi-Strauss, the anthropologist whose views are much discussed today, calls for a diachronic study that will lead us to a better understanding of the collective unconscious of human cultures, an ethnopsychology that is written largely on the many-leveled layers of human mythography. This is a search that has great potential for helping us wrestle again with the religious commitments, unspoken but read between the lines, of the diverse worlds of mankind. We must see this history not as a two-fingered exercise on the piano but as a symphony.

THE FERMENT OF THE EIGHTEENTH CENTURY

The roots of the dialogue we seek to describe lie deep in the Enlightenment, a period that defies precise definition. The questions first addressed by Max Müller, E. B. Tylor, and others came from the application of Enlightenment methodology and concepts of the autonomy of human reason to the growing eighteenth-century interest in the world of religions, more specifically in the mythology of the classical world and the folklore of the new world.

> Fifteen centuries after the Church Fathers had valiantly routed the pagan deities and their philosophical apologists, Jupiter had returned in triumph to the realms of the most Christian kings of Europe. The château of Versailles was adorned with gracious images of the gods of Greece and Rome, while Christ and the saints were severely restricted to the chapel. Baroque friezes depicting an alien pantheon, Christianized with the wand of allegory to be sure, decorated the ceilings of the great chambers in the new monastery at Melk and the magnificent royal library in Vienna. The coaches of aristocratic travelers and princes of the church were bedecked with voluptuous Venuses.[16]

The ceramic masterpieces of Josiah Wedgewood displayed coy little nymphs or a cavorting satyr. Translations from the classics were illustrated with lewd engravings of the gods. The opera house resounded with the melodies of Gluck's *Orpheus and Eurydice*. The young prince, hero of Mozart's *Magic Flute,* endured his trials in order to be initiated into the wisdom of Isis and Osiris. The French *philosophes*, who belonged to the nobility, took mythological nicknames: Claude Adrien Helvétius was the son of Apollo, Jean-Philippe Rameau was Euclid-Orpheus, Voltaire himself was nicknamed Attis. There was a steady outpouring of popular mythological dictionaries in all European languages for the education of the layman. At the height of the French Revolution in 1793, Millin de Grandmaison sold a twelve-volume *Mythologie mise à la portée de tout de monde*.

Much of this material on mythography was intended to amuse. But an important body of related literature served other purposes.

> It was devoted to the explanation of ancient myth as a study of high seriousness. In these writings the 'pagan gods' were not limited to the classical world of the eastern Mediterranean; paganism encompassed the deities of nations civilized and savage, ancient and modern, on all five continents. The science

[16]Frank E. Manuel, *The Eighteenth Century Confronts the Gods* (New York: Atheneum, 1967), 3.

> of mythology broke the bounds of classical antiquity and came to be related first to the investigation of primitive religion and soon to the fundamental psychic problem of the age, the very nature of religion itself. . . . Even the more abstruse and esoteric researches into the origin of primitive religion and the meaning of myth disguised soul-searching inquiries into human nature.[17]

In addition, there was a profusion of empirical data on world religions and folklore. Travel books fed the popular interest in the religious behavior and doctrines of civilized and primitive peoples in all four corners of the earth. Sacred texts from the East were translated and commented on for the first time. Formal expeditions to Greece, Turkey, and Egypt were supported by academies to gather unpublished religious documents of the heathen into royal libraries.[18] The last two years of the eighteenth century were the years of Napoleon Bonaparte's Egyptian expedition. In the course of that expedition the Rosetta Stone was discovered, leading to the decipherment of Egyptian hieroglyphics. Out of this came, between 1809 and 1822, the twenty-volume *Description de l'Egypte*. A cataract of literary effusion engulfed the academic world with all kinds of speculation about the Egyptian origins of Western civilization and religion.

One response to this plethora of interest was the cult of the "noble savage," romantic primitivism, immortalized by Rousseau. Voltaire (1694–1778) became a student of China and saw as the heart of their religion the worship of one Supreme Being, without idolatry or superstition. Confucius himself was almost beyond praise:

> His ethic is as pure, as austere, and at the same time as human as that of Epictetus. . . . He enjoins forgiveness of injuries, gratitude for benefits received, friendship and humanity. His disciples were a community of brothers. The period

---

[17]Ibid., 6.

[18]For examples consult Eric Sharpe, *Comparative Religion. A History* (London: Duckworth, 1975), 21–22.

> during which his laws were followed was the happiest and most honorable this earth has ever known.[19]

Behind this applause was a deep regard for the innate beneficence of a life lived in harmony with reason. The thinkers of the Enlightenment attempted to find the meaning of world religions in terms of "reason" rather than in the authority of revelation. John Locke was hopeful that revelation would confirm the natural knowledge of God given by reason. "He governs his assent aright, and places it as he should, who in any case or matter whatsoever, believes or disbelieves, according as reason directs him."[20]

The philosopher who systematized the Enlightenment mentality was Immanuel Kant (1724–1804). Though virtually uninvolved in the century's vehement discussions about primitive religions and mythologies, he summed up and personified the Copernican revolution behind those discussions in terms of mentality and methodology. In 1784, he typified that mentality in a magazine article, "What is Enlightenment?" Enlightenment meant the maturity of man, man's emergence from his self-inflicted reluctance to use his own understanding. Mankind, not yet enlightened, is in the process of coming of age.

The road down which that enlightenment would proceed was the road of a proper use of reason. Science was science and religion was religion, each with its own sphere, each operating with its own legitimacy—the starry heavens above, the moral law within.

> In [Kant's] thinking, the Christian substance remained only as the hidden foundation of absolute obligation. The religious dimension was excluded from anything which had to do with the world of knowledge; religious concepts were so narrowed that no content remained which could possibly create conflict. Kant represents the final product of a direction in which the

[19]Voltaire, *Oeuvres* 15:275; quoted in E. L. Allen, *Christianity Among the Religions* (Boston: Beacon, 1960), 46.

[20]John Locke, *An Essay Concerning Human Understanding* (London: 1690) 4.17.24.

> issues between science and theology were solved by the virtual abandonment of the distinctive claims of the latter.[21]

Kant verbalized the judgment of an Enlightenment jury. The God of the Christians had been impeached.

It was, says a critic, "as if a rumour, originating one knew not where, had at length grown too persistent to be ignored any longer. The rumour was to the effect that God, having departed secretly during the night, was about to cross the frontiers of the world and to abandon humanity."[22]

ENLIGHTENMENT'S REAPPRAISAL OF PAGANISM

In this context, the Enlightenment mind asked enduring questions that were inherited by anthropology as it arose in the nineteenth century: Is there a unique primitive mentality different from that of rational, civilized man? What is the relationship between the man of reason and the man of the mythic world? Are there unique qualities in this mythic mind which the man of reason loses as the inevitable result of growth and maturity? Should we rejoice in the imminent sloughing off of our prehistoric coils?

These questions were part of the current debate about Christianity, attempts to answer questions raised by that debate. Even theologians

> were not interested in other religions as such, nor in engaging in serious dialogue with their adherents (as opposed to attempts to persuade them of the error of their ways). They were interested in other religions because and in so far as they saw in them ways

[21]John Dillenberger, *Protestant Thought and Natural Science. A Historical Study* (Nashville: Abingdon, 1960), 186.

[22]Paul Hazard, *European Thought in the Eighteenth Century* (Middlesex: Penguin, 1965), 59.

> of justifying their own understanding of authentic belief, of overcoming objections to it and of defeating opposing beliefs.[23]

Out of this storm, Christendom produced four ways of referring to other religions. Some appealed to other religions as providing evidence for their own position; thus, deism affirmed the possibility of a natural knowledge of God, a "natural religion," so that an authentic knowledge of God was available before and outside the Christian faith. Others used non-Western systems of faith as theological mud to sling at opponents: An opponent's beliefs and practices could be discredited by indicating the similarity of those opposed beliefs with those of a "heathen" religion. Third, "there was a need to show that the arguments advanced to confirm a set of beliefs could not be held to confirm, perhaps even more strongly, the beliefs of another religion; this need arose particularly when Christian and Islamic claims were compared. Finally, it was widely felt that the truth of one set of beliefs could be significantly confirmed by showing the rational unsatisfactoriness of the other religions."[24]

The Origins of Myth: Allegorism and Euhemerism

A center of the debate, and one that demonstrates the shifts that were taking place, was the origin of myths. Two views in particular had been popular until the Enlightenment. One was the allegorical approach, which held that myths were symbolic of some hidden wisdom. Myths were allegories of specific human gifts and properties, such as reason, simplicity, love, etc. They were emblematic of the struggle of the elements among themselves. Poets were said to have embellished these allegories and thus contributed to the creation of a pantheon. Thus, in the Greek system of religion the gods become personifications of certain

[23]David A. Pailin, "Some Eighteenth-Century Attitudes to 'Other Religions'," *Religion. Journal of Religion and Religions,* vol. 1, pt. 2 (1971): 83.

[24]Ibid., 85.

aspects of nature or of human attributes and occupations. Poseidon and Neptune were associated with the sea. Diana was the goddess of hunting, Pallas Athena the personification of wisdom. This approach had long been a popular one among Christians, dating from the Church Fathers.[25] It served the Christian polemical purpose well, demonstrating as it did the childishness and obnoxiousness of pagan religion. The Renaissance, with its keen interest in the classics, gave it a revival. Boccaccio refined the approach in his handbook of mythology, *De Genealogia Deorum* (1375), considered "a work of unsurpassable erudition" in its day.[26]

A second approach to the origins question was labeled Euhemerism. It took its name from Euhemerus (c. 330–c. 260 BC), who wrote a novel, *Hiera anagraphé,* describing the fictional discovery by the author of a stele on a remote island in the Indian Ocean. The pillar, found in a temple of Zeus, was described as setting forth the human birth of the major gods and the manner of their deification. Euhemerus argued that he had seen evidence that these classic deities were originally humans who had deified themselves. So Aphrodite had been the first courtesan, worshipped by her lover; Cadmus was cook to the king of Sidon; Harmonia was a flutist.

Euhemerism had been a great favorite with the early church apologists. Its most scholarly representative on behalf of Christianity was Isaac Newton. In his work *The Chronology of Ancient Kingdoms Amended* (1728), he traced the brute worship of Egypt to a misunderstanding of the animal hieroglyphics of that land. The animal forms of the king-gods were merely pictorial, symbolic representations of actions for which the kings had become famous. The genealogies of the Greek gods were really national political histories. Men apotheosized heroes out of gratitude for great deeds

[25]Jan de Vries, *Perspectives in the History of Religions* (Berkeley: University of California Press, 1977), 13–18.

[26]Ibid., 22.

on behalf of the community, and the reward of the community was posthumous deification.[27]

As a complete theory, Euhemerism had few advocates. To many scholars it may have seemed too similar to the ideas of the allegorists. But in the hands of Enlightenment skeptics, the Euhemerist emphasis on the corruptive process of historicization in creating myth began to be applied to the Bible as well as to the myths of Greece and Rome. Samuel Shuckford, for example, explained the miracles of the Pentateuch as ordinary natural events. The miracle of the storm of hailstones and the Joshua account of the sun standing still were reconciled with astronomical evidence.

Old Testament critics began to look for disfigurations and modifications that might be traced back to historical processes of corruption. A Roman Catholic priest, Richard Simon (1638–1712), questioned in print the Mosaic authorship of the Pentateuch. Unlike Simon, Jean Astruc (1684–1766) still clung to the Mosaic authorship; but he argued in a book on Genesis published anonymously thirteen years before his death that the material upon which Moses drew had been transmitted either orally or in written form over several centuries. This could be substantiated, he argued, by the duplicate accounts of creation and the use of the divine names Elohim and Jahweh that distinguished these duplicate accounts. Behind Simon's and Astruc's program was the influence of Euhemerism, pointing to the corruptive process of historicization in the Bible itself.

One of those who first assaulted these theories, and Christianity with it, was Pierre Bayle (1647–1706), a French *littérateur* from a Protestant background, turned Cartesian and skeptic. The crown of his work was a vast *Historical and Critical Dictionary* (1697).

The object of Bayle's attack was the allegorical approach. Agreeing with Hobbes that religion was born of fear, he saw all

[27]Manuel, *Eighteenth Century,* 103–25.

allegorical interpretations of myth as beside the point. Myths were neither allegorical nor symbolic. They depicted the beliefs of people in a direct and realistic manner. Allegorists had been responsible, he argued, for a neoplatonic moralizing of the vices of the Olympian gods. The accounts of divine rapes, adulteries, lies, deceptions, and robberies had been made into symbols of the moral conflict between virtues and vices leading to the final triumph of goodness. Bayle assaulted that understanding and insisted that these were commonplace narratives. He contended that the pagans of antiquity believed in a commonsense way that these actions actually took place as described in the poetic tradition. The incest, cannibalism, and murder of the gods were just that—incest, cannibalism, and murder.

Bayle's assault on allegorism, however, was also an assault on Christianity. In a number of daring comparisons between paganism and Catholic beliefs and practices, he pictured the prejudices of paganism passing relatively unchanged into Christian Europe (an argument later to be used and refined by Hume). The transition from paganism to Christianity he did not see as a sharp break but as a fluid phenomenon. The same skepticism he brought to the Greek mythologies he brought also to the Bible. With powerful satire he attacked the miracles, comparing them to pagan wonder-working. H. E. Barnes calls him "the first writer to treat sacred history with thorough skepticism. His handling of Old Testament characters was one of the most devastating examples of skeptical satire in all literature. In the midst of the most burning ridicule Bayle would interject ostensibly pious comments and protestations of orthodox reverence."[28]

In keeping with the growing mood of the Enlightenment, he considered all religions to be irrational and psychopathological in nature. In this he foreshadowed Freud. Myths became social phenomena, "charters of reality" as Malinowski would say later.

[28]Harry Elmer Barnes, *An Intellectual and Cultural History of the Western World,* 3 vols. (New York: Dover, 1965) 2:807.

Somewhat different conclusions were reached by Bernard Fontenelle (1657–1757). He also examined Greek and pagan mythology and saw them as patently false. But his focus was on another theory of myth long popular in the church.

From the days of the Church Fathers it had been argued that demons, working through human agencies, had devised and maintained pagan oracles. Supported by Augustine, this argument had been the standard way to explain how philosophers like Plato and Aristotle could be persuaded to adopt false beliefs. A complementary patristic doctrine taught that the coming of Christ and the power of the true Word had finally silenced these demonic oracles. With an air of piety, Fontenelle charged that the demon theory had shown undue leniency towards idolatry. It had exculpated man of any evil intention. Paganism was simply the creation for gain of priestly tricks by priestly rascals. The final demise of the oracles was not due to Jesus but to a variety of historical causes—the exposure of the priestly craft by philosophers, the steady growth of reason, the political triumph of the Christians. Superstition declined as a result of the advance of science, not because of Jesus.

Fontenelle also suggested a new source for the making of mythology and the origin of the gods. Primitive mentality, he said, always has a tendency to exaggerate, to image rather than to observe, to render everything marvellous. The earliest myths of the gods were thus unintentional errors, the faulty perceptions of infantile reason. "They were simply erroneous understandings of causality, because primitives were like children that had not yet had the experience of adult life, and were thus unable to think in abstract terms."[29]

How did such myth-making generate the gods? Because of their fear of the powerful agitations of nature, the primitives had to conjure up creatures great enough to explain earthquakes, fire, and wind. Thus the gods came into being as magnified anthropo-

[29]Annemarie De Waal Malefijt, *Images of Man. A History of Anthropological Thought* (New York: Knopf, 1974), 70.

morphic projections. Fontenelle rejected the notion that the idea of God could be derived even from a rational contemplation of the natural order of the universe. A primitive in the infancy of reason was incapable of such discernment.

In the last stages of mythology's creation, he continued, "fables" (his term) were traceable to the natural corruptions of language and to the faulty translation of names and ideas from Phoenecian and Egyptian into Greek. But as mankind's mythopoeic nature yielded to reason, the sources of myth dried up.

Much of Fontenelle's influence would be felt in later theorizing. His idea of myth as a creation built on "the disease of language" would be used by Max Müller. Auguste Comte would draw on his picture of the evolution of man from primitive to rational in his metaphysics of positivism. The concept of primitives possessing a "prelogical" mind would be taken up by Lévy-Bruhl. Freud would expand Fontenelle's ideas on fear as the source of myth into a whole new psychology. In Frazer, Durkheim, and Andrew Lang one will find more than echoes of his picture of myth as a kind of mistaken science.

Natural Religion

With the traditional approaches to religion demolished by Bayle and Fontenelle, old questions became even more important: How do we explain the variety of religious experiences reflected in travel literature and in translations of the Chinese, Indian, Persian, and Vedic sacred writings? How do we account for the striking conformities among heathen ancient and modern? How do we explain the marked resemblances between pagan rituals and Christian revelations?

At this point a prolonged battle emerged within Christendom. The idea of "natural religion," introduced in a previous century by the British deists, became the center of the debate. On the deist agenda, "natural religion" as a theorem affirmed not the uniqueness of Christianity but its commonness. Primitive Christianity was, said Ralph Cudworth in *True Intellectual System of the Universe* (1678), the unadorned teachings of Jesus. And this was the essence of religion, universally acknowledged in all times and places. Lord Herbert of Cherbury published these same sentiments in his *De Religione Gentilium* (1663). Five common notions bind all the religions of rational man together: (1) belief in a supreme deity; (2) belief that this deity ought to be worshiped; (3) belief that virtue combined with piety is the chief part of divine worship; (4) belief that men should turn from their sins and repent; and (5) the concept of reward and punishment, following from the goodness and justice of God. These five principles, it was argued, constituted primitive religion before people "gave ear to the covetous and sacerdotal order." What is contrary to these five points is contrary to reason and therefore false. What is beyond reason but not contrary to them may have been revealed. All actual religions, insofar as they go against these five points, are simply corruptions of the pure and primitive rational worship.

Lord Herbert's ideas had their eighteenth-century supporters. John Toland, in *Christianity Not Mysterious* (1696), proclaimed reason to be the only principle of authority. There may be revelation as a means of providing information, but this revelation must satisfy man's reason. For Toland, an avowed pantheist, "natural religion" referred to the religious beliefs that all men could in theory determine from nature and humanity by the use of reason. Later in the century, Matthew Tindal, in his deist classic *Christianity as Old as the Creation* (1730), argued again that Christianity can have no articles of faith that are not in agreement with reason. Anything taught in addition to natural religion belongs to the realm of superstition or the corruption of the true religion.

The debate was confused but vehement. Part of the confusion, contends David Pailin, came from the lack of agreement about the precise meaning of the phrase "natural religion." In addition to the deist meaning, there was the understanding of natural religion as simply the beliefs that are innate in all men.

> For others 'natural religion' was the religion which God revealed to Adam and, from Adam, was transmitted in theory or in practice to all mankind; for others it denoted the beliefs and practices of those who were 'natural' men—unaffected, that is, by civilization; for others it meant the religion of those who were unaffected by divine revelation—that is, usually, those outside the influence of Judaism, Christianity and Islam (since Mahomet was held to have adapted many of his ideas from Jewish and Christian teaching). For some, talk about natural religion has a theoretical context, while for others it has primarily an empirical use. For some, natural religion was the pure and sufficient religion for all men; for others it was a human product which showed that valid religion can be derived only from a divine revelation accepted by faith. Confusions arose because the protagonists in the theological debates were often not at all clear about the different meanings that were attached to the phrase.[30]

The Christian response took various forms. There were those who questioned the empirical claims that all peoples of the world were basically monotheistic. Others doubted the existence of a body of truth shared by, or naturally available to, all mankind. Long lists of moral evils among "the heathen," some provided by missionaries, others by travel documents, backed claims of the corruptions and insufficiency of a natural religion wholly determined by human reason. Still others claimed that the virtues of "natural religion" were derived from the Jewish and Christian tradition of revelation.

Effects on the Church and on Missionary Motivation

Deism lost its battle, and "natural religion" as a focal point of debate faded quickly. But the results were devastating for the

[30]Pailin, "Eighteenth-Century Attitudes," 87.

church. The sufficiency of reason was confidently affirmed and Scripture was assigned a subordinate role. Christianity was on the defensive and found itself adopting some of its opponent's tactics.

The clearest example of this came to be the apologetical works of Bishop Joseph Butler (1692–1752), *The Analogy of Religion, Natural and Revealed, to the Course and Constitution of Nature* (1736). It was "symptomatic of the time that Butler tried to vindicate revelation by its analogy to natural theology (which he assumed was so widely accepted as not to need defense)."[31] Reasonable people, Butler contended, must see that all objections that might be raised against revealed religion could equally well be raised against natural religion. We cannot, as human beings, expect a rational demonstration of natural religion any more than we can expect one of revealed religion. Probability is the very guide of life—probability that makes a "reasonable use" of reason. For the adherents of natural religion as well as for Butler, God had become a debatable hypothesis. But the effect of Butler's argument was the adoption of reason as the instrument of probability. His *Analogy,* together with David Hume's *Dialogues on Natural Religion* (1779), marked the end of the natural-religion argument. But in the process he gave up ground the evangelical was not to regain.[32]

Missionary motivation in the eighteenth century was not untouched by the spirit of the age. In examining the origins of the missionary awakening in Great Britain between 1698 and 1815, Johannes van den Berg notes that

> the "calm broadminded optimism, characteristic of the Eighteenth Century Briton" saw no distance between civilization and the bringing of the Christian message, and it saw the

[31]Ian G. Barbour, *Issues in Science and Religion* (New York: Harper Torchbooks, 1971), 61.

[32]For a theological evaluation of Butler's failure, consult Cornelius Van Til, *A Christian Theory of Knowledge* (Presbyterian and Reformed, 1969), 215–17. A full exposition of Butler's apologetic method is found in Bernard Ramm, *Varieties of Christian Apologetics* (Grand Rapids: Baker, 1965), 107–24.

> Kingdom of God in alignment with the culture of Western Europe. So the cultural motive, which had always been present in British missions, received a new accent as a result of the general aspect of religious life in the period of the "Aufklärung." Yet the religious context was strong enough to prevent the cultural motive from becoming an independent factor in the missionary development. It was always in the background: the terminology pointed to it (Christian *knowledge* had to be spread, the 'poor natives' had to be converted from *barbarism*), a feeling of cultural superiority pervaded the whole attitude towards the heathen nations with which British missionary activity came into contact.[33]

John Sergeant, missionary among the Indians in Massachusetts, saw as one of his aims "to cultivate humanity among a people naturally ingenuous enough, but who, for want of instruction, live so much below the dignity of human nature." William Carey, writing out of a deep sense of the superiority of eighteenth-century English civilization, comments: "Can we hear that they are without the Gospel, without government, without laws, and without arts and sciences; and not exert ourselves to introduce amongst them the sentiments of men and of Christians? Would not the spread of the Gospel be the most effectual means of their civilization? Would not that make them useful members of society?"[34]

There were obviously many other motives in addition to the cultural one cited above. Van den Berg lists six and tries not to maximize the one to which we have drawn attention here. He is supported, with reservations, by Max Warren;[35] and Pailin, with less balance and discretion, cites a large body of supporting material for the cultural motive.[36]

At the same time there is a link between the rational spirit of

[33]Johannes van den Berg, *Constrained By Jesus' Love* (Kampen: Kok, 1956), 61.

[34]Quoted in Max Warren, *The Missionary Movement From Britain in Modern History* (London: SCM, 1965), 46.

[35]Ibid., 41–55.

[36]Pailin, "*Eighteenth-Century Attitudes,*" 98–102.

the age and the missionary awakening. It is possible, as van den Berg argues, to discern a correlation between rationalism and the propagation of Christian knowledge. A certain influence of "the Age of Reason" upon the reawakening of the missionary ideal cannot be denied. Colonialism was often seen by these early missionaries as the handmaid of the process of civilizing. And it could easily be defined as the grand movement of Europe that promoted the cause of rational behavior in the face of barbarous superstition. Thus, one missionary leader could plead in defense of the renewal of the East India Company's Charter in 1813 (an issue intensely bound up with the struggle to secure free entrance for missionaries into India):

> Shall sixty million heathen subjects of the British crown . . . be abandoned to a cruel and debasing superstition, when prudent measures and holy men will, with the blessing of God, be the means of enlightening their minds, elevating their characters, attaching them to British interests, and everlastingly saving their souls?[37]

RATIONALIST STUDIES OF THE DEVELOPMENT OF RELIGIONS AND CULTURES

In the nineteenth-century debate it was rationalism, not Christianity, that shaped the agenda. Apart from Wilhelm Schmidt and his school of diffusionism, primitive monotheism as a source theory for world religions was rejected. The role of reason as a judge of religion in isolation from revelation was retained and reinforced. The deist bifurcation of reason and revelation supported new efforts to isolate the study of religions and cultures from Christian theologizing. Three men in particular added to that future agenda the idea of developmentalism, structured around

[37]Warren, *Missionary Movement,* 55.

rationalist assumptions, as a way of making progress: Vico, Hume, and De Brosses.

Vico

Giambattista Vico (1668–1744) in many ways occupied a unique place in these shifts. His principal work, *Scienza Nuova* (*The New Science,* 1725), went almost unnoticed in his own time. Vico was rediscovered in the early nineteenth century. In contrast to many of his contemporaries, his Christian scruples still remained strong enough for him to attempt to exclude the Christian conception of history from his investigations. He spoke of revelation but confined it to the Hebrews. In the spirit of the Enlightenment he wished to determine the natural laws of history, independent of miraculous or revelatory intervention. As a Platonist he sought the eternal order of the universe in those eternal and ideal laws operating in the life of every nation.

Vico combined the Enlightenment interest in mythology with the Platonic quest for patterns of change in human societies. To discover the "perennial springs of change" in human societies, he set out to reconstruct all human history, because change, as he argued, was regular and subject to laws. Turning to ethnographic literature, "he was among the first to take nonliterate peoples into account as full members of the social tradition."[38]

Vico saw each culture evolving through three stages: the age of the gods, the age of heroes, and the age of men. The first and most primitive age was the age of theocracy, of rule by gods. It was the age of postdiluvian man, begun when some of Noah's sons, dispersed after the flood, wandered in the vast forests of the earth. They descended to zero point, forgetting all cultural learning, even language. At this point the civilizational process began. Terror of thunder and lightning drove mankind into caves

[38]De Waal Malefijt, *Images of Man,* 76.

and to the setting up of families. Fear created the myths of the heathen gods. And to placate these wrathful deities, the first act of man was the suppression of bestial lust. The promiscuous copulation with women was replaced by the institution of life in the cave with one woman alone. This first act of will toward a rationalization of human behavior was born of passion and terror.

From this age man moved to the age of heroes. Here the fathers of families became an aristocracy of virtue and ability. Two types of people now appeared, "one noble because intelligent, the other common because stupid." The former attained the full stature of human nature and made the latter their subjects. The heroic elite was responsible for the progress of the arts, agriculture, industry, colonization, and morals. The Roman Republic was the apex of this age.

The third stage was the Age of Man, the Roman Empire, displaying civilized rationality, a comprehensive system of laws, and alphabetic writing. Here the second cycle began, as the softening of laws led to a reversion to an earlier stage of savagery. Now, said Vico, we have entered the second Age of Man.

In all this, myth is the language of primitive man, a record of major developments in the history of humanity. Religion takes its shape as a revelation of broad cultural trends, a symbolic hieroglyphic of culture.

In some ways, Vico was the founder of the forthcoming science of social anthropology. He attempted to discover the intelligible order of history and tried to find the source of cultural changes within their own social settings. His notion of cyclic development through three stages resembles the later suggestions of Auguste Comte.

Hume

David Hume (1711–1776) was to add new skeptical dimensions to Vico's concept of development. And his study of the origins of religion was equally negative. His *Natural History of Religion* (1757) became the classic naturalistic interpretation of religion and its origin.

Hume rejected the deist view of natural religion as a purely rational process and with it he rejected the Christian dogma of innate primitive monotheism. Primitive man was not Rousseau's humanity asleep in a state of unreflective being—he was incapable of apprehending the rational mechanism of the world. Religion was born not of reason but of passion. It was the creation of an aboriginal man incapable of an abstract conception of the world.

Primal polytheism, Hume contended, was the original form of religion, born of a psychological process through which primitive man's imagination took those unknown forces that controlled life and projected them as personal beings. They were the projections of "sick men's dreams."

This tendency, however, was not restricted simply to polytheism. Hume saw the same processes operative in monotheism as well. It was just that the development of monotheism was more rational. Monotheism arose as people elevated their deities to the point where they conceived of them with attributes of unity and infinity, simplicity and spirituality.

And always there was the threat of a cyclic return to the beginnings. "Men," Hume wrote, "have a natural tendency to rise from idolatry to theism, and to sink again from theism into idolatry." Most of mankind would continue to behave like primitives in matters of religion. The only liberation lay in reason and philosophy. And even then "the whole is a riddle, an enigma, an inexplicable mystery. Doubt, uncertainty, suspense of judgment, appear the only result of our most accurate scrutiny concerning this subject."[39]

Hume's skepticism, even about developmentalism in religion, ultimately reinforced the patterns that were to be handed over to the nineteenth century. Natural religion's major thesis—the

---

[39]Quoted by Manuel, *Eighteenth-Century*, 183.

human mind as an orderly storehouse of religious truths—was gone. Science, agnostic about the metaphysics of religion, would have to turn to hard, empirical data for information. We were left with the observation of human behavior to make our way.

De Brosses

Charles de Brosses (1709–1777) picked up many of the themes of Vico and Hume and in methodology came very close to the forthcoming techniques of ethnography. His major work was *Du culte des dieux fétiches, ou parallèle de l'ancienne religion de l'Egypte avec la religion actuelle de la Nigritie* (1760). Much of the work of his predecessors was now synthesized. The ideas of progressive development, of the childish mind of the savage, of fear as a source of religion, of the primacy of emotions like fear and admiration over against rational considerations as sources of religious notions, even the idea of religion based on the fraud of priests, were to be amplified by him.

De Brosses's major contributions, however, were not made in his role as a synthesizer. Two other feats brought him to the edge of the beginnings of cultural anthropology.

His most distinctive contribution was the introduction of what he called *fetishism* to explain classical polytheism. By fetishism he meant the worship of deified animals and inanimate objects. A fetish can be anything selected for consecration by a priest—a piece of wood, a pebble or a shell, the tail of a lion, a plant, a tree. The fetish is not necessarily regarded as divine. It may serve merely as an amulet or a sacred object.

Contrary to Hume, De Brosses saw the origin of religion in fetishism. But with Hume and the rationalists before him, he saw the origins of fetishism in fear and irrational barbarism. The uncultivated and unreasoning mind of the savage prevents him from seeing the true relations between certain causes and their consequences. Savages are like children who imagine that their dolls are animated and who treat them accordingly. For this same reason the savage finds religion everywhere. All peoples are aware of some supreme power because human weakness is common to all.

De Brosses's term *fetishism* would fade into the background. But its function would be picked up by E. B. Tylor, the father of cultural anthropology, and baptized with a new name, *animism*.

Perhaps of more lasting significance for the coming science of cultural anthropology was De Brosses's methodology.[40] He made extensive use of what sources were available at the time to present as broad a picture as possible. For virtually the first time, African religion was introduced as an object of study, as well as the Iroquois Indians of America and the Siberian religions. And though restricted to extant written materials, his work closed with an appeal to scholars to analyze the cultures by direct observation and study rather than by imagining what they did. Hume's call for empirical reflection had found another supporter. Tylor was to quote de Brosses on this very point in the motto on the title page of his classic, *Primitive Culture* (1871).

In many ways, de Brosses adumbrated much of the nineteenth-century beginnings.

> The theory of primitive stupidity returned in the writings of Lévy-Bruhl, Freud, Frazer, Tylor and Radin; and his views about the unilineal direction of progress were more dogmatic than those of later "unilineal" evolutionists. His conviction that the evolution of the mind had culminated in his own enlightened society was a sentiment not wholly unknown to nineteenth-century anthropologists either.[41]

And beyond these ideas were the distinguishing features of Enlightenment's "religion": the triumph of rationalism and reason, the stress on empirical scientific methods, the deploring of primitive life and mentality, the belief that progress could be accelerated by enlightened education.

---

[40]Ugo Bianchi, *The History of Religions* (Leiden: Brill, 1975), 61.
[41]De Waal Malefijt, *Images of Man*, 92.

THE END OF THE BEGINNING

The eighteenth century set the course for the interaction between theology and anthropology. In a deep-level sense, it was a course of warfare and conflict, in which ultimately Christianity was the loser: it lost its central place as the system of thought that unified culture and life. And yet the sharp conflicts masked some rather striking parallels. In the years ahead similar parallels would combine to create the commonness of interests and questions we choose to call Consciousness One and Consciousness Two. Fred Voget, drawing on Carl Becker's work *The Heavenly City of the Eighteenth Century Philosophers* (1932), calls attention to these parallels in the context of the history of ethnology.

1. Both the Christian and the Enlightenment mentality believed that human history moved according to a universal plan. For the Christian, the human drama was God's. For the Enlightenment, man was nature or society's handiwork, with God sitting in the wings or excluded entirely.

2. Both religious systems were utopian. According to the Christian, God would arrest human corruption with the second coming of Christ. According to the Enlightenment, natural processes would carry mankind forward to the realization of a new humanity, to a new world organized by the tolerant sensibilities of reason.

3. Both worldviews were fascinated by contemplation of the fulfillment of the design. Christians looked forward with awesome exaltation to the coming to an end of human rule. Enlightenment thinkers, with exceptions like Hume, saw progress following inevitably from the sustained exercise of human reason in the course of human cultures and religions.

4. A fourth link was a view of metaphysics that united events into a chain of causes, divine or natural, and leading inexorably and irreversibly to a single and uniform end. Christianity and the Enlightenment were both committed to a nonreversible, unilinear, developmental process. The directions, of course, were different. Christianity saw mankind beginning at the summit of Eden and sliding to the bottom, with God in Christ intervening to save. The Enlightenment saw mankind beginning at the bottom and toiling up the slope; there would be faltering at times, but reason would help it regain its balance and humanity would move on.

5. Both movements applied absolute standards in their evaluative judgments. As sin and evil constituted the antithesis for the Christian, so unnatural acts in defiance of propriety and reasonable good order contradicted the path to progress for the *philosophe*.

6. Finally, the human drama constituted a war between conflicting forces, but a war whose outcome was determined (foreordained, to use the Christian term). The corrupting forces of evil would be overcome, either by divine or rational processes.[42]

Voget calls these parallels "coincidences." Are they simply that? Or are they more? Are they part of a religious agenda, adopted by two systems, waiting for a new scientific discipline to emerge and to begin the implementation of the agenda?

---

[42]Fred A. Voget, *A History of Ethnology* (New York: Holt, Rinehart and Winston, 1975), 49–50.

Chapter Two

Consciousness One

SUMMARY

Out of the nineteenth-century interaction between cultural anthropology and theology came a new paradigm for understanding human culture and the part missions should play in it. Shaped by a conflict of ideas not always accurately described as "warfare," Consciousness One, as a paradigm, saw the two streams of anthropology and theology converging in a set of common concerns: What does it mean to be human? What is the nature of religion? What is the nature of culture? What is the nature of language?

Anthropology proposed its answers to these questions through the models of developmentalism and diffusionism. And liberal theology borrowed freely from these models in its examination of the Bible. The evangelical reaction was one of fear and dismay.

Yet out of this dialogue came a suprising number of shared characteristics, which showed their effects in missions as well. *Depersonalization* reduced most of humanity to the status of "primitive man." And the missionary involvement in colonialism did not escape this danger. The "indigenous church formula" met strong opposition from those convinced of the inability of "the native" to lead his church without the help of the Westerner.

Among the anthropologists, *dichotomizing* isolated the person as a religious being from the person as a whole. Among the evangelicals, it operated to reduce the image of God in mankind to the attribute of reason. The missionary's task became the recovering of humanity's fundamental rationality through Christianity and civilizational processes.

A third characteristic of Consciousness One was its *static view of culture*. The colonial mentality of anthropologist and missionary pushed for a one-world culture in which the dynamic of each of society's cultures was lost.

This resulted in *passivity* as another by-product of Consciousness One. People became "quaint" objects of study for the anthropologist; and for the evangelical missionary, the gospel became a concentration on the benefits of salvation for the "barbarians" of the non-Christian world. The recipient of the gospel became a passive agent who "needed" the missionary.

Chapter Two

Consciousness One

THE WARFARE METAPHOR

Given the conflict between the worldviews of Christianity and rationalism in the eighteenth century, and given the thesis that these worldviews were worked out in separate paradigms and models in subsequent history, why have we chosen to talk about "Consciousness One" (singular), rather than about "Consciousnesses One" (plural)? Why would we stress commonality when we have been careful to point to struggle and antithesis on the deep level of presuppositions?

First of all, the reader will note that the sounds of battle are not altogether missing in the next two chapters. Even as we attempt to outline the shared characteristics of both disciplines, we continually point out how these characteristics are structured differently by the dialogue partners. Shared attributes do not always come from the same sources or lead in exactly the same direction. At the conclusion of the last chapter we drew attention to six parallels between the agendas of Christianity and the

Enlightenment. But at the same time we noticed also the radical divergencies within the parallels. The further history of this debate will repeat that pattern.

In the second place, history may be distorted by overextending the "warfare" metaphor. James R. Moore, in his valuable work *The Post-Darwinian Controversies,* points out the dangers in employing military metaphors. Catchy phrases and colorful labels often reshape history into their own image; they come with their own built-in value judgments and thus make a history of their own.[1] Moore is concerned with the effect this sort of language has had in characterizing the religious debates over evolution in the latter nineteenth century. It can be similarly manipulative in the dialogue between anthropology and theology. Implicit in this historiography of "conflict" and "warfare" can be the assumption that science and religion, more specifically cultural anthropology and Christian theology, can or should be divorced. Is the current evangelical concern about these interrelationships partly the residue of this kind of "corruption of language"?

We are not questioning the legitimacy of metaphors as indispensable figures of speech or even as useful to the scientific enterprise. The theological discussions about "anthropomorphism" are, in a sense, efforts to understand the divine use of metaphors in the Bible. Missiologists have made much helpful use of judiciously chosen metaphors as a heuristic device in research. Don Richardson's concept of "redemptive analogies" and Alan Tippett's discussions of "power encounters" are examples of this.

But in history, and especially in history from a diachronic perspective, metaphors may mislead. They may perpetuate false conceptualizations. And this may be particularly harmful if we are to make progress in understanding the dialogue to which we now proceed.

Three general "commonplaces" (Moore's language) are implicit in the military metaphor: the ideas of sharp polarization,

[1]James R. Moore, *The Post-Darwinian Controversies* (Cambridge: Cambridge University Press, 1979), 19.

distinct personnel, and violent antagonism. Each of these needs clarification in connection with our topic.

Polarization: Worldview and Paradigm

A typical war has two sides. In the eighteenth century, Hume emphasized the polarization of empirical science and religion. Kant attempted a harmonization, but in doing so created other walls of compartmentalization. We have argued, by contrast, for antithesis on the deep level of presuppositions. But this level is pretheoretical rather than theoretical; it is the worldview level of often inarticulate faith-commitment.[2] The conflict we have noted functions on this "uncritical" level, the level of the commitments of the heart that remain hidden behind the paradigms and models of scientific endeavor until science (whether philosophy or anthropology or theology) awakens from its self-imposed slumber to admit they are there. These commitments are, so to speak, apriorities of a religious sort.

Evangelicals confound their understanding of the dialogue between anthropology and theology if they cannot keep the realm of worldview distinct from that of paradigm. To speak of Consciousness One and Consciousness Two is to speak of paradigms: they are theoretical agendas created by the interaction of our worldviews with a particular field of science in a particular culture and time by a particular community.

Paradigms flow out of our worldviews. They come closer to the surface-level of reality and, of necessity, exist farther away from the worldview core. Their links with the particular worldview are clearer in one thinker than in another, read between the lines more easily in one place than in another. Paradigms are organizations of a theoretical sort in terms of which their proponents perceive reality.

[2]For a fuller exposition of this general position, consult Herman Dooyeweerd, *In the Twilight of Western Thought* (Philadelphia: Presbyterian and Reformed, 1960), 1–26.

Thomas Kuhn offers some useful insights into the role of paradigm, specifically as it functions in science. By paradigm he means something like a constellation of group commitments. It constitutes a scientist's conceptual world and is composed of such things as shared symbolic generalizations and values. It decides for the scientist which questions are important, what things really are, and what the results signify. Scientists who work within a given paradigm work on common problems with common methods toward agreed upon kinds of results. The paradigm is tacitly imposed, argues Kuhn, upon those entering the science. The paradigm is theoretical, yet it is more: It is metatheoretical. Those who function within its orbit perceive their work as altogether rational, self-evident, and obviously true.[3]

Our discussion in chapter 1 focused on the worldview level. It was an attempt to explore the hidden dimensions of "faith" that motivate both Christians and rationalists in their search for paradigms out of which they construct their models. On this worldview level the warfare metaphor is legitimate. Neutrality, at the heart level, is never possible for the sons and daughters of Adam, whether they function as anthropologists, missionaries, or theologians.

However, when evangelicals carry this battle language over into the realm of paradigms they may easily be saying more than they should. While recognizing the legitimate link between worldview and paradigm, they also make judgments on paradigms, judgments that assume these paradigms are simply or wholly worldviews. Theorization is not so simple. Here lurks the danger of what we earlier called "naive realism." The humanist is guilty of it when he or she defines religion as barbaric ignorance born of fear. And the Christian is no less guilty when he or she absolutizes a theory into a religion.

---

[3]Thomas Kuhn, *The Structure of Scientific Revolutions* (Chicago: University of Chicago Press, 1962, 1970).

Personnel and Organization

Battles are not fought without personnel and organization. And here too, the metaphor needs limiting. The struggle we portray is not simply a struggle between theologians on the one hand and anthropologists on the other. As our history of the two paradigms, Consciousness One and Consciousness Two, will show, theologians often found themselves on the side of anthropologists, either wittingly or unwittingly. A large number of theologians has supported the diffusionist model. Tylor's and Frazer's models of magic found their way into the evangelical *International Standard Bible Encyclopaedia*.

It is also true, to add to the picture, that

> the comparative study of cultures is posterior to and an offshoot of missionary work. The Spanish missionaries of the 16th century studied native American cultures and languages the better to convert native Americans to Christianity. Sahagún is the classic example; his ethnographic studies stood in service to his faith. Likewise, the problem of reconciling the Old Testament version of the origin and distribution of the world's races with the existence of the New World Indians was the stimulus behind early ethnological writings. The divorce of scholarly interest in non-European cultures from religious conviction is a more recent development, as are concepts of cultural relativism. Historically, anthropologists are latecomers with respect to missionaries.[4]

Christianity might be regarded as the father of anthropology.

None of this is meant to minimize the judgment of someone like Claude Stipe who argues that the majority of his contemporaries in the field of anthropology are either atheistic or agnostic. "Having been involved in the discipline for over 25 years, I would be very surprised to discover that over half of my fellow

---

[4]Adriaan C. Van Oss, "A Response to Claude Stipe," *Current Anthropology* 21 (April 1980): 176.

anthropologists were theists."[5] Nor is this a contemporary situation only. Much of the theorizing of the great pioneers of anthropology, key figures in our understanding of Consciousness One, came out of a sense of the meaninglessness of religious beliefs. And scholarship traces this commitment to eighteenth-century rationalistic philosophy.[6]

This picture would seem to be different from what James R. Moore seeks to prove. And indeed, he may be more justified in questioning the use of the military metaphor in connection with reactions to Darwin than we are in our study of anthropology. Nevertheless, we must warn against overdoing it.

Antagonism

The last major implication of the military metaphor is the idea of violent antagonism. Warfare commences when there are hostile clashes of opposing armies. Here too we must be careful.

Part of the reason for caution is simply the lack of research in this area. In connection with his own studies on Darwin, Moore mentions the monumental study of Alvar Ellegard, *Darwin and the General Reader: The Reception of Darwin's Theory of Evolution in the British Periodical Press, 1859–1872* (1958). Ellegard surveyed 115 British periodicals (including forty-five religious serials) to analyze the reactions to Darwin's theory. No comparable work has been done, to my knowledge, in the area of cultural anthropology for any period of its history. Until this is done we must speak with great tentativeness.

My own perceptions in this area lead me to suspect that if we do find evidence of conflict, it will be ill informed on both sides.

---

[5]Claude Stipe, "Anthropologists Versus Missionaries: The Influence of Presuppositions," *Current Anthropology* 21 (April 1980): 178.

[6]Robin Horton, "African Conversion," *Africa* 41 (1971): 85–108; Peter Lawrence, *Road Below Cargo: A Study of the Cargo Movement in the Southern Madang District of New Guinea* (Manchester: University of Manchester Press, 1964).

Though Christianity may, in a sense, be called a father of anthropology, it appears to have disowned its child for many decades. Our survey will indicate that many theological judgments have rested on anthropological assumptions for well over a century. However, very few theologians have been aware of the origins of those assumptions and even fewer have been trained as anthropologists. And it is equally appropriate to note the anthropologist's lack of theological expertise.

The greatest theoretical antagonism on the part of theology came during the period we associate largely with Consciousness One. The anthropology of this paradigm was closer to its eighteenth-century rationalist roots and less disciplined as a science. It provided a wider, more diffuse target for theologians to shoot at. As anthropology refined its methodologies and reduced its interest in the question of the origins of religion, theology, already disenchanted, withdrew its armies from the battlefield. Not until the rise of "applied missionary anthropology" in the 1950s was there enough sustained interest on either a popular or academic level for theology and missiology to move from antagonism to discussion. By then a new mentality on the part of the evangelicals, who pioneered in this subdiscipline, sought to minimize the belligerent posture of the past.

An Alternative to the Warfare Metaphor

As we contemplate the overall history of the interchange we find ourselves wondering whether it may not be best understood, not in terms of a military metaphor, but by means of a model provided by social psychology and the ideas of Leon Festinger.[7]

According to Festinger, the human response to opinion-making information proceeds in four stages. At first there is a *conflict* as new knowledge or new theories challenge the old.

[7]Leon Festinger, *A Theory of Cognitive Dissonance* (London: Tavistock, 1959), 3–13. A good summary of the theory is found in Moore, *Controversies,* 111–12.

Incompatible alternatives are established in the mind and there is a state of tension that can lead to frustration, anger, and aggression. Could this be analogous to the mentality both disciplines brought with them into the nineteenth century and the early stages of the interchange?

The normal way to eliminate this tension and regain one's intellectual composure is by making a *decision*. Conflict is either eliminated or minimized by committing oneself to one or the other of the incompatible alternatives. We can very easily overlay this pattern on the history of Consciousness One and the conflicts and struggles that gave it dynamic vitality.

At this point, following the decision, there is often another kind of conflict which Festinger calls *dissonance*. Here the discrepancy is not between incompatible alternatives but between what one chose and what one might have chosen. Would this explain the refinements going on in Consciousness Two as the partners in the dialogue tinker with past postures and attempt to stretch toward other ones while still tethered to their pasts?

The last stage is *dissonance reduction,* in which the individual seeks to reduce the dissonance by reinterpretation, changing either one or more of the dissonant elements or their relationship. Could it be that the present state of the dialogue has reached this stage? Could it be that we are observing the formation of reinterpretations from both the side of anthropology and the side of theology?

Festinger's model is fascinating when placed alongside Kuhn's analysis of how new paradigms are constructed by science. Revolutions in human thinking are not created by new information but by new paradigms that allow more information to be fitted more fully and adequately. And revolutions in scientific paradigms can be awesome moments of cognitive dissonance. Will Festinger's model help us to understand our "future shock" better than a military metaphor that sums up the dialogue as "a history of the warfare of anthropology with theology in Christendom"?

SHARED CONCERNS OF ANTHROPOLOGY AND THEOLOGY

The world that spawned Consciousness One was a lopsided one. It was the last full century of Western global colonialism, a period someone has described as "the longest, most determined, and most brutal gold-rush in history." Gospel and gold, ointment and gun, oppressor and oppressed—these were the twin agents of Western empire in the nineteenth century. Out of this world and the agenda shaped by the previous century came the set of questions that molded Consciousness One.

What does it mean to be human? people were asking. Both missionaries and anthropologists had come face to face with an enormous variety of peoples from different races and cultures. How will we define them in relation to ourselves? What constitutes their "peoplehood"? Too often both categories of investigators saw the world as nonwhite and therefore noncivilized (that is, largely nonliterate). The societies subjugated or dominated by the West were relatively unchanged, fairly isolated, and largely immobile societies. Anthropologists called them "primitive" and meant "uncivilized, irrational, not like us." Missionaries called them "savage" and "barbaric" and meant much more than simply "gentile." Even the great Robert Moffat, after twenty years in South Africa, could declare that the aboriginal peoples of the subcontinent had no religion at all.[8]

What is the nature of religion? was another area of concern. The earliest stages of professional anthropology were deeply influenced by developmental optimism; writers like E. B. Tylor, James Frazer, and Emile Durkheim had little use for either sophisticated

[8]Peter Hinchliff, "The Selection and Training of Missionaries in the Early Nineteenth Century," in *The Mission of the Church and the Propagation of the Faith,* ed. G. J. Cuming (London: Cambridge University Press, 1970), 134.

or primitive religion. The early pioneers were dominated by a mentality that regarded all religions as outmoded superstitions, suited to a prescientific age. Religion was seen as a roadblock on the way to the rational social regeneration of mankind and to cultural progress.

E. B. Tylor (1832–1917) may be typical of this mentality. He saw human cultures moving on a scale from the simple, or "primitive," to the complex. One moves up the scale through the use of reason. Progress requires unfettered reason. For Tylor, the deficiency of the "primitives" was their inability to distinguish adequately between reality and myth. Thus, they were said to find spirits and souls (*anima* was the term he coined) in all of nature—mountains, trees, rivers, etc. To the primitives, he concluded, spirits were simply personified causes.

From animism, continued this argument, evolved polytheism. And polytheism was said to give way to monotheism. All of this was a perfectly rational process, part of the continuum from the simple to the more complex. But even monotheism never divests itself totally of this animistic spirit. The world's great religions still retain clear traces of former stages of development and evolution. These traces confirm the developmental character of religion. So too, the argument ran, one could find elements of the higher religions also in the lower products of "natural religion." Primitive man and modern man are both looking for causation.

What is the nature of culture? they also asked. How will we understand the formation of culture, its origins, growth, and diffusion? Consciousness One anthropologists very soon began to grapple with the social character of culture. The creator of this awareness was Emile Durkheim (1853–1917), the father of sociology, who saw culture and religion not as a rational construct but as a social construct: "Society" prescribes to the individual the dogmas that must be believed and the rites that must be used to express these dogmas.

How does society construct religion? Fundamental is society's basic separation of all things into two categories—the sacred and the profane. The sacred is the interdicted, that which may not be touched. Mixing the sacred and the profane is sacrilege. Religion then is a "unified system of beliefs and practices relative to sacred things, that is to say, things set apart and forbidden."[9] It is created in communities bound together by a common attitude toward certain "sacred" objects (or totems), places, and persons.

Durkheim put the *totem* at the heart of this process; it was symbolic of the god who was a personification of the clan. The life of the totem represented the life of the society itself. The totem was for the social group a type of the sacred, the visible symbol of a supernatural power. And it was a symbol of the clan, the mark by which the clan distinguished itself from all others. The "totemic" principle was the clan or society represented and transfigured in the visible form or symbol of a supernatural power.[10] The soul then is simply the totemic principle incarnate in a society member. In the totemic principle the individual carries a part of the society or clan inside him or her in the form of beliefs or sentiments.[11]

Much of the thinking of Durkheim and of the school that followed him has long since been questioned by anthropologists and by historians of religion. His totemic principle in particular came under attack. If totemism is directly related to the origins of religion as a collective clan creation, should one not expect totemism among all tribes? And yet, said A. A. Goldenweiser for example, the simplest tribes do not have totems. Nor do they have clans. Where then do nontotemist people get their religion? Furthermore, Durkheim argued that the religious sentiment originated in the collective enthusiasm typified by the Australian ritual. But, continued Goldenweiser, if the assembly gives rise to

[9]Emile Durkheim, *The Elementary Forms of the Religious Life: A Study in Religious Sociology* (New York: Macmillan, 1915), 47.

[10]Ibid., 236.

[11]Ibid., 297.

the sentiment of religion, why is it that the secular dances of North American Indians were not transformed by this same social process into religious occasions?[12] Wilhelm Schmidt also assaulted the data base of Durkheim's thesis. He pointed out that Durkheim limited his information to the central Australians, especially the Arunta. But he ignored the southeastern Australians who apparently form the earliest developmental stratum, according to Schmidt—yet this group does not have totemism.[13]

Also criticized was Durkheim's use of exclusively social categories to fully explain religious phenomena. Such a model was unable to explain why, in the construction of myth and ritual, so much use is made of the nonhuman, nonsocial outer world. There is a specific preference for the use of natural and cosmological symbols in the creation of clan myths. However, if religious concepts are merely derivatives of the social category, why do they not express themselves predominantly in social symbols?[14]

Notwithstanding these objections, Durkheim's emphasis on the societal role of religion was picked up and became the source of new questions for Consciousness One. What is the role of kinship in a culture? Where is the integrating core of culture? How do cultures relate to one another? What is the social structure of culture?

What is the nature of language? people also began to ask. Early anthropologists and missionaries were faced with learning unwritten languages. The methods developed by classical linguists were for written, largely Western, languages. A new approach to language was required.

At this stage there was interest in the relationship of language

[12] A. A. Goldenweiser, *Early Civilization: An Introduction to Anthropology* (New York: Knopf, 1922), 360ff.

[13] Cf. also Robert Lowie, *Primitive Religion* (New York: Boni and Liveright, 1924), 153ff.

[14] J. van Baal, *Symbols for Communication. An Introduction to the Anthropological Study of Religion* (Assen: Van Gorcum, 1971), 124–26.

to culture. But this interest focused on the origins of language, partly due to the pressure of the developmentalist model of evolution. Max Müller (1823–1900) typified much of this interest. A philologist, he held that etymological research can discover the meaning of religion for early man. "It is," he argued, "as impossible to use words without thought as to think without words."[15] The mythology created by the primitive was not traced simply to man's irrational apprehension of natural phenomena. The personification process that deified lightning and the stars was due to "a period of temporary linguistic insanity" in the human mind, what Müller called a "disease of language." In the process, the noun "dawn" became "she of the dawn" about whom stories could begin to be told. Poetic renderings of events lost their original metaphorical meaning and became proper names of the objects concerned. *Nomina* became *numina*. Greek euphemisms for "the sky as our father" (Zeus-pater) were linguistically corrupted into "Jupiter."

Müller's naiveté about religion and human languages was monumental. His popularity was short lived, its demise helped along by the relentless and powerful criticism of his views by Andrew Lang (1844–1912).[16] Most of his theories met sudden anthropological death—his hypothesis that roots are the first elements of language; his thesis that the oldest forms of language were inadequate expressions of the experiences of their speaker; his understanding of myth as a disease of language. But he had created an agenda for linguistics and for the study of religion—though it flowed from a man whose theories made "abundantly clear that he never fathomed Belief."[17]

---

[15]F. Max Müller, *The Science of Language Vol I* (New York: AMS Press, 1978 reprint of 1861 ed.), 72.

[16]For a summary of the criticisms and the career of Lang, consult Eric Sharpe, *Comparative Religion. A History* (London: Duckworth, 1975), 58–65.

[17]Jan de Vries, *Perspectives in the History of Religions* (Berkeley: University of California Press, 1977), 90.

ANTHROPOLOGY'S PART IN THE FORMATION OF CONSCIOUSNESS ONE

The answers of Consciousness One to these shared questions came, where theology was concerned, from two basic directions: the profound reflection of anthropology's moods in the agenda of liberal theology and the retrenching response of evangelical thought. In a few cases, the impact of anthropology was direct and the theologian would credit his indebtedness to anthropology in footnotes. But in most cases it was more covert, more caught than taught. John Rogerson summarizes the picture in his book *Anthropology and the Old Testament*:

> It has been rare for an Old Testament scholar to be trained as an anthropologist (an exception was the late S. H. Hooke). Yet for at least two hundred years, Old Testament scholars have made judgments about the Old Testament which rested on anthropological assumptions, and they possibly have at least as many areas of common concern with anthropologists as with Egyptologists or Assyriologists. Indeed, the matter is complicated by the fact that Egyptologists and Assyriologists also make assumptions which are essentially anthropological assumptions, and the Old Testament scholar may be in danger of applying to the Old Testament, anthropological conclusions reached in these other fields by specialists who may know no more about anthropology than he does.[18]

The same comments could be made about New Testament research. There was ideological and methodological interaction on a grand scale. Some samplings of the dialogue should illustrate the process.

What Does It Mean to Be Religious?

In response to the question, What does it mean to be religious? anthropology in Consciousness One moved in at least

[18]John Rogerson, *Anthropology and the Old Testament* (Atlanta: John Knox, 1979), 2.

two different directions, represented in developmentalism and diffusionism.

DEVELOPMENTALISM

Developmentalism was linked as much with the concept of progress as with the ideas of Darwin. The "pre-understanding" was that all races had passed through identical stages of social, mental, and religious development. The ancestors of civilized peoples were said to have once lived, thought, and behaved like contemporary primitives.

Theology was quick to reflect this temperament. Julius Wellhausen (1844–1918) did more than simply systematize theological reflection when he began to collate his version of the documentary hypothesis. He incorporated the mindset of Consciousness One. He assumed a developmental structure, as Tylor had done, and applied it to Hebrew religion. That religion became a historical movement from simple to complex, from polytheism to monotheism. Three stages marked the evolution: (1) the animistic stage, which the Hebrews were said to have inherited from their nomadic background; (2) the Mosaic development of a form of monolatry (not a denial of all other gods but a choice of one God alone for Israel); (3) the monotheistic stage, reached through the interaction of monolatry with the cultic practices of the Canaanites. The formative power in this final transformation was not the Mosaic law as traditionally assumed, but the teaching of the prophets: in the course of their polemic against ritual worship, there was said to have arisen the concept of a transcendent deity. The deity's relationship to man was thus changed in this process from a national into a universal and ethical one. This prophetic conception of monotheism led, Wellhausen continued, to further complexity. There was the centralization of the cultus at a single shrine, the temple in Jerusalem, where we find the beginning of a process of ritual development that climaxed in the elaborate rites of the so-called Priestly Code.

Another exponent of progressive developmentalism was the Old Testament scholar W. Robertson Smith (1846–1894). Smith applied some of Tylor's ideas to the Old Testament and this, combined with other theses, placed him in the center of the struggle of Consciousness One. But particularly the influence of Durkheim on Smith was significant and direct. Smith saw the most primitive stage of Semitic religion in the concept of sacrifice as a public ceremony of the whole clan. At this primitive stage, he claimed, communion was established with the totem god. And this was accomplished, as Durkheim had argued, when the totemic group ate the totem object after which it was named. Out of this grew the atonement, or "at-one-ment" as Smith called it. It was simply an act of communion designed to wipe out all memory of previous estrangement. The community was to be brought again into harmony with its alienated god.[19]

Smith and Wellhausen differed on how the continuity in ritual from the earlier to the later Israel was to be understood. But for both, the idea of development was crucial. The last stage of development, said Smith, was Christianity and its concepts of atonement, communion, and holiness. In this stage, the concrete terms were gradually freed from their material connotations. Thus they became the "spiritual truths" of Christian doctrine.[20]

DIFFUSIONISM

Developmentalism, however, was not the only anthropological model seeking answers to the question of the nature of religion. Another was Diffusionism. The developmental model approached religion as a history of upward theological mobility. Diffusionism

[19]W. Robertson Smith, *The Religion of the Semites,* 3rd ed. (London: Black, 1927), 319–20.

[20]Ibid., 439–40.

and its high priest Wilhelm Schmidt (1868–1954) looked elsewhere.

Similar customs and beliefs are found scattered all over the world. How do we account for their origin and relationships? The developmentalist model supposed that all races had passed through similar stages of cultural development. Schmidt, a Roman Catholic priest, tried to explain similarities and relationships by diffusion from one or more centers of culture. He found three such basic centers (*Kulturkreise* he called them). And in each, he continued, there existed a primordial form of monotheism (the high-god concept), which degenerated through diffusion. Animism, polytheism, mana belief, and magic are later accretions through corruptions of imagination.

Schmidt's intent was to discredit the evolutionary ethnologists. Evans-Pritchard concedes that "undoubtedly he proved his case against them."[21] However, it was done by accepting their evolutionary criteria. His cultural history is in many ways merely a variant of the conjectural developmentalist history he despised. The main difference was that the developmentalists based their theories on an analogy with biological evolution, whereas Schmidt used a geographical model.

It is no surprise that his ideas were eventually discarded in spite of the massive amount of his research. Some charged him with doing polemics, not science. Others, then and now, questioned his high-god concept. Still others charged that the theory of culture centers (*Kulturkreise*) could be used to prove anything or nothing and that the hypothesis of a primeval monotheism at the beginning of religious history was completely arbitrary. And there were those frightened by his rigid rationalism. Eliade notes with much concern his assertion that "primitive man discovered the idea of God through a logical quest for a cause."[22]

[21]E. E. Evans-Pritchard, *Theories of Primitive Religion* (London: Oxford University Press, 1965), 103.

[22]Mircea Eliade, *The Quest. History and Meaning in Religion* (Chicago: University of Chicago Press, 1969), 25.

But though Schmidt found few anthropologists to follow his trail, there was a readier market among the theologians before his ideas dissipated their strength with them as well.

Panbabylonianism was one of the earliest of the spin-offs. Beginning in the early 1870s, newly discovered cuneiform texts from Mesopotamia were published. The shock waves of the Babylonian flood narrative and creation accounts began to appear in the academic world. The Tel-el-Amarna tablets revealed the whole ancient Near East in the fifteenth and fourteenth centuries B.C. as one great civilization, embracing a number of peoples but united by deep political and cultural ties.[23] Israelite history began to look more and more like only one part of an influential pool of religious symbols and history. Wellhausen's developmental model of simple to complex no longer looked quite so simple. Hugo Winckler (1863–1913), publisher of the first critical edition of the tablets (1889–1890), proposed a theory to explain the interrelationships. The panbabylonian model of diffusionism was born. All Near Eastern religions, mythology, and especially astrology were said to have originated in the Babylonian worldview. Many of the cultural and religious forms of the Old Testament were said to be dependent on this common intellectual and spiritual corpus. It was not simply a question of borrowing from an older civilization. It was a question of participation in a highly developed culture common to the whole ancient Near Eastern world. By 1902, even a conservative like Friedrich Delitzsch had accepted the model.

Diffusionism also influenced New Testament research. Scholars turned to Hellenistic and pre-Christian Jewish backgrounds in their study of the origin of New Testament religion. Hermann Gunkel (1862–1932) outlined the agenda of what was called the *Religionsgeschichte* (History of Religions) school. He saw Christian-

[23]For a translation and discussion of the more significant tablets, consult Alexander Heidel, *The Babylonian Genesis* (Chicago: University of Chicago Press, 1942); idem, *The Gilgamesh Epic and Old Testament Parallels* (Chicago: University of Chicago Press, 1946).

ity as a syncretistic religion, containing strong religious themes derived from abroad, both Oriental and Hellenistic, which it has transformed to advantage. These foreign religious themes, he argued, must have infiltrated the community of Jesus immediately after his death.

Wilhelm Bousset (1865–1919) used the diffusionist model to explain the titles of Jesus. *Kurios* became a title first applied to Jesus in the Hellenistic world. Paul was said to have added this to his Christology, along with the Palestinian contribution, *Son of Man;* his own creative addition was considered to be the title *Pneuma* (Spirit). The mystery religions and their emphasis on a dying and rising god became the diffusionist sources of New Testament Christology.[24] Wilhelm Wrede (1859–1907) offered another variation of the diffusionist program. The Pauline conception of Christ, he argued, was derived from the Jewish apocalyptic conception of the preexistent, heavenly Messiah, a conception Paul already had before his conversion. Paul's addition was said to be the belief that the heavenly Messiah had already come to earth and carried out a plan of redemption.

What does it mean to be human?

Anthropology in the Consciousness One phase assumed that primitives experienced the world very differently than modern Western peoples. Two models exemplified this paradigm theme and again had their parallels in theological circles.

Sir James Frazer (1854–1941) originated one of the conceptions. With E. B. Tylor, he presupposed the idea of development and progression. Both men were primarily interested in the construction of a conjectural history of the human mind. Frazer, in

[24]Charles C. Anderson, *Critical Quests of Jesus* (Grand Rapids: Eerdmans, 1969), 66.

fact, once proposed to discard the term *social anthropology* in favor of the phrase *mental anthropology* .

According to Frazer, mankind everywhere passes through three stages of intellectual development: from magic to religion to science. Magic, he asserted, has nothing to do with religion. Religion arises when magic fails. Magic was seen as an early expression of science based on the false notion of the regularity of cause and effect. Religion, he continued, was a higher achievement than magic. It arose in cultural history when shrewder intelligences discovered that magic did not really achieve its ends. Humanity, as yet unable to counter the crisis precipitated by this failure of magic with a refined philosophy, fell into another illusion—religion. It began to believe that there were spiritual beings who could aid us. In the course of time, the argument went, the shrewder intelligences saw that the notion of spirits was equally as false as the original magic. This enlightenment heralded the dawn of experimental science. Behind this transition from magic to religion to science was the inherent tendency of thought to perfect itself. The primitive mind was irrational, and the history of human development was progress from irrationality to rationality.

How did Frazer's ideas appear in theological form? This is not an easy question to answer: "Frazer's explanations have become so much a part of what many people think about the workings of magic, that almost all the modern textbooks on the Old Testament which speak of magic do not even bother to define the term magic."[25] A glance at the article on magic in the original *International Standard Bible Encyclopaedia,* will provide a quick sample. Frazer's distinctions are used to define magic and to sketch the relation between magic and religion.[26]

Another example is found in the work of Sigmund Mowinckel (1884–1965). In his study on the Psalms, he welded Frazer to the

[25]Rogerson, *Anthropology,* 52.

[26]James Orr, ed., *International Standard Bible Encyclopaedia, Vol. III* (Grand Rapids: Eerdmans, 1955), 1963–64.

panbabylonian diffusionist ideas. He saw reflected in many of the Psalms a primitive belief in the effectiveness of magic ritual. And on this basis he rejected the postexilic dating proposed by other critics. He placed their origin in the early historical period. The enthronement Psalms in particular he saw as cult drama, representing the enthronement of the divine king. And this was seen in direct analogy to the Babylonian system. The rituals of accession corresponded to ancient vegetation and fertility rites. These rites, he contended, were originally believed to have magical potency to insure the fertility of the soil and to induce abundant rainfall. Frazer had found similar rites among primitives and interpreted them as "magical in intention." Their purpose was always to induce the desired outcome by imitation. Accordingly, Mowinckel saw the annual enthronement of Jahweh as "magical in intention."[27] In imitation of the Babylonian rites, it actualized through ritual Jahweh's annual resumption of his royal power and his recreation of heaven and earth. Following the ark of the covenant annually into the temple was repeating "the creation event through magical intention."

The British "myth and ritual" school refined these concepts again. It also made use of the general idea of a culture pattern diffused throughout the ancient Near East and focused in particular on the Hebrew rituals connected with sacral kingship and the so-called "enthronement festival." S. H. Hooke, one of theology's few trained anthropologists, saw the ritual as particularly centered in the person of the king. According to Johnson, the king in Israel was the symbol of national virility, the responsible agent for communal prosperity.[28] Frazer, in his book *Lectures on the Early History of the Kingship* (1905), had cited many cases from around the world of the institution of divine or sacral kingship. The

[27]For an elaboration of these convergences, consult Herbert F. Hahn, *The Old Testament in Modern Research* (Philadelphia: Fortress, 1966), 64–67.

[28]A. R. Johnson, "Divine Kingship and the Old Testament," *Expository Times* 62 (November 1950): 36–42.

descent of the king was traced back to the worker of magic. Hooke's and A. R. Johnson's concepts intersect with Frazer's at several points.

A second approach to the question of humanity came later than Frazer with the work of Lucien Lévy-Bruhl (1857–1939) and his concept of "primitive mentality." With the Durkheim school, he attempted a sociological explanation of the mental processes of primitive society. Unlike Frazer, he did not see magic and religion as products of the primitive's intellectual reasoning or even lack of it. Primitive man was not a "primitive philosopher." Rather, he was what Lévy-Bruhl called "pre-logical and mystical."[29] The primitive was not yet familiar with the normal functions of logical reason. His was a type of thinking indifferent to logical contradiction; it was thus "pre-logical." But it was "mystical" as well. There was a belief in forces and influences imperceptible to the normal senses. Primitives perceived things as being mystically connected with other things. If his child is ill, a father might drink the medicine intended for the child. A man might see his shadow and believe it to be his soul. There was also, the argument continued, a blurring of the boundaries between objects. A man's personality could merge with his sick child's. His name, his shadow, his hair clippings could be thought of as an extension of his personality. Thus Lévy-Bruhl considered the primitive mentality to occupy some middle ground between animal instinct and normal human logic. This middle ground preceded logical thought and was characterized by mental short circuits.

In all this, the influence of Durkheim's model of the social origins of religion can be seen. In this model, primitive thought was collective thought. It obeyed a "mystical" principle that understood selfhood or personality as the result of some "law of participation" in invisible cosmic forces. Lévy-Bruhl's ultimate purpose was to distinguish between various levels of developing or

[29]Lucien Lévy-Bruhl, *Primitive Mentality* (New York: Macmillan, 1923); idem, *Les fonctions mentales dans les sociétés inférieures* (Paris: Alcan, 1910), 344–345.

evolving culture on the basis of greater or lesser dependence on the law of participation and communal consciousness.

There is some evidence that before his death Lévy-Bruhl was radically reconsidering the wisdom of some of his language.[30] But it was too late for most anthropologists. His model was strongly criticized by those in the Tylor school who saw primitive man as a "philosopher." Others wondered about his assumption that "civilized" man is always logical and "primitive" man always "prelogical." Rather, are not examples of primitive mentality to be found everywhere, even among apparently civilized people? Further, if the thesis was correct and the mind of the primitive was so radically different from ours, how could civilized anthropologists ever fully grasp its workings? How could we communicate with primitives or even learn their languages?

Yet, at the same time, the model was picked up by theologians and applied particularly to Old Testament research. Rogerson sees it behind the notion of "corporate personality" introduced in 1911 by H. Wheeler Robinson.[31] The Hebrew mentality, like the primitive mentality described by Lévy-Bruhl, was said not to distinguish clearly between what the modern mind would regard as separate objects. In the Hebrew mind a personality might merge with that of a larger group to which the individual belonged. Or it might merge with other personalities in the group. Robinson used this to interpret the idea of the suffering servant in the Isaiah songs.[32] Some had seen the servant as an individual, others as a corporate idea. Robinson said both views would be correct if one took account of the distinctive Hebrew mentality.

Others also picked up the theme. A. R. Johnson used the idea

---

[30]Maurice Leenhardt, ed., *Les carnets de Lucien Lévy-Bruhl* (Paris: University of Paris, 1949); English translation: *Note Books on Primitive Mentality* (London: Oxford University Press, 1976).

[31]Rogerson, *Anthropology*, 55.

[32]H. Wheeler Robinson, *The Christian Doctrine of Man* (Edinburgh: T. and T. Clark, 1911), 8.

of the "extension of personality" in his studies and explicitly mentioned Lévy-Bruhl as his mentor.[33] William Foxwell Albright (1891–1971), the noted biblical archeologist, also borrowed from the model in his analysis of the intellectual development of ancient Near Eastern man. In the intellectual history of Egypt and Mesopotamia, he said, men start "with a prelogical, corporate tradition." After the third millennium, this prelogical thought is progressively discarded and men enter the empirical stage of logical thinking. Polytheism represents this prelogical mentality; monotheism, rational advance beyond it.[34] The same concept appears again in S. H. Hooke and is used to explain the pattern of thinking that made divine kingship the link between human society and the world of cosmic forces in nature.

What is the Meaning of Culture?

Consciousness One was preoccupied with a developmentalist approach to culture. Durkheim, for example, did not simply emphasize the societal role of religion. He was dominated by the desire to reduce the phenomenon of religion to a societal necessity. Many were not ready to agree with him on that emphasis. But his focus on the societal character of culture was picked up and modified and became a very important element in the rise of functionalism.

This societal model had sweeping impact in the area of theological studies. The diffusionist themes of Gunkel and the Scandinavian school zeroed in on ritual and communal kingship. This was fed by Durkheim's emphasis on the social origins of religious rites. Others searched the social patterns of Babylon or Egypt, Hellenism or Jewish apocalyptic for the roots of Hebrew and Christian origins.

---

[33]A. R. Johnson, *The One and the Many in the Israelite Conception of God* (Cardiff: University of Wales, 1961), 2 n. 4.

[34]William Foxwell Albright, *From the Stone Age to Christianity* (Garden City: Doubleday, Anchor, 1957), 168ff.

What Is the Nature of Language?

Consciousness One approached language primarily from a historical and comparative perspective. How does language help us understand the developmentalist progress of religion and society? Are the ambiguities of language open doors for peering into the growth of culture's many mythologies? Under Durkheim's influence, linguistics added the societal dimension. It began to focus on kinship terminology. What were the semantic elements used to link or separate sets of kin?

Behind all these questions was a rigid, static view of language that paralleled the static view of culture also characteristic of Consciousness One. There was a focus on words rather than on speech-acts-in-context. A sharp contrast was assumed to exist between thought and its symbolic expression. Words existed as brute facts, straightforward formal correspondences of reality.

Flowing from this static view of language emerged several givens for Consciousness One. (I use elements from the list provided by Anthony Thiselton in another connection as illustrative of these presuppositions.[35])

1. "The word, rather than the sentence or speech-act, constitutes the basic unit of meaning to be investigated." Müller had made this thesis his cornerstone. It was, in fact, basic also to lexical work done in connection with the Christian Scriptures through the early part of the twentieth century, perhaps the greatest example of which is the monumental *Theological Dictionary of the New Testament,* edited between 1930 and 1973 by Gerhard Kittel and Gerhard Friedrich.

James Barr, in his work *The Semantics of Biblical Language* (1961), ruthlessly criticizes the Kittel multivolume work on this very point. The assumption behind the articles was that words as

[35]Anthony Thiselton, "Semantics and New Testament Interpretation," in *New Testament Interpretation: Essays on Principles and Methods,* ed. I. Howard Marshall (Grand Rapids: Eerdmans, 1977), 76.

single units, not phrases or sentences, carry theological meanings. The end result is what he calls "illegitimate totality transfer." This occurs when the semantic value of a word as it occurs in one context is added to its semantic value in another context.[36]

2. "Questions about etymology somehow relate to the real or basic meaning of a word." Again, this thesis has been virtually a standard assumption of much biblical study. The arrangement of the Hebrew lexicon of Brown, Driver, and Briggs encourages the arriving at conclusions about meaning on the basis of etymology. Many of the articles in Kittel's *Theological Dictionary* operate on this same assumption. The earlier work of Richard Trench, *Synonyms of the New Testament* (1855, continually in print since then), is also governed by this methodological assumption.

3. "Logical and grammatical structure are basically similar." On this assumption, the form of a word thus inherently possesses the meaning of the word. And in the Christian community of exegetical scholarship, commentaries on the biblical text made a virtue of moving through a text "word by word" to find meaning. Later developments in language study would begin to remind scholarship that biblical language as language can only be understood with reference to its extralinguistic situation. But those lessons would not really be learned till much later in our history.

4. "The basic kind of language use to be investigated (other than words themselves) is the declarative proposition or statement."

5. "Language is an externalization of inner concepts or ideas, sometimes a merely imitative and approximate externalization." This was the linguistic principle through which Max Müller saw

---

[36]James Barr, *The Semantics of Biblical Language* (London: Oxford University Press, 1961), 218.

"the disease of language" as it externalized irrationality and slipped into the creation of mythology.

Theology, as we have already suggested, quickly tasted the linguistic fruits of Consciousness One. Liberal higher criticism was no more exempt than the evangelical. Words were studied in a search for primitive survivals in the Bible. Albrecht Alt in 1929 examined phrases in the book of Genesis. He focused on terms like "the God of Abraham" (28:13), "the Fear of Isaac" (31:42), "the Mighty One of Jacob" (49:24). These were said to be survivals from inscriptions dating from 50 B. C.to A. D.350. The inscriptions talk about "the God of X," X being a person's name. It was assumed that such phrases imply a type of religion in which X founded a religious cult. X's posterity, argued Alt, thereafter continued to worship the God whose name was bound to that of their forebear, X. Thus, Alt said, Abraham, Isaac, and Jacob were founders of cults. Their posterity worshiped the divine under the names connected with their ancestors.[37] Earlier, Wellhausen had made use of these same linguistic principles when he dated the various parts of the Pentateuch on the basis of the names of God used in the text. Different names must indicate different origins—the assumption was the linguistic one of Consciousness One. Supposed differences of conceptual thought were based on incidental differences in grammar and words.

EVANGELICALISM'S RESPONSE: APPREHENSION

In this context evangelical theology shaped its Consciousness One paradigm. Its often frightened mood was reflected in a deep fear of cultural anthropology, which resulted in missionary neglect of the behavioral sciences. A 1957 survey of retired Protestant

[37]Albrecht Alt, "The God of the Fathers," in *Essays on Old Testament History and Religion* (London: Oxford University Press, 1966).

missionaries shows this. It indicated that 83% of them had gone to their fields of labor without any cultural orientation training, while 72% of them had no training in a foreign language.[38] This same problem may be reflected in the curriculum of Christian colleges. In March 1980, *Moody Monthly* published a survey of 135 Christian institutions of higher learning; only two indicated the offering of cultural anthropology as a major.

A number of reasons lay behind this mentality of fear. Theology perceived anthropology as evolutionism. The conflict of the church with W. Robertson Smith was typical of these feelings. Smith had been appointed to the chair of Old Testament studies at the Free Church College in Aberdeen in 1870. Within ten years his developmentalist views had twice been subjected to disciplinary study by his church, and by 1880 he was dismissed from his post. For Smith and his supporters the issue was simple: were the Holy Scriptures to be studied on genetic and historical principles or were they forever exempt from such treatment? For the Smith group the debate was a question of academic liberty: Was the individual scholar to be free to interpret his faith along the lines of free inquiry? Or only in relation to an unquestioned principle of authority?

The church perceived Smith's views as a threat to the gospel, as compromising the uniqueness of biblical authority and revelation. The church won and lost at the same time. When the dust clouds had settled, Smith was gone and the church emerged as champion of the gospel. The faith had been defended. But in the process the church had also reinforced a negative posture, a posture of battle against any scientific research into non-Christian religious traditions. The theologians saw anthropology as representing that research.

The battle over these questions was fought over and over again in the late nineteenth and early twentieth centuries. As the

[38]Richard W. Brislick and Paul Pedersen, *Cross-Cultural Orientation Programs* (New York: Gardner, 1976), 149.

church's battle losses mounted with the passage of time, the negative mentality grew.

Evangelical theology perceived anthropology, linked as it was with progressive developmentalism, also as crass, absolute relativism. Ernst Troeltsch (1865–1923) epitomized that relativism for many. In his most famous work, *Die Absolutheit des Christentums* (1903; English translation, *The Absoluteness of Christianity and the History of Religions,* 1971), Troeltsch systematized that relativism into a radical form of historicism. Christianity was, after all, a historical religion. And to Troeltsch "historical" meant "relative," "subject to all the limitations and relativity of other human phenomena." Christianity was still the supreme religion in the world. But this was chiefly because of its civilizing contribution, as evidenced by its many close bonds with Western culture. That culture was seen as the best of all possible worlds. Even this, however, was not an absolute. It is quite possible, he argued, that a new revelation of a still higher form of religion might be given to us. In that unlikely case, the Christian religion would vanish completely.[39]

By 1923, he had moved even further: Christianity's supremacy was valid only for the Westerner. The inhabitants of Southeast Asia can accept the same degree of finality and absoluteness for their proper religion, Buddhism. Troeltsch insisted that we must respect other people and not impose our religion upon them. God alone knows whether one religion possesses greater validity than another. Our call must not be for conversions but for mutual understanding.

Troeltsch's work as the systematic theologian of the *Religionsgeschichte* school demanded a response. The missionary movement was seen as threatened at its roots. Part of the reply came from Gustav Warneck (1834-1919), the father of missiology. Troeltsch argued that the missionary must refrain from attacking or

[39]For a good summary of Troeltsch's views, consult Benjamin A. Reist, *Toward a Theology of Involvement: The Thought of Ernst Troeltsch* (Philadelphia: Westminster, 1966), 174–97.

supplanting established religion. Warneck saw "Christianity as the complete and final revelation of God . . . and [the] absolute religion." Troeltsch saw the right and duty of missions in its civilizing contribution—its hospitals, its schools, its resistance, for example, to the Indian caste system. Warneck shared with Troeltsch a colonialistic view of Western (and specifically German) culture, and saw Western culture as far superior to the cultures of Asia and Africa, even superior to the advanced Hindu and Chinese systems.[40] World trade and the policies of colonial annexation had ushered in "a period of the opening of doors to the gospel."

But Warneck, in opposition to Troeltsch, did not see this as the principal or exclusive task of missions. That task was both "the extension of the kingdom of God" and also "the founding of the church." Christianity alone possesses the full truth and salvation: Jesus, the Christ who became man, is a "universal person with the blood of universal salvation coursing through his veins, so to speak." "Being sinful and therefore in need of salvation and yet redeemable because human nature bears a divine likeness," all of humanity depends on Christ for that life-giving stream that flows from him and penetrates the whole. Using the language of Troeltsch, Warneck comments, "As the herald of this message of salvation, mission is the naturally necessary consequence of the absolute character of Christianity."[41]

Unfortunately, voices like that of Warneck were few and far between at this time. The mentality that reacted against relativism overreacted. Research into the contemporary religions was too often regarded as at best worthless, at worst the work of the devil.[42] Evangelicalism, concerned about the cloud of developmental optimism, turned away from academic interest in the budding skills of anthropology. Missionaries were by no means

[40]Hans Kasdorf, "The Legacy of Gustav Warneck," *Occasional Bulletin of Missionary Research* 4 (July 1980): 106.

[41]Quoted in Johannes Verkuyl, *Contemporary Missiology. An Introduction* (Grand Rapids: Eerdmans, 1978), 27.

[42]Sharpe, *Comparative Religion,* 144.

indifferent to the study of the cultures they wooed for the gospel—their research was often the basis for anthropological studies. But we are not speaking now of specific studies but of a general mindset. Typical of that mindset is an incident involving Bartholomew Ziegenbalg (1682–1719), one of the first Protestant missionaries to India. He brought his studies of South Indian Hinduism home to Europe. And there he was informed that "his business was to root out Hinduism in India and not to propagate heathen superstition in Europe."[43] The home reaction could easily have been the voice of the nineteenth- century evangelical.

Colonialism had a great deal to do with these reactions. Another factor was the widespread lack of education among early missionary forces. The selection and training of early missionaries was extremely haphazard. The London Missionary Society in the early nineteenth century had sent four missionaries to South Africa. One of them was encouraged to continue his studies—in spelling![44] Many of these early pioneers were barely literate. Max Warren notes that "most of the missionaries who left Britain for service overseas in the first half of the nineteenth century were hardly figures to hit the headlines."[45] They were largely members of the working class—skilled mechanics, carpenters, day workers. With this kind of personnel, how could one expect a sophisticated attitude toward culture?

SHARED CHARACTERISTICS OF CONSCIOUSNESS ONE

Out of this dialogue came a surprising number of shared characteristics—the attributes of Consciousness One.

---

[43]Ibid., 145.

[44]Hinchliff, "Selection and Training," 132.

[45]Max Warren, *Social History and Christian Missions* (London: SCM, 1967), 50.

Depersonalization

Depersonalization was one of these characteristics.[46] The developmentalist framework of the anthropologist dehumanized. Debates were held on whether the newly discovered pygmies of central Africa were humans or apes. Lévy-Bruhl's portrait of the primitive mind spoke of tribal peoples as prelogical. The Anthropological Society of London was the outgrowth of a debate over whether African blacks were mentally and morally capable of civilization. The Society doubted it. To the anthropologist, "primitive man" became something closely resembling pre-man.

The evangelical theologian resisted this reductionism on a biblical and theoretical level; humanity everywhere displayed the image of God. But on other significant levels the evangelical did not practice what he preached. Theologian and missionary alike "were convinced of the superiority of their culture. And they did not always differentiate this from their faith in the superiority of Christianity."[47]

The end result was missionary involvement in the process of depersonalization. Cultural ethnocentrism did not always allow the missionary to separate Christianity from the process of Western civilizing. "I beg to direct your attention to Africa," David Livingstone had said on the eve of his return to the African continent in 1858. "I go back to Africa to make an open path for commerce and Christianity." He took with him a mining geologist

> to tell us of the mineral resources of the country, an economic botanist to give a full report of the vegetable productions, an artist to give the scenery, a naval officer to tell of the capacity of river communications, and a moral agent to lay a Christian foundation for anything that may follow. All this machinery has for its ostensible object the development of African trade

[46]Paul Hiebert, "Missions and Anthropology: A Love/Hate Relationship," *Missiology* 6 (April 1978): 166.

[47]Ibid.

> and the promotion of civilization. . . . I hope it may result in an English colony in the healthy high-lands of Central Africa.[48]

Colonialism devastated the missionary's biblical assertions. It created a missionary task force uncertain as to whether "the native church" left to itself could flourish and grow. It minimized, in the eyes of the missionary, the capabilities of "natives" to lead and to create their own clergy. In response to this ideology Rufus Anderson (1796–1880), administrator of the American Board of Commissioners for Foreign Missions, and Henry Venn (1796–1873), general secretary of the Church Missionary Society, created and developed the so-called "indigenous church formula"—the church as self-supporting, self-propagating, self-governing.

The formula was a radical innovation in its day. It sought selfhood for the "native church" and legitimacy for the new concept of a "native clergy." A bold assault on the impact of colonial depersonalization, it carried its own set of problems.[49] And it met with stiff resistance from the missionaries who repeatedly delayed the organization of local churches. Gustav Warneck warned that the indigenous formula, if applied in a doctrinaire way, could become a mere expression of independence and autonomy that could ruin the whole work of missions.[50] There is much truth in Warneck's argument. But in view of his own inability to extricate missions fully from colonial ethnocentrism, one wonders how much of his thinking was motivated by his genuine fears for the church and how much by a colonialist ideology that pled for transition time for the missionary churches to move to full selfhood. Does colonialism in its deprecation of full

[48]Geoffrey Moorhouse, *The Missionaries* (Philadelphia: Lippincott, 1973), 135.

[49]For some excellent analyses of the assets and liabilities of the indigenous church formula, consult Charles H. Kraft and Tom N. Wisley, eds., *Readings in Dynamic Indigeneity* (Pasadena: William Carey Library, 1979), 15–86.

[50]Ibid., 17–18.

humanity for anyone other than the colonizer ever yield full maturity for the colonized?

Dichotomizing

Dichotomizing also bound anthropologist, theologian, and missionary together in Consciousness One. All three ended up isolating the person as a religious being from the person as a whole. The anthropologist did it by treating religion as irrational aberration. Little attention was paid to the peoples' own explanations of their activities. Anthropology was a search for truth. But truth in its central significance had little to do with religion.

Even in his methodology the anthropologist dichotomized. People became dehumanized objects of study. Research aimed at objective, value-free judgments. In Australia, Europeans conducted aborigine hunts and slaughtered the tribespeople in order to possess their land. The anthropologist denied help to those in need and simply hoped that "a better knowledge of [anthropology's] deductions and principles would have instilled some feelings of prudence and pity into the murderers."[51]

The evangelical theologians dichotomized in another direction. They had been molded by the same commitment to the primacy of reason that motivated the anthropologist. But instead of polarizing reason and religion they paired the two together. All too frequently they understood the image of God in man as mankind's rational capacities. And the end result was dichotomizing of another sort—not between reason and religion, but between mankind's essence as image of God and the reduction of that image to the rational. The image of God was reduced to an attribute— it was no longer seen as the essence of peoplehood. Again, a holistic view of persons was not possible.

The missionaries followed in that same spirit. They could use

[51]Hiebert, "Missions and Anthropology," 168.

the same terms the anthropologists had coined—primitive man, irrational man, savage. And, like the anthropologists, they meant more than simply "gentile," "the natural person without Christ." They meant "irrational man." The current term "primal religion" is not much of an improvement. The missionary's goal became the recovery of that rationality and thus the recovery of the reductionistic *imago Dei*.

The missionary dichotomized in methodology as well. The theologians had created a distinction between natural and supernatural in the battle against the deists of the eighteenth century. It was ultimately a distinction intended to preserve the uniqueness of the supernatural from displacement by rational, natural theology. But it functioned also to dichotomize the two realms into rational and superrational. In the mission field, it often led to a missionary distinction between the "essence" of people, their supernatural, superrational character, and the "accidents" or cultural forms in which that essence was imprisoned. Holding to this dichotomy, the missionary could become oblivious to the tremendous effect the gospel might have on culture, carefully watching only for changes in the more openly and flagrantly religious forms of culture—ancestor worship, for example, or idolatry. The dichotomizing abstracted the gospel from culture's specific human shapes.

Still another effect of this dichotomizing was felt on the mission field. The rational core of the gospel, the "gospel essence," was seen as untouched by human cultural forms. It would remain the same in its superrational form. The missionary task then was a simple one. The gospel message was reduced to the simplistic task of translating from the biblical forms into the cultural forms, from Hebrew and Greek to Kikuyu and Korean.

A Static View of Culture

A static view of culture also bound the various participants together. Anthropology in Consciousness One was still an armchair science. It was deeply rooted in the rationalist mentality of the eighteenth century. More deductive than inductive, it viewed society as a static organ. It did not yet speak of "primitive cultures" but of "primitive culture." Culture had a monolithic character, even within a developmentalist framework. Tribalism, as examined by Durkheim, had a static structure, as if it had no capacity for change. Even diffusionism operated from this perspective. Culture contact was perceived in terms of culture clash, a powerful society from outside crashing against a static or passive one. The static culture thus disintegrates under the impact and the intruder stands alone. Culture contact was interpreted as exchange, not assimilation.

Evangelical theology also approached culture as an armchair science. Its monocultural world had no tools to do otherwise. It understood itself as a rational search for propositional theorems. And this minimized the possibility of allowing any meaningful place to the reality of cultures as contexts. Theology was done from the point of view of traditional metaphysical philosophy. And that locked theology into both the strengths and the weaknesses of philosophical attempts to describe cultural realities. It created one monolithic ultimate out of what it saw as one monolithic human culture.

The effects of this viewpoint on missionary practice were profound. Colonialist ethnocentrism was already pushing for a one-world culture. This was reinforced by the static view of culture and combined with the early North American evangelical notion that identified the millennial expectations of the kingdom of God with the expansion of English-speaking civilization.[52] The mission station became more than a place of residence for the missionary and of shelter for the new convert. One commentator sees them as "little colonies from the American religious commu-

[52]Charles L. Chaney, *The Birth of Missions in America* (Pasadena: William Carey Library, 1976), 9–47; J. A. DeJong, *As the Waters Cover the Sea. Millennial Expectations in the Rise of Anglo-American Missions, 1640–1810* (Kampen: Kok, 1970), 1–2, 157–58, 228.

nity, designed to practice evangelical ideals in the sight of the heathen."[53] They were to be substitute cultures, intended not simply to penetrate and influence alien societies but to replace them.

Against this background, John Eliot started Christian towns for his North American Indian converts. Against this background, the antimissionary movement of the early twentieth century in China was not simply a protest against missionary indifference or insensitivity to Chinese culture; it was in a sense an implicit protest against the early missionaries' views of culture as a static essence, which made Christianity appear to be a Western form of culture alien to the Chinese culture, rather than a religion for China.

The same pattern was repeated, for example, in Ghana. Missionary compounds persisted long after their physical need had expired. They were not necessary simply for the missionary's health; converts also made their home there. And when the compound was vacated by the missionary, the national successor occupied it. The compounds represented more than even a kind of cultural triumphalism. The Akan people called them *Oburoni kurom,* "White man's town." A static view of culture turned them into alternative views of society and culture. Becoming a Christian for the Akan people became a physical, cultural act, involving the bodily removal of one's person from the heathen to the Christian town, from the heathen culture to the Western, Christian culture.[54]

A static view of culture produced a structural foreignness to the Christian's substitute culture. In Ghana the missionaries ignored lineage concepts—the social organization in traditional religion—and introduced the church and the school as organiza-

[53]Clifton L. Phillips, *Protestant America and the Pagan World: The First Half Century of the American Board of Commissioners for Foreign Missions, 1810–1860* (Cambridge, Mass.: East Asian Research Center, Harvard University Press, 1969), 244.

[54]Harris W. Mobley, *The Ghanaian's Image of the Missionary* (Leiden: Brill, 1970), 73–80.

tions for worship. Moreover, the missionaries tabooed the recurrent events of the lineage rites of passage, ceremonials, participation in state functions, and marriage forms. Western forms of marriage and the family were made compulsory. Material objects used in traditional society were rejected. The missionary substituted the institutions of Western Christianity. The indigenous arts—music, drumming, dance, architecture—were forbidden. A Western organization with all its paraphernalia was imposed upon the societies.[55]

Passivity

Passivity was another by-product of Consciousness One. Anthropology looked at a static world from the armchair. Mankind had been depersonalized into an object of study, and a rather "quaint" object of study at that. The absence of fieldwork pushed that objectifying process one step further. The anthropologist investigated mankind in books and not in the flesh. Colonialism's impact allowed the anthropologist to look more down the nose than through the eyes. All of this reduced humanity's role in culture to a passive one. Durkheim's emphasis on society reduced the role of personality even further. Developmentalism focused its interest on such a broad picture that the personality of "primitive man" was lost in the absorbing pattern of human society.

Evangelical theology typified this passivity from another direction. Pietistic revivalism concentrated on the individual in its message of redemption. But even here the focus was on the individual *as a recipient of blessing*. Whether Calvinist or Arminian, the evangelical focus was on the benefits of redemption. What does Christ do *for us?* The structures of salvation and its sequences became molded into logical patterns whose object was mankind as receiver. Justification, adoption, and sanctification lost their

[55]Ibid., 119.

biblical sense of eschatological history, their reference to the sweep of God's dramatic history in the coming and coming again of Christ. The center of their reference became individualized by the push of Western individualism. And in the process the global dimensions of the gospel were reduced to "Jesus loves me," and the divine initiative of grace was translated into mankind-as-passive-recipients.

The effects of this on missionary methodology were far-reaching. Colonialism helped us to create a "double standard" that divided home from foreign missions, "sending church" from "receiving church." "The field which is the world" became reduced to "everywhere outside Europe and North America." And the "Third World" was always the "receiving" world. The missionary struggled with the question whether and when a native clergy should be formed. And behind that struggle was more than concern over theological adolescence. There was a hidden assumption of the gospel recipient as a passive agent, as someone who needed us by virtue of his or her very nature as receiver.

Why else has the call for Third World churches to participate in world missions delayed so long? Why did the Ugandan pastors I challenged two years ago to send foreign missionaries from their churches laugh when I made the suggestion to them? Why? Because they had learned to accept their passive role as Christians. Why else did Henry Venn experience so much difficulty in promoting his idea of an "indigenous church"? Why was the three-self formula (the church as self-supporting, self-propagating, and self-governing) needed in the first place?

It was in part the beginning of an assault on this presupposition of "primitive man" as a passive agent who needed "us." There is no sense of self-respect in someone who perceives himself or herself always as a passive recipient. Behind the current clamor of the Third World church for its own theological integrity and creativity lies in part a protest against a self-image imposed in the past by Consciousness One and a call for theological resistance.

Chapter Three

Consciousness Two

SUMMARY

In the first half of the twentieth century a new mentality arose to refocus and adjust the old agenda—Consciousness Two. A growing awareness of the multiplicity of cultures and a movement away from generalizations and universals, from rationalism to the human subsconscious, left anthropology in a less antagonistic mood toward religion and its study. Functionalism arose to claim at least a functional legitimacy for religion. The development of field work as a technique underlined the diversity of human cultures in which religion operated. Language studies explored the interrelationships between language and human cultures.

The rise of applied anthropology during this time opened the door to its ready appropriation by missions. But evangelical theology's response was one of retrenchment. The isolation of missions from theological concerns prevented mission discussions, still oriented toward methodological strategy, from breaking down this isolationism. No evangelical theology of cultures was formulated.

All of this produced significant modifications in the characteristics of Consciousness One. They were significant enough to speak of a new mentality but not significant enough to overcome old problems. There is a shift from depersonalization—but toward functionism. The indigenization discussions in missions may reflect this. Culture as a bounded, functional set is "Christianized" by replacing one computerized unit (music, architecture, forms of rule and leadership) by others more functionally oriented to the Scriptures.

There was also movement away from dichotomizing toward particularizing. Evangelical missions may not have escaped this problem either. Religion, among some missionary anthropologists, still sounds like only one aspect in culture rather than the integrating center of cultures. Similarly, Consciousness Two rejected a static view of culture but replaced it with an equally static plurality of cultures. And missions, for this reason, may currently be having trouble recognizing the legitimacy of a black theology or an African theology.

Finally, Consciousness Two turned its back on passivity and moved toward determinism. Missions may be seeing the fruits of that shift in Third World antagonism to manipulation by Western money and in calls for moratorium. Mission controls are not easily loosened in areas where the believer still is seen as the "object" of missions.

Chapter Three

Consciousness Two

Waves of change engulfed the relationship between anthropology and theology, especially during the first half of the twentieth century, waves that collided with the wave of Consciousness One. They overlapped. There was conflict and tension. And out of this arose a new model of perception—what we are calling Consciousness Two. Consciousness One had left us commonalities but no resolution. In Consciousness Two the original problems remained—only new dimensions were now added to complicate our life.

THE REVISED AGENDA

What does it mean to be human? The question remained, complicated increasingly by a wealth of field data and new paradigms. Consciousness One asked, In what way are people one? Consciousness Two added, How do we relate this to the variety of human societies and cultures? "Culture" became "cultures." Exceptions multiplied as fast as the previous generalizations. Functionalism arose as a new model for thinking. It gave up the old search for universals and origins. All we can wrestle with now are the particulars: What are they? How do they function in society?

Adding to the new dimensions of the old dilemma was the disappearance of the old foundations. The presuppositional underpinnings of the original tensions were now being temporarily dropped. The developmental conception had been built on what some might call irrational rationalism. The scientific pendulum now swung over to a rationalistic irrationalism. Rudolf Otto would describe it in terms of the numinous, the *mysterium*. Freud and Jung would look for the irrational in the human subconscious and its religion-making propensities. Mircea Eliade would join in rebuking the rationalism of the past, and its quest for a logical cause. "Religion is a very complex phenomenon," he would tell us; it is "first of all, an experience *sui generis,* incited by man's encounter with the sacred."[1]

What is the nature of religion? scholars asked once more. The dichotomizing of Consciousness One was questioned. Diffusionism devastated evolutionism as a dominant possibility for explaining religious development, but its own generalizations were no substitute. Nationalism added its strength to the assault on developmentalism; combined with diffusionism, it called for more attention "to questions concerning individual religious traditions, each in its uniqueness."[2] Consciousness One had placed in the foreground questions of "religion-as-such." Consciousness Two saw religion not as a singular but as a plural.

Durkheim's emphasis on the formative place of society in the structure of religion fostered this shift. His notions of social solidarity were picked up in the new sounds of functionalism. The

---

[1]Mircea Eliade, *The Quest. History and Meaning in Religion* (Chicago: University of Chicago Press, 1975), 24–25.

[2]Eric Sharpe, *Comparative Religion. A History* (London: Duckworth, 1975), 174.

functionalist saw social structures as basic to the creation of human categories. How did mankind function in the diversity of social structures? What functional arrangements did they create to maintain an orderly social life? Here functionalists like Malinowski and Radcliffe-Brown turned to religion. Religion was a functional response of mankind to one of society's essential needs. In Consciousness One, religion was regarded as a bastard child. Consciousness Two found a home for it.

What is the nature of culture? Consciousness One left us with a monolithic, static view of culture. Now that perspective was assaulted by the plethora of human cultures in all their diversity. The early stages of Consciousness Two asked, How will we explain this diversity? The later stages added still another question: How will we explain the phenomenon of change in culture? Out of this interest in cultural diversity and change came a new phase of anthropology especially important for missions. We refer to applied anthropology.

Applied anthropology was born in the 1930s, passed through adolescence in the 1940s, and faced the threat of premature old age by the 1950s. Until the 1930s, most anthropologists had viewed the study of "primitive" societies as a key to comprehending modern societies. Then, along came Robert Redfield to study folklore in a contemporary Mexican village. The Western Electric Company of Chicago hired a Harvard University anthropologist, Lloyd Warner, to find the "reasons behind fatigue" among its factory workers. The stage was set. Suddenly factory workers in Chicago had become the object of study, rather than the Trobriand Islanders.[3] Concern with contemporary problems began to increase. Anthropology started looking for links with other behavioral sciences—especially with sociology, social psychology,

[3]William L. Partridge and Elizabeth M. Eddy, "The Development of Applied Anthropology in America," in *Applied Anthropology in America,* ed. E. M. Eddy and W. L. Partridge (New York: Columbia University Press, 1978), 15–18.

and psychology. Functionalism was adding a new dimension or extension to anthropology, which was becoming also a science of human relations and interactions within social groups.

Government now added financial support to the movement. In the 1930s the Indian Bureau of the U.S. government began to employ anthropologists to study the American Indian and to make policy recommendations. But the real change came during World War II. Anthropologists were hired to train officers for military duty overseas. They advised on public policy and technical assistance programs. In 1941 the Society of Applied Anthropology was formed. The upstart had become part of the establishment.

The postwar years were hard on this fledgling discipline. Research money from the government began to dry up in the 1950s. There was less need for the anthropologist. Applied anthropology can be done, after all, only if somebody is going to apply it. It has to have a consumer.

But applied anthropology left its mark. It moved anthropology from the theoretical realm into the practical arena of contemporary human life. It helped to shift the focus of concern from traditional, geographically bounded cultures to contemporary, macrocosmic society. It opened up new areas of research for anthropology—economics, technology, politics, and social change on a macro and even a mini-micro scale. It placed on the agenda the analysis of social systems in terms of their interdependence.

What is the nature of language? was still being asked in the Consciousness Two mindset. Consciousness One had centered many of its language questions on the subject of origins: What were the circumstances that caused man to need and develop language? Did language come from some psychological necessity, from the innate need for vocal and nonvocal forms of self-expression? Or did it come from sociological need, the demands of social contact and cooperation? Is thought possible without language? Or is thought in essence a linguistic phenomenon? Is thinking dependent on speaking?[4]

Consciousness Two saw the fruitlessness of that agenda. A new awareness of the world's languages was growing rapidly. And the scholar could no longer presuppose the static view of language and culture. Comparative linguistics was said to be an overemphasis on languages written in the past. It ignored languages spoken today. It ignored also the dynamic character of language. The new agenda for language came from the Swiss linguist Ferdinand de Saussure (1857–1913). His *Course in General Linguistics* (1915) was likened to a Copernican revolution in the subject. Historically, de Saussure opened up three new areas of investigation, each with different repercussions.

In the first place, he retained an earlier interest in the history of language. But he succeeded in limiting it to the question of development without reducing it to a search for the origins of that development. He did this by formalizing the two fundamental dimensions of linguistic study: the synchronic and diachronic dimensions. From the synchronic perspective, languages are seen as self-contained systems of communication at a given point in time. The diachronic dimension is the historical side of language study, a look at language in terms of its chronological development and history. Each has its own methods and principles. Each is essential to language study.

Second, he reinterpreted the role of society in the shaping of language. He distinguished between what he called *langue* and *parole,* terms that remain in use today. *Parole* is a reference to the actual phenomena or data of linguistics, the brute facts of utterance. *Langue* refers to the social context of communication; it is the lexicon, grammar, and phonology implanted in each person by his or her upbringing in society. On the basis of *langue* one

[4] J. O. Brew, ed., *One Hundred Years of Anthropology* (Cambridge, Mass.: Harvard University Press, 1968), 164–65.

speaks and understands his language. De Saussure emphasized the importance of *langue* over *parole,* revealing Durkheim's influence.

Third, he argued that any *langue* must be described synchronically. It is a system of interrelated elements—sociolexical, sociogrammatical, and socio-phonological. It is not an aggregate, a collection, of self-sufficient entities. Linguistic terms are to be defined relative to one another, not absolutely.

This structural approach to language, which ran parallel to the development of functionalism in other areas, underlies virtually the whole of modern linguistics. It sees language as finding its meaning in functional service to the needs of the social community, providing a vital avenue of communication within the social context. Communication is in fact impossible, it argues, without this societal character of language.

ANTHROPOLOGY'S NEW MOOD: REVISION

Consciousness One was a mentality of conflict between anthropology and theology. Anthropology now moved toward modifications that created a new wave, Consciousness Two. The mood became one of revisionism rather than toe-to-toe confrontation.

Two figures stand at the crossroads of this anthropological transition to revisionism: Rudolf Otto and Franz Boas. Neither developed a school, nor are there any theories attached to their names. But they signaled the beginnings of new approaches.

Several things isolated Rudolf Otto (1869–1937) from continuity with any of the movements we are sketching. He was not an anthropologist but a theologian. Consciousness One had seen man's central religious experience in rational terms. Otto created a new vocabulary that would be used to reinforce the break with that mindset. Terms like *mysterium tremendum, majestas, das Ganz Andere* (the wholly Other) were his contribution.

It is hard to fit Otto into any specific category. Eliade links him with the psychological school of Freud and Jung,[5] but the link is tenuous. With the psychological school, he stressed the nonrational character of religious experience. But unlike Freud, he did not seek to discredit the religious experience by tying it to the nonrational. Others have related him to phenomenology and the work of van der Leeuw.[6] But again there are differences. Otto's work is more philosophically oriented than phenomenology. And the interests of religious phenomenology are more centered in a theoretical exposition of methodology than Otto was. He remained transitional.

Otto, in harmony with Consciousness Two, sought for some legitimacy to the cultural experience of religion. He found it in what he called the a priori category that defined religion: the idea of the "holy," the numinous.

He saw two aspects to the numinous. First, it is the *mysterium tremendum,* a fear-and-trembling-arousing mystery. It includes everything that induces awe and terror in man: the strangeness and fearfulness, the majesty, the wrath and the energy of God. It is that which points to the divine as "the Wholly Other." At the same time, it is *fascinans,* fascinating. It is something uniquely attractive, something that confers blessing. These two aspects produce two reactions in mankind. Humanity feels itself at one-and-the-same time mysteriously repelled and mysteriously attracted. Thus, in the deity wrath and grace are revealed side by side. Here is the "real, innermost essence," without which we would not be religious at all. Here is the essential element of all piety, the "creature feeling." It is the "experience of sinking down and vanishing in one's own nothingness in the face of what is wholly superior to every creature."[7]

---

[5]Eliade, *The Quest,* 23.

[6]J. van Baal, *Symbols for Communication. An Introduction to the Anthropological Study of Religion* (Assen: Van Gorcum, 1971), 89.

[7]Heinz Zahrnt, *The Question of God* (New York: Harcourt, Brace and Javonovich, 1966), 49.

Otto's ideas "made a more enduring impact on the Western, especially German, cultivated public than on historians of religion proper or theologians"[8] (or anthropologists). Nevertheless, they did achieve a number of significant things as far as the transition to Consciousness Two was concerned. Otto's definition of religion as an irreducible category *sui generis* was unacceptable. But it made it possible to study religion as more than merely an error that had to be explained. It placed religion back into human culture as a normal human experience. It allowed academic scholarship to use intuitive as well as rational faculties in the analysis of religion.[9] It helped to open the way for research into religion as a ceremony of the personality and the subconscious.

The other transitional figure was Franz Boas (1858–1942). He reigned as professor of anthropology at Columbia University from 1896 till his death in 1942. Among his students were practically all the anthropologists of significance between the two world wars—Kroeber, Goldenweiser, Lowie, Sapir, Herskovits, Mead, Underhill, Benedict. Yet there was no Boasian school that would link him with the new paradigms of Consciousness Two. And there are no theories closely associated with his name.

He did not belong to Consciousness One. He was an antievolutionist even during the heyday of developmental optimism. He saw the major error of developmentalism in its assumption that cultural similarities always arose from the same causes. That assumption, he argued, no one had ever bothered to prove. At the same time he spurned the functionalist model that was growing in popularity during his teaching career. He criticized it because of its presumed antihistorical bias.[10] In fact, he showed an extreme dislike of any theory.

[8]Eliade, *The Quest,* 23.

[9]Jacques Waardenburg, *Classical Approaches to the Study of Religion: Aims, Methods and Theories of Research* (The Hague: Mouton, 1973), 1:60.

[10]Annemarie De Waal Malefijt, *Images of Man* (New York: Knopf, 1974), 230–31.

How then was he a transitional figure? What were his links with Consciousness Two? Boas shifted attention from the general idea of "culture" to the reality that every society possesses its own culture. Each culture is an integrated way of life, not merely an aggregate of separate elements. There are no "higher" and "lower" cultures, only integrated wholes. In keeping with this, he became the apostle of anthropological field work. He did not originate the practice. But he refined it, he advocated it. And he accomplished more in terms of collecting vast amounts of data than almost anyone else. He set the whole tone for Consciousness Two in his insistence on careful and precise observation.

ANTHROPOLOGICAL AND THEOLOGICAL CONCERNS IN CONSCIOUSNESS TWO

How did Consciousness Two deal with the four basic questions: What is the nature of man? What is the nature of religion? What is the nature of culture? What is the nature of language?

What Is the Nature of Man?

In Consciousness Two, at least two paradigms circulated in response to this question—the psychological paradigm and functionalism.

The psychological paradigm exploded onto the anthropological scene in 1915 with Freud's book *Totem and Taboo*. The book had many links with Consciousness One. It focused on the problem of religious origins. It drew heavily on the work of men like Robertson Smith and James Frazer. It made explicit comparisons between "primitive" peoples and modern man.

At the same time, Freud's model does not fit into a Consciousness Two paradigm. Freud was not even an anthropologist. Indeed, the subtitle alone—*Resemblances between the Psychic*

Life of Savages and Neurotics—would have been enough to infuriate Consciousness Two anthropologists.

Then there were the ideas in the book, rejected time and again by anthropologists. Freud posited the existence of a primal horde. The leader, the oldest male, assumed exclusive sexual rights over all females in the group. Frustrated, the sons murdered and ate their father. But overcome by guilt afterward, they decided to obey his commands and abstain from sexual intercourse with their mothers and sisters. A totem animal is chosen as a symbolic father substitute. And the males declare that it must be protected during the year, to be consumed only on ritual occasions. These ritual totem meals reenact the original deed and reenforce their self-imposed incest prohibitions. All culture originates from this sacrificial meal.

The roof fell in on Freud. Boas said the theory was one-sided and could do nothing to advance understanding of cultural development.[11] Malinowski, the functionalist, looked at the Trobriand Islanders to test the supposed universality of the Oedipus complex. He found the love-hate sentiments directed toward maternal uncles rather than fathers and incestuous wishes aimed at sisters rather than mothers. "A notable confirmation" of the major thesis, he decided—but the Oedipus complex was certainly not universal. No one was particularly happy with the Viennese thinker's thesis.

What then did Freud give to Consciousness Two? A new way to approach humanity and religion. Freud had virtually discovered the uncharted realm of the subconscious. The psychological dimensions of culture and humanity could no longer be ignored, in spite of Freud's reductionism. Freud had said that personality molds culture. Now anthropological fieldwork set out to test that thesis. Margaret Mead began her great career with a study of sexual patterns among adolescents in Samoa. Was the rebellion of Western adolescents a product of their sexual drives or a result of

[11]Franz Boas, *Race, Language and Culture* (New York: Macmillan, 1940), 288–89.

culture? Samoan children were her basis for comparison. Freud lost out. Human nature is not rigid and unyielding. The biophysiological determinism of psychoanalytic theory would not cut the Samoan mustard.[12]

More positive direction came from Edward Sapir. He saw the emphasis on the psychical as a corrective to the evolutionary mechanism of the past. People were not robots carrying out the rules of their culture. Culture was not the simple sum of patterns of behavior. Ruth Benedict's classic *Patterns of Culture* (1934) reinforced the new direction. Consciousness Two was off and running.

Carl Gustav Jung (1875–1961) added a new dimension to the approach. Freud had dismissed religion as a neurosis. Jung affirmed its place as a key to a vital understanding of mankind. In the ferment of growing interest in mythology, his emphasis on religious symbolism and myth helped open other doors. Myth, to Jung, was the intermediate stage between consciousness and the unconscious. From the unconscious, man draws on the archetypes and verbalizes them into the great images and symbols of myth. They lead the individual out of time into timelessness.

The influence of Jung in anthropology was widespread. Using Jung's ideas, Joseph Campbell attempted a total interpretation of world mythology.[13] Much less doctrinaire and more influential has been the work of Mircea Eliade (b. 1907). From Jung he has drawn the ideas of a collective unconscious and of religious experience as an integrating, goal-providing function of the self. The study of the history of religions for him was not simply a historical discipline. It was the study of man as a living symbol, a "metapsychoanalysis." Man must be understood as a myth—making creature. Man seeks meaning in a "nostalgia for eternity," a mystical equivalent to a journey back to origins, *illo tempore,* to

[12]Margaret Mead, *Coming of Age in Samoa* (New York: Morrow, 1928).

[13]Joseph Campbell, *Creative Mythology* (New York: Viking Press, 1968).

the Golden Time. "Archaic man only exists, only lives in being, by a continual process of negating concrete time and space; he constitutes his world, his 'cosmos,' by a dialectic of repetition."[14] Existence is continually re-created in the image of its archetypal model.

Theology listened carefully to these new sounds. Pastoral psychology as a theological discipline emerged from Freud's discovery of what he called "unconscious" psychical processes. The shift from the rationalism of Consciousness One to the irrationalism of Consciousness Two had wide-ranging effects in various areas. Paul Tillich, for example, praised Otto and his philosophy of revelation. Revelation, no longer seen as a supernaturalistic invasion, has become the intuition of the mysterious at the boundary line of natural experience.[15] Tillich saw those intuitions as being intimately linked with discussions of symbol and myth. Among contemporary theologians, Tillich interacted deeply with psychology's agenda. Myth became the language of man and the language of ultimate concern. And that language is always the language of symbols. The only univocal statement man can make is that God is being itself. Everything else is symbolic. To assign reality to a mere symbol is to make it ultimate. And that is idolatry.

Existential theology echoes with the concerns of psychological anthropology. Tillich's idea of God as the ground of being is not abstract logical ontology. Talking about being is talking about human significance. It is talking about anxiety and finitude, about the shock of possible nonbeing. It is talking about the wonder of being that this shock awakens. The central points in all this discussion have a psychical tilt to them—estrangement, the healing of conflict, the "depth" dimension.

[14]Thomas Altizer, *Mircea Eliade and the Dialectic of the Sacred* (Philadelphia: Westminster, 1963), 274.

[15]Paul Tillich, *The Religious Situation* (New York: Holt, 1932), 178–79.

Another paradigm arose that was much more influential in the area of anthropology. Its scope was larger, and it was rooted more deeply in anthropology than in other disciplines. It offered Consciousness Two a model that was comprehensive and far-reaching. In a real sense, it might almost be called the dominating thrust of Consciousness Two from the 1920s on. The model was functionalism, and the leading names associated with it are those of Bronislaw Malinowski (1881–1942) and A. R. Radcliffe-Brown (1882–1955). Malinowski's dominance lasted roughly from 1924 to 1938. It was superseded by a sociological wave, led by Radcliffe-Brown, that carried into the 1940s.[16] For the sake of the larger picture I put the two men together. They themselves were far from happy bedfellows.

At the core of functionalism was man, viewed in terms of his biological and psychological needs. Tylor had placed his emphasis on man as a rational creature. Social order and cohesion, cultural institutions, and human behavior basically flowed out of mankind's rational faculties or lack of them. For Malinowski, they were produced by a humanity governed by bioemotional tendencies or forces. Man was seen as essentially a biological and emotional creature, not as a rational one.[17] Thus, for example, primitive man has an intense fear of death, and from that emotional fear comes a theory of immortality. The theory is neither a primitive philosophical doctrine nor an expression of rational thought. It is the expression of "the deepest emotional fact of human nature, the desire for life." Similarly, magic is an institutionalized manifestation of a spontaneous emotional response in people. Magic arises when there is a gap in knowledge. Anxieties, fears, and hopes induce an emotional tension. And that tension drives us to the activity of magic. Science is based on more

---

[16]Adam Kuper, *Anthropologists and Anthropology* (New York: Pica, 1974), 92.

[17]Elvin Hatch, *Theories of Man and Culture* (New York: Columbia University Press, 1973), 298.

or less intellectual processes; magic, on emotion. The mainsprings of behavior are shrouded in emotion.[18]

What Is the Nature of Culture?

Out of these convictions, Malinowski and functionalism approached the topic of culture. Malinowski saw society as an integral whole. He defined culture as a system of objects, activities, and attitudes in which every part exists as a means to an end. In these cultural schemas everything has its place. And that place is dictated by the *individual's* "instrumental needs." Here he diverged increasingly from Radcliffe-Brown, who placed stronger emphasis on the social origins of need.

His focus, and that of Radcliffe-Brown, remained, however, on the functional character of human response. All standardized cultural forms have positive functions. "In every type of civilization, every custom, material object, idea and belief fulfills some vital function, has some task to accomplish, represents an indispensable part within a working whole."[19] Thus, out of the basic biological need for reproduction was said to emerge the cultural function of kinship. The need for relaxation is mirrored in the function of play and repose. Safety is a basic biological need; protection is the cultural response. Hunger must be satisfied, so man, in cultural response, makes his cooking utensils and builds his MacDonalds and Taco Bells. He does not consume his food alone but shares it with others. And he develops ritual attitudes toward this communal consumption. His fire, his implements, and his rituals relate culturally to the satisfaction of primary biological and psychological needs.

Malinowski saw this principle as a corollary of the evolutionary viewpoint. The developmental scheme posited nonfunctional cultural survivals from previous stages in the evolutionary process.

[18]Ibid., 302.

[19]Robert D. Baird, *Category Formation and the History of Religions* (The Hague: Mouton, 1971), 61–62.

For Malinowski, these survivals merely pointed to a better adaptation of an institution to its function. Social survivals were customs that supposedly could no longer be explained in terms of their social functions. They could be explained only in terms of their past history. At the same time, as his work progressed, he admitted that he had "grown more and more indifferent to the problem of origins."[20] His focus increasingly was on methodologies.

To these emphases Radcliffe-Brown added Durkheim's notion of social solidarity. His brand of functionalism recognized mankind's social structure as basic to the creation of categories to meet those social needs. How does humanity function in the diversity of social structures? What functional arrangements do people create to maintain an orderly social life? How do belief and ritual work for social integration, for culture as a whole?

In the 1940s and 1950s disillusionment with functionalism grew, partly as a result of the rise of applied anthropology in the United States. The new focus on the here and now forced anthropology to deal with the reality of culture change. Malinowski's functionalism had helped to devastate the old idea of a static culture. But had he put in its place a static concept of structure? What realistic place did functionalism allow the dynamic aspects of social change? Functionalism placed its emphasis on cultural equilibrium; was it essentially a theory of no change rather than a theory of change? Durkheim saw change conflict as basically a form of social *pathology*. Did functionalism, either from the Malinowski or the Radcliffe-Brown side, allow for structural change as a *normal* part of social development, or were the followers of functionalism merely uninterested in change? Or more basically, were they unable to explain it?

Before theology caught up with this problem, however, it had followed the functionalist hints in several directions. Anthro-

---

[20]Kuper, *Anthropologists,* 21.

pology had shifted its concern from the unity of culture to the diversity of cultures. It had begun to specialize in differences. Theology took the same direction. H. H. Rowley commented in 1957 that "when the writer began his theological studies it would have seemed a hazardous thing to announce a course of lectures on the Unity of the Bible."[21] Studies focused on the fragmentation and splintering of the Biblical message into countless sources, traditions, and redactions. In 1936, C. H. Dodd was calling in agony for a "centripetal movement to succeed the centrifugal."[22] In Old Testament studies, scholars searched for the antithesis between the legal and the prophetic books, between priestly and prophetic religion. The New Testament research picture was no different. Scholars looked for gaps between the religion of the Gospels and that of the Pauline epistles. Even within the Gospels, the historical Jesus was set over against the Christ of faith. The bonds between the two Testaments were also being investigated and severed. Jesus was no longer the fulfillment of Old Testament hopes. He had become the setter-aside of the Old Testament faith. The preacher came to be at a loss to know what to do with the Old Testament. Too frequently it was ignored.

On the level of methodology, the influence of functionalism was even stronger. Radcliffe-Brown had underlined the sociological dimensions of culture that Durkheim had set forth before him. Max Weber (1864–1920) became the bridge that crossed over the chasm between sociology and the Old Testament.[23] He saw the early history of the Israelites as an expression of a tension over the separate economic interests of the seminomadic clans on the one hand and the settled agricultural clans on the other. These two basically different groups united on occasion for military purposes.

[21]H. H. Rowley, *The Unity of the Bible* (New York: Meridian, 1957), 15.

[22]Brevard Childs, *Biblical Theology in Crisis* (Philadelphia: Westminster, 1970), 36.

[23]Herbert F. Hahn, *The Old Testament in Modern Research* (Philadelphia: Fortress, 1966), 159ff.

The idea that brought them together was the covenant. Not only did the covenant define Israel's relationship to its God, it also established the political unity of the tribes in the premonarchial period. The confederation of tribes was "a military league united under and with Jahweh, the warrior God of the league, the guarantor of its social institutions, and provider of its material needs."[24]

Without permanent political institutions, Weber continued, the tribal league was united in time of war by a "God-inspired warrior hero." Even after the establishment of the kingship and the rise of autocratic rulers, the tribes yearned for that charismatic leader. As new economic pressures arose, this original social system became submerged but was not forgotten. The old solidarity was lost in the growing tension between a landowning aristocracy and the landless, debt-ridden peasants. Through the prophets came the call for justice and humaneness in the ruling classes' treatment of the poor and helpless. That ethical element had once been a reality in the old covenant relationship. The prophets reemphasized it as the central element.

Weber's ideas are mirrored in the theories of Albrecht Alt and Martin Noth. Alt too saw a wide difference between the political and social structure of the Palestinean peoples and those of Transjordan in the eleventh century B.C. He contrasted these with what he called the "charismatic" leadership of Israel during the period of the Judges. The tribal organization of Israel consisted of twelve "clan groups" bound together in an amphictyony. And the basis for this social organization was the covenant ideal. Alt was reinforced by Martin Noth in his conclusions. Sociology was being used to capture the "essence" of the Old Testament religious structure. The prophets became sociological pioneers, hammering out a higher meaning for the egalitarian ethics of the earlier nomadic society. This sociological interpretation added one more

---

[24]Quoted in Hahn, *Old Testament*, 162.

blow to the Wellhausen assumptions that rejected the antiquity of the basic principles of Israel's religion.[25]

Rogerson comments that the theory of the amphictyony in Israel has come under recent attack. The bulk of that attack has been based on the argument that the Old Testament itself lacks evidence that there ever was an Israelite amphictyony on the Greek model as assumed by scholarship.[26] Why then has it become such a popular resort of research? Could part of the answer lie in the thesis we are seeking to point to now—the failure of Old Testament scholars to analyze carefully borrowed anthropological concepts such as tribe and kin relations? Rogerson suggests that there is a need "to examine all the traditions about tribes and genealogies, etc., in the Old Testament in the light of anthropology."[27] That suggestion is helpful. But we must add another. There is also a need to be wary of the anthropological theories of kinship and tribe that shape our understanding of the biblical data concerning kinship and tribe. Structural functionalism does not always serve us well.

What Is the Nature of Religion?

Two models have shaped Consciousness Two's answer to the question of religion: functionalism and phenomenology. The former we have already touched on. Malinowski made no exception to the functional service of all standardized cultural forms—including religion. Religion was not something one looked forward to discarding culturally à la Freud or Frazer. It was a significant part of the cultural worldview and integral to it. One could not understand human cultures, even primitive cultures, without understanding their religious dimensions.

But what is the functional dimension of religion? According

---

[25]Martin Noth, *History of Israel* (London: Black, 1960), 85–108.

[26]J. W. Rogerson, *Anthropology and the Old Testament* (Atlanta: John Knox, 1979), 91.

[27]Ibid., 101.

to Malinowski, it sacralizes, reinforces, and maintains customary practices and beliefs.[28] In magic we see a specific act intended to achieve concrete and definite ends. The end is attained by the rites themselves. The rites have no higher purpose. While magic is a technique, religion is more complex; psychologically, however, the two are alike.[29] The function of both magic and religion is cathartic. Humanity is faced with life's crises, especially death. In their fear and anxiety they release their tensions and overcome their despair by the performance of religious rites. Magic seeks manipulative control of the forces of nature for personal ends; religion seeks to enter into a communal relation with spiritual beings who are more than impersonal forces. One establishes an I-it relationship, the other an I-Thou relationship.

Phenomenology as a radical alternative to functionalism in religion appeared in 1933, when Gerardus van der Leeuw (1890–1950) published his *Phaenomenologie der Religion* (English translation, *Religion in Essence and Manifestation*, 1938). Others were to add their contributions to the model—Mircea Eliade, George Widengren, William Brede Kristenson, S.G.F. Brandon. But van der Leeuw, building on Husserl, took phenomenology out of the philosophy class and put it on the anthropological map.

With Husserl, he rejected any attempt to reduce the study of religion to the merely psychical or sociobiological or rational. All these efforts were based on naturalistic prejudices, seeking to explain religion by something other than itself. The main task of the phenomenology of religion was to illumine the inner structures of religious phenomena. Religion is a legitimate human property by itself, not to be measured simply by functions. To van der Leeuw, the task of phenomenology was to uncover the timeless essences of religion, to create a typology where those essences might best be evaluated. "Essence" is what "appears" to someone

[28]Bronislaw Malinowski, *Magic, Science and Religion* (New York: Doubleday Anchor, 1948), 54–69.

[29]E. E. Evans-Pritchard, *Theories of Primitive Religion* (London: Oxford University Press, 1965), 39.

in the interplay of subject and object. The religious scientist must seek an eidetic vision, must "transpose himself into his object . . . and re-experience it." From this process of understanding will come "meaning."

Van der Leeuw saw power, the "mana" of primitive religion, as the key to religious meaning. Religion arises at the point where man's own power is met by another Power. "A strange, wholly other power obtrudes into life."[30] The language is strongly reminiscent of Otto. The science of phenomenology cannot grasp this power-in-itself. It is grasped only in the phenomena in which it is experienced. The experience in itself remains intangible, inapprehensible to us.

Van der Leeuw's definition of religion was not well received either in anthropological circles or among his fellow historians of religion. The phenomenologists claimed that they could grasp the essence and the structure of religious phenomena. This gave religion a transhistorical value that sounded too much like a search for Platonic ideals. The functionalists had succeeded in demanding that more attention be paid to religion in terms of observable social complexities, to religion as functional rather than essential. Van der Leeuw, on the other hand, sounded too much like a theologian with his own theological agenda to be acceptable to the anthropologist. He argued that "phenomenology can assist theology to organize facts, to penetrate their sense, to find their essence, before theology is able to evaluate them and use them for its doctrinal conclusions."[31] And no anthropologist was ready to reduce his or her own discipline to a course in theological propadeutics.[32]

But it was the methodology of van der Leeuw, and more specifically his idea of the *epoché,* the suspension of judgment, that had a strong effect on anthropological and religious studies. *Epoché*

[30]Gerardus van der Leeuw, *Religion in Essence and Manifestation* (London: Allen and Unwin, 1938), 681.

[31]Gerardus van der Leeuw, "Confession Scientifique," *Numen* 1 (1954): 13.

[32]Sharpe, *Comparative Religion,* 233.

is more than simply an "intellectual suspension of judgment for the sake of objectivity."[33] To be sure, that is an important part of the concept. The observer of the phenomena is to free himself from private prejudices and preconceptions. One has to take the detached observer's point of view. But there is more involved. One also "brackets" those elements that do not belong to the universal essence. Phenomenology demanded that the study of religion "cannot concern itself with the question of the truth of religion. Phenomenology must begin by accepting as proper objects of study all phenomena that are professed to be religious."[34] One does not seek to explain away the religious phenomenon, nor does one refer it to some transcendental standard. In that sense the study of religion is presuppositionless. It is the work of the "uninterested spectator" who seeks to avoid the dispersion of the "subject" into the multiplicity of the factual course of things.

Did any of these discussions touch theology? That question is hard to answer in terms of specific footnote references. But in terms of general trends there were overlappings. Classical liberalism would have breathed deeply of any atmosphere that focused on the social functionalism of religion. Albrecht Ritschl had already called theologians to a vision of the kingdom of God that had deep socioethical colorations. Much later, in the United States, the social gospel movement would put functional teeth into this tiger of idealistic optimism.

The historicism of Troeltsch had raised questions about the uniqueness of Christianity. Phenomenology would shrink the category of revelation even further. Christianity, to the classic liberal, looked more and more like a creation of human history, one among the other great world religions. "Religion was shown

---

[33]Dean Gilliland, "Phenomenology as Mission Method," *Missiology* 7 (October 1979): 456.

[34]C. J. Bleeker, *The Sacred Bridge* (Leiden: Brill, 1963), 3.

to be, not a creation of the human mind by a rational process, but an uprush from a subliminal region."[35]

The full impact of all this, however, was never felt. Karl Barth's work from the 1920s on slowed the flood. Barth's aim was to break with the structure of liberal theology, a structure that, in the judgment of William Nicholls, had founded everything upon the phenomenology of faith. As such it could be analyzed by the interested nonbeliever in every detail. But that unbeliever could regard it as descriptive of an outlook not shared by the observer. For Barth that was man-centered. It inevitably exalted the inherent religious capacities of man beyond what Barth thought proper or plausible limits.[36] Thus, during the high tide of neoorthodoxy there was little conversation between theology and cultural anthropology. Barth allowed no common world of discourse. Our faith starts with revelation, not naturalized religion.

Barth did not kill phenomenology's impact on theology. Heidegger built a road from phenomenology to existentialism, and people like Tillich and Bultmann have demanded that we follow it. Tillich stated that "theology must apply the phenomenological approach to all its basic concepts." But unlike Husserl and others, he saw this as preliminary to "discussing their truth and actuality."[37] "Pure phenomenology" must yield to a "critical phenomenology." The intuitive-descriptive element must unite with an existential-critical element. According to Bultmann, hermeneutic must study essences revealed in the phenomena of Christianity's past; interpretation looks for the original mythical essences hidden behind New Testament language. But it does more: it reclothes the essences in new language. The essences found by the first-century writer before their conceptualization in language are

[35]John McConnachie, *The Significance of Karl Barth* (London: Hodder and Stoughton, 1931), 16.

[36]William Nicholls, *Systematic and Philosophical Theology* (Baltimore: Penguin, 1969), 92–93.

[37]Paul Tillich, *Systematic Theology,* vol. 1 (Chicago: University of Chicago Press, 1951), 106–7.

reconstructed. Phenomenology rises again in the quest of the new hermeneutic.

What Is the Nature of Language?

In this maelstrom of interest in the function of culture and its social dimensions, the study of language was reshaped into new answers and new questions. De Saussure had started the reconstruction; the United States was to become a center for the follow-up.

Edward Sapir had pioneered in the area of ethnopsychology. Now he turned to language. How does language function as an aid in penetrating the conceptual world of a society? What is the relation between language and the psyche? Until Sapir, language epitomized the model of culture as a structured, conventionalized system of habit. Yet change did occur in language. How could one explain this discrepancy? Sapir did it by questioning the static, passive character of the language model. Language he saw as more than merely some sort of systematic inventory of human, individualized experiences. Language is not a prisoner of humanity. Humanity is a prisoner of language. Our view of reality is an abridged version of the world that has been edited by our language. "Human beings do not live in the objective world alone, nor alone in the world of social activity as ordinarily understood, but are very much at the mercy of the particular language which has become the medium of expression for their society."[38] The worlds in which different societies live are distinct worlds, not merely the same world with different labels attached. Language, which was now seen as also a self-contained, creative symbolic organization, makes them distinct.

Drawing on Sapir's ideas, Benjamin Whorf (1897–1941) reinforced the idea through an intensive study of the Hopi

[38]Edward Sapir, "The Status of Linguistics as a Science," *Language* 5 (1929); 209.

language. He saw our verbal labels as reflecting modes of perception. An English speaker views a field of corn and comments, "That corn was planted in May, is now two feet tall, and will be ready for harvest in September." The Hopi speaker by contrast has no verbal tenses, no past, present, or future. He sees only corn advancing toward fruition.

The Sapir-Whorf hypothesis continues to stir discussion among anthropologists. There are still unanswered questions. It is extremely difficult to generalize about an entire culture's habits of thought. And it is equally difficult then to prove that they are caused by language.[39] Whorf, some suggest, has overemphasized one point: that language programs us to think only along certain prescribed lines, closing off alternative ways of looking at the world.

But after the corrective and qualifying statements are made, linguistics and anthropology have been left with an exciting new way of understanding culture and the process of understanding. There is a profound interrelation between language and culture. A people's language does provide a map of their culture. It tells us what each culture considers important and what it sees as trivial.

The impact of Sapir's work on theology was a longer time in coming than that of almost any of the other models we have studied till now. The traditional lines of Consciousness One were enshrined and went unchallenged in the lexical works of theology in the early twentieth century, in the attempts to draw inferences about the distinctive thought of a people, for example, "Hebrew thought" or "Greek thought." The methodological procedure of Kittel's *Theological Dictionary of the New Testament* captures the frustrations of the delay. It seeks to be a "concept-history" but is in practice a dictionary of words. It seeks to find dynamic meanings by encapsulizing concepts into etymological histories

[39]Fred Plog and Daniel Bates, *Cultural Anthropology* (New York: Knopf, 1976), 87.

and reducing meaning levels of language to verbal symbols cut loose from their cultural moorings.

It was the missionary who tried to help theology catch up at this point. The contributions of Sapir and Whorf were mediated through missionary linguists such as Eugene Nida and William Wonderly. Evangelical study programs like the Summer Institute of Linguistics, the pioneering work of Wycliffe Bible Translators, tried to force theology on one level to grapple with the relationships between language and culture. The task of Bible translation into non-Western languages revealed the utter impossibility of leaving language wedded simply to the idea of logical, historico-grammatical correspondence. Nida sounded the message loud and clear: "Words do not carry with them all the meanings which they may have in other sets of co-occurences."[40] He called for the use of field semantics in biblical lexicography: "Critical studies of meaning must be based primarily upon the analysis of related meanings of different words, not upon the different meanings of single words."[41]

Even at this level, however, I do not yet see radical progress. Extensive discussions about the value of various English-language Bible translations still betray antiquated ideas of language and its usage. Some of this left-over Consciousness One mentality may explain also the negative reactions of the Christian community to Charles Kraft's usage of these models for theologizing. This may come in large part from the cultural colonialism of the mindset—a monocultural theology that cannot recognize its own linguistic conditioning.

The clearest theological fruit from this linguistic challenge to the past came from James Barr and his book *The Semantics of Biblical Language* (1961). With Saussure, Barr has spoken against

[40]Anthony Thiselton, "Semantics and New Testament Interpretation," in *New Testament Interpretation: Essays on Principles and Methods*, ed. I. Howard Marshall, (Grand Rapids: Eerdmans, 1977), 84.

[41]Eugene A. Nida, *Language Structure and Translation* (Stanford: Stanford University Press, 1975), 248ff.

the priority of diachronic linguistics, against giving preeminence to the etymology of a word as a safe guide to meaning. Does "person" basically mean "mask," since the English word "person" derives from the Latin term *persona* ("mask")? When Englishmen say "Good-bye," do they "basically" mean "God be with you"? The etymology of a word, says Barr, is not a statement about its meaning but about its history. Synchronic linguistics must have priority.

EVANGELICAL THEOLOGY'S RESPONSE: RETRENCHMENT

Consciousness One had left the evangelical community with a negative knee-jerk reaction to the perceptions of anthropology. Overall, there was little to change that reaction in Consciousness Two. The rise of applied anthropology opened up new possibilities for missionary application. But theology still lived in isolation from the world beyond Europe and North America. Negative reaction slipped into retrenchment.

Many of the old factors continued to create this mentality. Until the mid-twentieth century, anthropology continued to be associated in the popular and academic mind largely with "primitive" societies. The scope of missionary concern did little to change this image. The "bias of the exotic" reinforced theology's concern with the "modern," i.e. "Western" world. In addition, there was the pressure of Western theology's own past, its concern with the thinking that dominated the "Christian" countries and the *corpus Christianum* of the medieval period. Where missions began to function as a discipline in the seminary curriculum, it functioned in isolation from the real work of theologizing.

Missions itself did not help in breaking down this isolation of theology. Its own agenda included items like the question of indigeneity, leadership development on the "mission field," biblical justification for its own existence. Little or no time was given to the missiological dimensions of the work of theology. Theologizing as an activity of the Third World church was a question missions did not raise. Its struggles were with institutional questions—the organization of missions, the relation of missions to the national church, the future structure of the national church. The debate over the indigenous church formula did not cover the question of indigenous theology; its concern was methodological strategy.

All this did was reinforce the comfortable dichotomy between theology and anthropology, between theology and mission. Theology could underline its self-conception as a universal ontology *sui generis*. It needed no historical, geographical, or social qualifier.[42]

The church's history during this period also contributed to the retrenching mentality of evangelical theology. In the United States, evangelicals found themselves doing battle over the essence of the gospel itself. Fundamentalism arose and was forced to defend the claim that its theology is somehow the essence, the core, of the gospel. The gospel as a normative given was certainly at stake. But in the process of guarding the gospel, fundamentalism assumed also the universality of its own theologies. Interest in the broader questions of the gospel and human cultures was minimized for the duration of the theological war. The drift of the liberal/fundamentalist encounter forced evangelical theology into focusing on that which was regarded as the same for all human beings. In the meantime, the focus of anthropology was increasingly on the discovery of human diversity. This further dated evangelical theology.

During this time, Dutch Calvinism was particularly rich in its exploration of culture. Abraham Kuyper stimulated a movement that has not stopped yet. But his concern was with culture as a monolith and with culture's by-products. He opened up new questions in a Christian exploration of aesthetics and statecraft.

[42]Charles Taber, "Contextualization: Whose Ox is Being Gored?" *Gospel in Context* 1 (October 1978): 2.

But nowhere did he pay extensive attention to understanding the cultural, contextual contingencies of the world's diverse theologizing. Perhaps as a result of all these factors, we are left in Consciousness Two with an evangelical theology that has no theology of cultures.

Paralleling this lack is evangelical theology's insensitivity to its own culture-boundness. In the name of biblical givenness, it immunized itself to its own contextual misreading and cultural misrepresentation of the biblical message. This is not to say that theology was silent on political, social, economic, or philosophical issues, or even on issues like natural revelation, religious pluralism, or demon possession. It is simply saying that our theology assumed it was everyone's theology. It reenforced a model of self-understanding that demanded the extraction of the non-Western theologizer from his or her familiar frame of reference. Theology's pastoral concern for the felt need was maximized into the conceptual work of the experts. Theology became the work of the Hodges and the Chafers, not the Nyamitis and the Kims.

SHARED CHARACTERISTICS OF CONSCIOUSNESS TWO

1. There is movement away from *depersonalization* toward what I call *functionism*. Consciousness One anthropology dehumanized by reducing our nature as image of God to the prelogical or the irrational. Consciousness Two moves in a similar dehumanizing direction. But the reason now becomes its reduction of culture and religion to the level of the usable. The most widespread model of Consciousness Two was that of functionalism. Its paradigm was that of a functioning organism existing (ideally) independently of other organisms. The organism had an inherent bias towards stability. Fundamental change was not expected nor did it have to be studied. The focus was on function,

not people. Phenomenology added to the dehumanization process by objectivizing the process of understanding.

A recent essay by Al Krass suggests to me that this drift to what I call functionism may be detected in the indigenization discussions of the 1950s.[43] Indigenizers described cultures as wholes made up of different institutions. These cultural systems were seen as closed and self-contained. And it was assumed that in our approach to them as missionaries, all we need to do to begin the transformation process is to replace Christian functional substitutes for any given functional unit within their system. We replace one computerized unit with another more functional one. The end result would then be that the bounded cultural set would be "Christianized." For one functional set of music, architecture, liturgy, forms of organization, we slip in another. In evangelical discussions of contextualization today there is often a tendency to confuse indigenization with contextualization. I suspect that part of it may come from the unrecognized presupposition of functionalism, incorporated in the Consciousness Two mindset.

The year 1973 saw the demise of the periodical *Practical Anthropology*. Charles Taber, in an editorial in the first issue of *Missiology*, after the latter absorbed *Practical Anthropology*, left an unfinished agenda for us to work on. One item on that agenda is important here. He said, "I would like to see much more thought given to the question of what actually happens when an idea originating in one culture is presented to people of a quite different culture."[44] At the heart of this question is the problem of accommodation and syncretism. Is our continued raising of this question related to our continued resort to functionism? We have not paid enough attention to the quality of the communication of the gospel across cultures because our methodological focus is on structural, static function, rather than on dynamic transformation.

[43]Alfred Krass, "Contextualization for Today," *Gospel in Context* 2 (July 1979): 28.

[44]Charles Taber, "Change and Continuity," *Missiology* 1 (January 1973): 12.

Our problem is not primarily the narrowness and inadequacy of our empirical data base. Our problem is the paradigm through which we analyze the data.

2. There is movement away from *dichotomizing* toward *particularizing*. Consciousness One isolated man as a religious being from man as a totality. The anthropologist reduced religion to the irrational and the theologian reduced the gospel to a core-essence.

Consciousness Two has assaulted this dichotomizing tendency. The psychological paradigm points away from the irrational to the emotional; and the further it gets away from Freud, the less pejorative the word "subconscious" becomes. Phenomenology, as Eliade practices it, repeatedly warns of the collapse of modern man, who isolates the sacred from the secular. Our "deep structure" calling to return to the *illo tempore* is a noble calling.[45] Even functionalism grants a legitimacy to religion as a functional response to biopsychological needs.

Nevertheless, Consciousness Two itself does not escape a form of reductionism. Only, in this case it more resembles particularizing than dichotomizing. Particularization always focuses on one set of aspects only, screening out others. It robs us of wholeness.[46] And that is what Consciousness Two has done with the religious dimension of our lives: It has reduced it to one aspect only, has robbed it of its character as integrator of the whole.

The functionalist model of Malinowski is an example of this particularization. Religion is simply one response of the more basic biopsychological nature of man among many as he responds to need with cultural creativity. It ranks along with providing food, protection against external threats, transmission of knowledge, and maintenance of the social system. Given this view of mankind,

[45]Eliade, *The Quest,* 50–53; compare also Mircea Eliade, *Cosmos and History: The Myth of the Eternal Return* (New York: Harper & Row, 1959).

[46]Ulrich Duchrow, "The Spiritual Dimensions of the Scientific World," *Gospel in Context* 1 (October 1978): 5–6.

religion is particularized into less than what it is—the instrument of integration in culture. Religion cannot be, as J. H. Bavinck calls it, central to cultural formation.[47] That place Malinowski gives to the biopsychological. Faith is reduced to a functionalist box, "religion—a part of culture."

There is some reason to believe that the "missionary anthropology" movement has not totally escaped this danger of particularization. By no means can one say that it "remained synonymous with functionalism done by Christians."[48] No evangelical could be accused of reducing religious response solely to the satisfaction of biopsychological felt needs. And when someone like Eugene Nida embraces it as an explanatory model, it is generally for the sake of emphasis on the utilitarian values of religion. And even then Nida adds the warning, "but religions sometimes turn out to be malfunctioning."[49] Further, it is also a functionalist model modified by later interests in the process of culture change. Even Louis Luzbetak, who designates his own approach as "to a large extent 'functional',"[50] devotes approximately half his book to the question of dynamic culture change.

But having said all this, I still fear the ogre of particularization. I fear it when Eugene Nida mentions "traditional approaches to religion, which have often classified it as one of the cultural capstones—a kind of overarching worldview of the supernatural." And then he adds, "religion is essentially not this at all. Rather it constitutes a componential feature of all the basic motivations thus providing 'meaning with supernatural sanctions.' "[51] Am I looking too closely or with not enough charity? Or is that the voice of modified particularization?

---

[47]J. H. Bavinck, *The Impact of Christianity on the Non-Christian World* (Grand Rapids: Eerdmans, 1949), 57.

[48]Contrary to the argument of Krass, "Contextualization," 28.

[49]William A. Smalley, ed., *Readings in Missionary Anthropology II* (Pasadena: William Carey Library, 1978), 21–24.

[50]L. Luzbetak, *The Church and Cultures* (Pasadena: William Carey Library, 1975), 141.

[51]Smalley, *Readings*, 22.

What do Marvin Mayers and Stephen Grunlan mean when they say "religion is found in all societies because it meets universal (social and psychological) needs"?[52] Is not Charles Kraft on much firmer ground when he modifies Malinowski and uses the term 'religion' to designate that part of culture increasingly recognized by more contemporary anthropologists as "worldview"?[53]

Yet, am I too fussy if I also ask Kraft now: Can the perspective of religion as worldview be consistently recognized by adding religion as number seven to Malinowski's list of six other basic human needs?[54] I acknowledge Kraft's insistence that it has a vertical dimension none of the other items on that list possesses. It is different in that sense from obtaining food or providing shelter or producing or providing for children. Even contemporary anthropologists are generally loath to see the centrality of the supernaturalism Kraft advocates. My question is only one of consistency with his own construction.

What are the possible effects of such particularization? I said it robs us of wholeness. Is this why Krass feels missionary functionalism hinders us from a more fully holistic approach to human beings? The Christian faith is consigned to the realm of mind and spirit rather than to the broad stream of the history of societies and civilizations where it belongs. As a result, our missionary agenda proposed by Paul Hiebert still remains unexplored: power and powerlessness, missions out of affluence and out of poverty, art, music, drama and literature, ritual and symbolism.[55] Missions still needs a theology that encompasses all of life. Is particularization one of the reasons why we still do not have it?

---

[52]Marvin Mayers and Stephen Grunlan, *Cultural Anthropology* (Grand Rapids: Zondervan, 1979), 236.

[53]Charles Kraft, *Christianity in Culture* (Maryknoll: Orbis, 1979), 54.

[54]Ibid., 90–91.

[55]Arthur Glasser et al., eds., *Crucial Dimensions in World Evangelization* (Pasadena: William Carey Library, 1976), 81–82.

3. There is movement away from a *static view of culture* toward a *static view of cultures.* Consciousness One perceived culture as a singular, not a plural. Colonialist ethnocentrism left us with a monolithic picture of the world that even the missionary often promoted.

Consciousness Two wrestles deeply with the plurality of human cultures. But its dominant model, that of functionalism in its earlier forms, has not in the process escaped the charge of a static view. Its focus on cultural equilibrium has been pluralized to cover the global cultural patterns they studied. But we still struggle with the model of all these human cultural formations as a basically stable phenomenon.

Is this mindset the reason behind what Kraft calls a preference on the part of the evangelical missionary for "static models" versus a preference for "dynamic models" of reality?[56] Is this mindset the reason why someone like J. Robertson McQuilkin can recognize that cultural tools are essential for the task of the interpreter, while immediately calling for other "common-sense principles for understanding human language"?[57] What lies behind constant warnings against cultural forms being used "to change the meanings of plain words and expressions or relativize the plain teaching of Scripture by replacing direct statements with general principles"?[58] Does appeal to "plain sense of the text" and "plain words and expressions" come from more than simply a desirable effort to prevent the setting aside of biblical authority for cultural authority? Does it not also come in part from a static view of human cultures? Does the verbal symbol "plain" in this case not really mean "static"?

Is this mindset also partly behind the evangelical effort to

---

[56]Charles Kraft, "Conservative Christians and Anthropologists: A Clash of Worldviews," *Journal of the American Scientific Affiliation* 32 (September 1980): 142.

[57]J. Robertson McQuilkin, "Limits of Cultural Interpretation," *Journal of the Evangelical Theological Society* 23 (June, 1980): 114.

[58]Ibid., 116.

understand contextualization while often confusing it with the old indigenization discussion? Indigenization, as Charles Taber reminds us, tended to define culture in rather static terms. The various aspects of culture are "given" and they sit there while the gospel works around them. There is an insufficient appreciation for the flexibility and changeableness of culture, for its dynamic character.[59]

Flowing from this may come also our evangelical difficulties with talk about an "Asian theology" or a "black theology." Do our Consciousness Two assumptions regarding the static nature of cultures, combined with our continued ties with a Consciousness One view of language, increase the superficiality with which we affirm the "expression" of the gospel as "the same" all over the world's cultural horizons? But we do not see clearly enough that "that universal dimension is much more remote from the surface level of verbal and symbolic expression than was previously acknowledged. Every language is inextricably part of a culture, and is used in an irreducibly particular context."[60] A static view of cultures and of language reduces our range of visibility and our acceptance of developing theologies as a legitimate response of the Bible to the problems within each culture. The evangelical is willing to assert that "understanding helps both in interpretation and in application," but he immediately adds, "the two activities are distinct."[61] A static view of cultures helps in keeping distinct the line between interpretation and application. Interpretation gives us "theology." Application makes it "black" or "African" or "Asian."

4. There is movement away from *passivity* toward *determinism*. Consciousness One reduced humanity's role in culture to a passive one, and "the field which is the world" to "foreign, non-Western

[59]Don McCurry, ed., *The Gospel and Islam: A 1978 Compendium* (Monrovia: MARC, 1979), 144.

[60]Ibid., 145.

[61]McQuilkin, "Limits," 121.

missions." Consciousness Two moved away from this in its growing focus on the personality. Even Malinowski conceded the importance of the emotional, though he disagreed substantially with the needs.

Yet even here the movement of Consciousness Two was not ultimately liberating. The rediscovered personality, for the functionalist, operated in a culture rigidified by the schematization of behavioral role playing and function. Consciousness Two's perception of culture was not yet modified by a full acknowledgment of cultural change as a process.

Missions reflected Consciousness One passivism in a colonialist mentality that regarded the national believer as the "object" of missions. Behind the popularity of the indigenous formula was a way of looking at gospel communication that was structure-centered. As Consciousness Two gained momentum, the colonial movement was losing steam. But new models were proposed that only reshaped the earlier passivism into a later determinism. People abuse now took place at a subtler level of power. Missionary string-pulling continued, wedded now to mission money bases rather than to simply colonialism.

Missions out of affluence had and has a great difficulty recognizing this new determinism, but it provides one example after another of the characteristic. "It manifests itself in our unconscious arrogance in dealings with Third World Christians, in our automatic assumption that *we* know best what the Gospel is and what methods should be used in Christian work; and that since we have the money and the technical know-how to operate in our capital-intensive and technology-intensive ways, we have a right to run the operations."[62]

Is this problem a real one? Why did John Gatu in the early 1970s call for a moratorium on mission money as well as on missionaries? Why does money play such a crucial role in the church-missions tensions that still trouble the world church? Is

[62]Robert Coote, ed., *Missions From the West in a New Key* (Abingdon, Pa.: Partnership in Mission, n.d.), 8.

financial determinism being seen more clearly from the oppressed Third World side of the blanket?

What lies behind the resistance of Third World people at the 1980 Lausanne Consultation on World Evangelization to the ideology of "people movements"? Is it simply a fear of Western pragmatism and ignorance of "church growth" thinking? Or do Third World evangelists also have deeper fears and concerns with which we are not dealing? Will renewed apologetic for the homogeneous unit principle adequately respond to this deeper fear? Is it not fear of Western determinism, of the dismantling of ethnic integrity through a more subtle use of power manipulation? Is this not what really lies behind the antagonism of a René Padilla toward concepts of "church growth" as they have been developed in contemporary missiology? Why does he fear what he calls "manipulative research" and translate his concern for strategy methods into his ironic dynamic-equivalent proverb, "If an evangelistic method is 'successful' in the U.S.A., it must also be successful anywhere else in the world"?[63] Why does he use this language as an illustration of what he heads, "Determinism and unlimited growth"? Is this a new call for us to begin relating church-growth thinking to the sociology of religion?

---

[63]René Padilla, "Comments on Spiritual Dimensions of the Scientific World," *Gospel in Context,* 1 (October 1978): 18.

Part Two

Challenged by the Present

Chapter Four

Converging Streams for a New Wave

SUMMARY

In the 1970s, missions began to focus attention on the topic of contextualization. This discussion gives hope that we may be moving toward Consciousness Three. There are some indications that the traditional dialogues—missions and theology, theology and anthropology—may be moving into a trialogue, the three traditional disciplines in simultaneous interchange. In our responses to anthropology's claims, we may have moved from the level of conflict through dissonance to dissonance reduction.

In the contextualization discussions, theology is being seen increasingly in terms of the demands of a world without Christ. Theology's metaphysical orientation is being replaced by a missiological one. Even the most reticent of the partners, anthropology, is undergoing shifts in mood and style that may indicate more openness to discussion with Christianity than in the past. Its notions of neutrality are becoming less steady as human needs allow it less and less to be a spectator science. The obligations imposed by the need for humanization draw it closer to the Christian agenda.

Of the three participants, it is missions that seems to have made the biggest step toward trialogue. Building on the discipline of applied anthropology and with deeply rooted linguistic interests flowing out of Bible translation, it has created a new discipline, missionary anthropology. As a result, evangelical attitudes toward anthropology have shifted from judgment and suspicion to cooperation. Two concepts especially have been helpful in this movement toward Consciousness Three—the idea of dynamic equivalence, associated with the name of Eugene Nida, and that of tagmemics, the interdisciplinary, bridge-building concept associated with Kenneth Pike.

Out of this movement has come a new agenda—ethnotheology. The work of Charles Kraft is especially important in this development. He has amplified the ideas of Nida and Pike and expanded them into a new model for doing theology. The object of sharp evangelical criticism, his work is a call to reexamine the nature of theologizing done across cultures. The process of doing theology, to Kraft, is the process of human interaction with divine truth perceived and defined according to cultural, contextual settings.

Chapter Four

Converging Streams for a New Wave

In 1978, Stanley Gundry, then president of the Evangelical Theological Society, put on his prophetic robes and inquired, "Evangelical Theology: Where *Should* We Be Going?" He saw missiologists addressing issues that many feel make the inerrancy question pale into relative insignificance. And yet, he continued, with only a few notable individual exceptions, North American evangelical theologians seem to be unaware of, and unconcerned about, the missiological discussion and literature. Gundry saw missiology and its questions as one way for the scholar to avoid theological provincialism. High on his proposed agenda was contextualization. "I wonder," he pondered, "if we really recognize that all theology represents a contextualization, even our own theology? We will speak of Latin American liberation theology, black theology, feminist theology; but without the slightest second thought we will assume that our own theology is simply theology undoubtedly in its purest form."[1]

[1]Stanley Gundry, "Evangelical Theology: Where *Should* We Be Going?" *Journal of the Evangelical Theological Society* 22 (March 1979): 11.

In a real sense, the contextualization discussions of the 1970s are markers that may indicate a new direction for the discussions we have outlined. In the past, much of the interchange has been ultimately dialogue of one sort or another—missions in dialogue with theology, theology in dialogue with cultural anthropology. At the crossroads of contextualization, the possibility of a trialogue now exists—missiology, cultural anthropology, and theology in simultaneous interchange.

A NEW SITUATION

Each of the partners in the exchange is seriously questioning old paradigms and examining the possibility of new ones. This alone would make a trialogue more possible. But for the theological partner in the trialogue there is now a new element that stimulates participation.

The Missiological Demands

In the eighteenth century, the dominant emphasis was philosophical. In the nineteenth century, the discipline of cultural anthropology was created, and this new partner in the discussion emerged as the dominant one. Now, moving into the latter half of the twentieth century, the agenda is shifting its focus again. It is no longer the metaphysical focus supplied by philosophy. We are not primarily interested in purely ontological or epistemological topics: What is the relation of the behavioral sciences in the theological encyclopedia? Where does theology fit, where does cultural anthropology fit?

Rather, our context is supplied by missiology, the discipline of cross-cultural evangelism and church planting. The ontological questions remain. And they must be examined. Our answers on this level will have a deep effect on what we do in the subdiscipline of applied missionary anthropology. But rightly or wrongly, the actual situation is more urgent and pressing than these questions. There are over 700,000,000 Muslims in our world. And they accuse us of more than slightly muddled theological communication. How shall we explain to them the doctrine of the Trinity or the substitutionary Atonement of Jesus Christ as the Son of God? And how shall we minimize the cultural blockades that are raised against our confession, "There is no God but Allah and Jesus is His prophet"? The first question we posed is traditionally called theological, the other anthropological. How will our answer reflect the strengths of both approaches and escape the mistakes of our past?

When the Communists came to power in China in 1949, the Christian church is said to have numbered about four million—360 years of Catholic and Protestant activity had won 2/35 of one percent of the people. Why?

Parts of the answer to that question are what most of us would call "theological." Thus, some have sought the reason in classical liberalism among the missionary advocates, a syncretism that advocated Christ as the crown of Confucianism and Buddhism. But could anthropology help us also in our search for an answer? Why did the Chinese react so strongly to Western colonialism and its partnership with the gospel in China? Is ethnocentrism too simple an answer? Was there a static view of culture behind nineteenth-century missionary ethnocentrism, a view that the missionary took for granted? Was there a confusion of romantic sympathy with anthropological empathy behind Hudson Taylor's pigtail and his insistence on eating with chopsticks?[2] Can current anthropology help us see sympathy's presuppositions of a superior/inferior, teacher/learner relation? Can it help us recognize our mistakes and plan for a better future?

What of an evangelical presence in the future of the Chinese mainland? Can the Christian function, with uncompromised zeal, in a Marxist-Maoist system? How? Westernized theology will be

[2]Alan Tippett, "Anthropology and Post-Colonial Mission Through a China Filter," *Missiology* 1 (1973): 478.

hard pressed to provide careful answers because of its past identification with capitalism. Indeed, should it provide these answers? Can a closer look at current anthropology's interest in ethnopolitics and a holistic perspective on societal structures help us again?

All these question clusters underline again the missionary focus of our new situation. The trialogue is shaped by our concern for the propagation of the gospel and for the full discipling of all the nations.

It is also missionary frustration that calls for a new interchange. Too many evangelists, both national and expatriate, are struggling with the problem of old wineskins and new wines. They have been taught in training schools around the world that theology is the wine and cultures are the wineskins. But they have discovered something in the ghettos of New York City and the favelas of Rio. As a matter of fact, the theology they have learned resembles the wineskins more than the wine. The post-Christian orientation of Western white theology has taught them about rational proofs for the existence of God and the need for demythologization in a scientific world. But they minister in a pre-Christian world where these answers, developed in another context, do not fit. The tribal, face-to-face culture needs to hear about the kingdom of God and Jesus' power over the world of spirits. The ideological government, whether of the right or the left, needs to see Jesus in conflict with "the principalities and powers." The black ghettos of Los Angeles and Philadelphia need to meet, not a honky redeemer, but a funky Christ.

Traditional schools for ministerial preparation are of little help. Theologians introduce terms like "common grace" and "general revelation" in their classes. But lectures on common grace are abstracted from questions about things like "redemptive analogies" in world cultures. And general revelation is a descriptor more often associated with Thomas Aquinas or glorious sunsets than with Sawi mythologies of a Peace Child or Chinese rites controversies. The pressures of the task of a world mission, the task faced by a world church, and the predicted shift of the geographical center of the church from the northern to the southern hemisphere by the end of our century demand a new shift in the exchange. Missions, not philosophy, demands a new agenda.

Changing Anthropological Moods

A second major contribution to new possibilities comes from the present state of cultural anthropology. As we have seen, until the last ten to twenty-five years it has been less a partner than an opponent. Evangelical missiologists and theologians have rarely listened to these negative vibrations.

To be sure, the negative vibrations continue. They are chronicled for us by Claude Stipe in the April 1980 issue of *Current Anthropology*. "Anthropologists in general," he writes, "have a negative attitude toward missionaries, especially when they conceive of missionaries as agents of culture change."[3] That negative attitude Stipe lays at the feet of two common presuppositions. First, anthropology's idealistic view of the organic nature of a culture: when you preach the integrity of a culture and give the impression that indigenous peoples are passive spectators in the acculturation process, it is easy to condemn culture change as necessarily bad for those people, and it is also easy to condemn the missionary as the change agent. Second, the assumption that religious beliefs are essentially meaningless. Stipe's conclusion?

> I suspect that, in at least some instances, the antipathy of anthropologists toward missionaries lies in the fact that missionaries take seriously and teach other people religious beliefs which the anthropologists have personally rejected. It would be difficult for most people to maintain a positive (or even neutral)

[3]Claude Stipe, "Anthropologists Versus Missionaries: the Influence of Presuppositions," *Current Anthropology* 21 (April 1980): 165.

> attitude toward a position they had personally rejected as being either invalid or meaningless.[4]

At least two other presuppositions have been suggested in addition to Stipe's two. First, anthropological attitudes toward missionaries are a reflection of missionary attitudes toward anthropology. It is a case of tit for tat. Prior to 1950, very few missionaries had any acquaintance with anthropology. Further, the missionary's hard-earned knowledge of a given culture has sometimes been exploited by an anthropological fieldworker looking for academic brownie points. In addition, missionaries may share in a heritage of anti-intellectualism that predisposes them to skepticism about the knowledge gained by anthropology.[5]

Second, the missionary fears implicitly that the study of anthropology leads automatically to a learning model that is potentially secularizing. If one agrees with Thomas Kuhn that becoming a member of a scientific community involves learning a paradigm, then it may be that the very nature of the paradigm for anthropology is potentially hostile to missionary work. In short, the evangelist fears that the call to "presuppositionlessness" may be the most dangerous of all presuppositions.

What is exciting about our present situation is that new shifts in anthropology are now raising questions about the thinking behind at least several of these problems. The air may not be getting any cleaner. But it is most certainly changing. What is happening to the presuppositions outlined above?

The old idealistic view of the organic nature of culture is undergoing assault from several quarters. One of Stipe's respondents comments that this theory "might have been plausible, if

[4]Ibid, 168.

[5]Ronald J. Burwell, "Comments," *Current Anthropology* 21 (April 1980): 169.

debatable, two centuries ago or at the latest in our grandparents' generation."[6] That may be stretching it a bit. But certainly the idealistic myth of pure and undefiled cultures has been demythologized even by anthropologists. The functionalist school tended to consider tradition and society as an integrated but fragile whole. But this school presumably is now in question for some, if not for many.

Further, since World War II, anthropology has stretched its field of vision. Its narrow interests in nonwhite, traditionalist (or so-called "primitive") cultures have been expanded. Anthropology has turned also to cultural questions on a macro-level. Society seems more pervasive and all-embracing than before.[7] The anthropological agenda now includes economics, social organization, politics, aesthetics, ideologies, and so forth. Its objects of study now include North American street-corner culture as well as the culture of the Australian aborigines. This also will have its effect on the way in which we view smaller culture units. The global problems of a global village leave no "pure and undefiled culture" untouched. The anthropologist, like the missionary, is talking about a holistic approach.

Are indigenous peoples passive spectators in the acculturation process? Again, the contemporary anthropological agenda raises new questions. Eric Wolf looks at the "new anthropology" and sees a major change in perspective on the role of personality in cultures. In the past, anthropology looked to the study of socialization, which became the lever in understanding the place of the individual in a cultural setting. Each individual was a replica of one's culture, a faceless diplomatic courier. Now there is a new call for ethnopsychology, a new interest in the cognitive processes of diverse cultures. Scholars turn to study the roles we play in society and the way in which these roles create an actor's or actress's social repertoire.

---

[6]Ibid., 169.

[7]Eric Wolf, *Anthropology* (New York: Norton, 1974): 14.

Bypassing for the moment Stipe's second charge, is there any possibility that the tit-for-tat argument may recede in the future? Are anthropological attitudes toward missionaries indeed mirror reflections of similar attitudes among missionaries toward anthropologists? Certainly, the two groups are similar enough to create this ping-pong reaction. They share a strong conviction that they have truth, and they both use a complex set of symbols and ideas which they strive to impose on people or through which they "observe." At the same time, they differ radically in how they view these symbols and value systems. The anthropologist still presumes too often that his or her methodology has "bracketed" preconceived ideas. Stipe suggests that such a scholar has more difficulty "seeing through" himself or herself than the missionary.

Yet, there may be a sign of hope on the anthropological horizon. It is a cloud already bigger than a man's hand. The "new anthropology" now wrestles earnestly with its own obligations for humanization. The image of God built into every humanist, no matter how distorted, begins to fear anthropological abstraction. The anthropologist asks questions about the coldness of a required neutrality in studying cultures where children cry from hunger. Can one look on and merely analyze the disintegration of traditional cultures in the face of technology and modernization? The rise of applied anthropology has drawn the anthropologist closer to the "object of study." Now the questions are asked, What is the place of anthropology itself in culture change? Is not anthropology a tool in social engineering? Do our objectifying methods make that tool into a weapon for destruction?

My personal hope is that these questions will lessen the antagonism. It offers one more area of commonality between missionary and anthropologist—one that is closer to the missionary's side of the fence than to that of the anthropologist.

What about Stipe's charge that for the anthropologist religion and religious beliefs are essentially meaningless? I combine this with the last presupposition on the list, the concern that anthropology's learning model is potentially secularizing. In these areas I am not at all optimistic (Stipe's response to his eighteen commentators is similarly cautious).

The history of anthropology has returned repeatedly to the question of religion in cultures. And repeatedly it has formulated theories that minimize the place of religion. My ultimate hope for change here does not come from getting together all the anthropologists I can find and busing them to a Billy Graham Crusade, although that might be quite helpful, of course. Earlier I quoted Stipe's comment that, having been involved in the discipline for over twenty-five years, he would "be very surprised to discover that over half of [his] fellow anthropologists were theists."[8] But Stipe's concern at this point, and mine also, is with structural methodologies that tend to minimize religion as meaningful, not with getting anthropologists to church. With Herman Dooyeweerd, I feel that we need a new critique of theoretical thought, in this case of anthropology. We need to take a hard, tough look at our constructions if we are to see change in these areas—and that will be a very long time coming.

At the same time, there may be a glimmer of light in the gloom of the "new anthropology." Wolf sees the anthropology of the pre–World War II period as disillusioned. The temper of the 1930s favored the idea that human nature is inherently flexible and therefore changeable. This optimism is evaporating in the colder realities of the postwar world. "The silhouette of the City of Man is seen in bleaker outlines against a colder sky. Human nature seems less malleable."[9] The new anthropology is recognizing more quickly "the apparently inherent dilemmas of human existence. . . ." Our cultural studies have uncovered "a world of dinosaurs in which the big lord it over the small, in which the facts of social and cultural dominance are inescapable."[10] Against this

[8]Stipe, "Anthropologists Versus Missionaries," 178.
[9]Wolf, *Anthropology*, 20.
[10]Ibid., 21.

mood, according to Wolf, there is a decreasing emphasis on cultural relativity and a new search for universals.

I have no hopes that this means a new look at the role of Christian ground-motives in the construction of new methodological options. But it may signal at least a new willingness on the part of anthropology to look again at its foundations. And we must be grateful for every crumb that falls onto our tables. Is anthropology facing a time of theoretical crisis, a time of structural anomie when things have a way of breaking up and the search is on for new models? If it is, I am glad we have our Claude Stipes, our Alan Tippetts, and our Paul Hieberts. We may be getting ready for a new wave, a new Consciousness.

A NEW PARTNER: MISSIONARY ANTHROPOLOGY

We have already spoken of the emergence of a new ally in the struggle: applied missionary anthropology. It deserves more detailed treatment at this point. Its history has not yet been written, but it is without a doubt a principal factor behind the new trialogue now emerging. It has been the major contributing element in shifting the evangelical attitude toward anthropology from one of judgment or suspicion to one of cooperation. It has made possible the emergence of a Consciousness Three in the future.

Missionary Anthropology: Its Roots

Historically, the roots of missionary anthropology lie in the mid-twentieth century. This is not to say that missionaries of previous decades were insensitive to anthropology.

> A number of them—R. H. Codrington of Melanesia, M. Leenhardt of New Caledonia, H. Junod and E. Smith of Africa, the Wisers in India and Father W. Schmidt and the Vienna

School of Anthropology, to name only a few—made significant contributions to anthropological knowledge and theory. Many others studied the ethnographic materials of their fields.[11]

APPLIED ANTHROPOLOGY

Its roots, however, were not in theoretical anthroplology per se but in the new subdiscipline of applied anthropology as it took shape in North America. Much of the design of the model for missionary anthropology was transferred from the concerns of this new mid-century discipline.

William Partridge and Elizabeth Eddy see three basic differences between "abstract" and "applied" anthropology, each of which reinforces our appreciation of the impact of the latter on mission studies. First, applied anthropologists study living cultures and contemporary people. Their research into history and the selective memory of the past is intended to direct them to important questions for applied research. How do people today form social groups? How do they accomplish tasks, survive in an environment, solve problems? Second, in addition to research among living peoples, applied anthropologists conduct research oriented toward living problems. Their research is people-oriented, structured around the needs of those they study. (Our brief introduction to the science in the previous chapter illustrated some of the needs out of which it arose.) Finally, applied anthropologists seek applications of their findings, data, and analyses beyond anthropology itself. Both abstract and applied anthropologists use the same process of research abstraction and theory building. But for the applied anthropologist, "these abstractions derive their

[11]Paul Hiebert, "Introduction: Mission and Anthropology," in *Readings in Missionary Anthropology II,* ed. William A. Smalley (Pasadena: William Carey Library, 1978), xxiii.

significance from their contemporary implications for living people."[12] Traditional boundaries between disciplines are more quickly crossed in this search. Problems ordinarily outside the anthropological traditions are examined. Data selected for analysis are gathered on the basis of their relevance to current issues.

All of these features would be strongly congenial to the missionary. Concerned with more effective ways to share the gospel among the peoples with whom he or she lives, the evangelist moves in the present rather than the past. Anthropology per se is minimized in the search for ways and means to answer people's deepest needs, the needs of the heart. The American cultural theme of pragmatism combines with the drive for evangelization to ask "how" rather than "why" questions. The mission field becomes a living laboratory in this quest.

Many of the areas of academic concern of the applied anthropologist also converged with those of the missionary to reinforce the connections. The focus on the contemporary, of necessity, placed the topic of culture change high on the anthropological list of interests. And the missionary saw himself or herself as change agent *par excellence* and the issue of culture change as preëminent. Unfortunately, until more recently, missionary naiveté about the complexities of culture change has been widespread. Planned change, as the anthropologist was learning, involved such things as

> awareness of local needs; limitations of the local ecology; complex interrelations affecting any innovation; problems of unanticipated consequences; utilization of tradition in the interests of modernization and avoidance of a conflictive opposition of old and new; importance of demonstrating pragmatically the advantages of an innovation; getting local people involved by translating their basic motivations into action; knowing the social order and the locus for decisions and

---

[12]William L. Partridge and Elizabeth M. Eddy, "The Development of Applied Anthropology in America," *Applied Anthropology in America*, ed. E. M. Eddy and W. L. Partridge (New York: Columbia University Press, 1978), 5–6.

> the mobilization of action; importance of prestige and personal satisfaction, communication and the timing of innovation; and the guarantee of success in the assurance that when responsibility for an operation is transferred to the local people, they will have a shared experience that will impel them to maintain it.[13]

Books could be written about missionary failings surrounding each of the items on this list. With the rise of ethnotheology in the 1970s the missionary has begun to catch up here also.

Missionaries have had to struggle to a far lesser degree than the anthropologist with one problem this concentration on social change creates—the problem of personal, humanitarian participation in social change. For the anthropologist, "neutrality is an essential factor in . . . effectiveness as a scientist and as an aid to informed government."[14] How then can one serve as a model for action, either as technical advisor, humanistic intervener, or catalytic discussant? Neutrality is compromised by that very act.[15] The missionary, theoretically, has no such internal struggle in the use of applied anthropology. No commitment to "neutrality" hindered evangelical participation in this humanitarian response.

At the same time, the missionary was harassed by a sense of "neutrality" in other areas affecting social change. Anthropologists developed a discipline that affected political and microsocial decisions. Though sometimes made with superficial understanding, their judgments carried the scientist into the worlds of cultural economics, community unrest, labor relations. In these areas the evangelical, developing an "applied missionary anthropology," did not follow. Sensitivity to the position of "guest" in a host country, pietistic withdrawal paradigms with regard to society and culture, concern for the future of the gospel in an antagonistic

---

[13]Fred A. Voget, *A History of Ethnology* (New York: Holt, Rinehart and Winston, 1975), 777.

[14]Homer Barnett, *Anthropology in Administration* (New York: Harper & Row, 1956), 177.

[15]Discussions of this problem emerge repeatedly in such books as Voget, *History of Ethnology*, 772–74 and Fred Plog and Daniel G. Bates, *Cultural Anthropology* (New York: Alfred A. Knopf, 1976), 304–5.

state—all these made the missionary "neutral" about the socio-political dimensions being explored by applied anthropology. In this area the expatriate church leader did not venture. And this mentality, by and large, still characterizes the missionary's use of the discipline.

APPLIED LINGUISTICS

A second tributary to the development of mission's new partner sprang from the growing use on the part of evangelicals of linguistic skills and understanding in the area of Bible translation. The Summer Institute of Linguistics (SIL), begun in 1934 as a sister organization of the Wycliffe Bible Translators, was to become the seed-bed for leaders and thinking in this whole area.

As with missionary attraction to applied anthropology, pragmatic goals became the instrument for coexistence and eventual interaction between linguistics and missions. Conceived by W. Cameron Townsend (1897–1982) and L. L. Legters, the Summer Institute sought to equip the student with the background and skills needed to approach an unfamiliar language, usually unwritten. Courses sought "to prepare the student to learn to speak, analyze, and manipulate the new language with a view to subsequent provision of a written literature in that language."[16] Bible translation for linguistic minorities was, and still is, one of the goals of the large majority of the students.

These goals drove the SIL staff during the early years deeper into the foundations of language theory and from there into questions revolving around the nature of communication. Among the five students who made up the second SIL session in 1935 was Kenneth L. Pike (b. 1912), who eventually became President of SIL (1942–1979). He was encouraged by Townsend to pursue graduate studies with Edward Sapir, who was then on the staff of

[16]Frank Robbins, "Training in Linguistics," in *The Summer Institute of Linguistics: Its Works and Contributions,* ed. Ruth M. Brend and Kenneth L. Pike (The Hague: Mouton, 1977), 57.

the University of Michigan. There, at a time of crucial change in the linguistics paradigm, Pike began studies that would serve as a bridge to deeper questions of meaning and hermeneutic.

A second major figure also began his studies at SIL in the 1936 session. Eugene A. Nida (b. 1914) followed Pike to the University of Michigan. Serving on the faculty of SIL from 1937 to 1953, he, more than even Pike, drew the evangelical community from the study of linguistics into the discipline of anthropology. Serving from 1943 to the present as Executive Secretary for Translations of the American Bible Society, he is a voluminous author and has not limited himself to linguistic material only.

In 1954, he broke new ground with his popular treatment of anthropology for missionaries, *Customs and Cultures*. Ten years as Secretary for Translations had made him "increasingly conscious of the tragic mistakes in cultural orientation shown not only in translation of the Scriptures but in the general pattern of missionary work."[17] That sensitivity moved him to write the book. He sought to bring "to bear upon [the missionaries'] problems the results of contemporary research in the field of anthropology." Nida's work through the years has continued to insist on the need for meaningful cooperation between missions and anthropology.[18]

The impact of SIL, and of these men in particular, on missionary attitudes toward anthropology is reflected clearly in the list of current scholars whose studies began with SIL and who remain today leaders of missionary anthropology. William Wonderly and William Smalley are two such men. Their work is foundational also to an understanding of more recent contributors to the field. Charles Kraft, Professor of Anthropology and African Studies at the School of World Mission, Fuller Theological Seminary, has produced the most innovative effort to date at

[17]Eugene A. Nida, *Customs, Culture and Christianity* (1954; reprint ed., London: Tyndale, 1963), xi.

[18]Compare Eugene A. Nida, "Missionaries and Anthropologists," *Practical Anthropology* 13 (1966): 273–77, 287–88.

synthesizing theology, missions, and anthropology. In his largest work, *Christianity in Culture* (1979), he refers to Nida a total of 41 times. Kraft's model of ethnotheology borrows extensively from Nida's enthusiasm for the dynamic equivalence paradigm that forms the basis of much of SIL's work.

This historical stream of influence has also shaped the early agenda of applied missionary anthropology. Louis Luzbetak notes in his own contribution to this area, *The Church and Cultures* (1963), that the "main contribution of American Protestant missionaries has been in the field of Linguistics rather than Social Anthropology or Ethnography, and their achievements have been considerable, thanks especially to the training program of the Summer Institute of Linguistics."[19]

This concentration on linguistics may explain in part why we cannot yet see this emerging discipline as a part of some already present Consciousness Three. The focus of the early mood was perhaps too restrictive in its interest in initiating or carrying on dialogue on the larger issues already on the agenda of theology and anthropology. In addition, the implication of linguistics for these larger areas, though increasingly recognized by missionary linguists, would not have been acknowledged by Western theologians. Bible translation skills, as practiced and taught in Western theological seminaries, remains basically monocultural (Greek to English, Hebrew to French, etc). The cultural questions raised by bicultural translations into "non-Western" languages by (then) largely Western laborers would increasingly sensitize the missionary to the question of meaning and cause him or her to inquire more deeply into the nature of meaning. The monocultural Westerner at work on monocultural theologizing had few of these motivations. It has been the study of analytic language philosophy, more than linguistics, that has partially opened this new avenue of understanding for the Western theologian.

[19]Louis Luzbetak, *The Church and Cultures* (Pasadena: William Carey Library, 1975), 49.

PRACTICAL ANTHROPOLOGY

At the same time, it is possible to overemphasize the focus of early missionary anthropology on linguistics. The connections between language and the larger anthropological questions were not forgotten. The links were being forged by the third major stream that entered into the formation of the discipline. We speak of the nineteen-year history (1953–1972) of the journal *Practical Anthropology*. In this bimonthly periodical a forum was provided for the expansion and communication of research into the anthropological side of the mission process. Hiebert notes that

> the quality of the articles published in the journal is reflected in the fact that they found acceptance in departments of anthropology on university campuses and that the first edition of *Readings in Missionary Anthropology,* selected reprints from this journal, found wide use in mission circles and has gone through several reprintings.[20]

The journal was created by a small group of people, most of whom served on the staff of the Translations Department of the American Bible Society. Until 1973, when *Practical Anthropology* was absorbed into the journal *Missiology,* its personnel continued to consist largely of Bible Society translation consultants. But its range was by no means limited to linguistic questions.

> From the beginning, *PA* took for its scope the entire field of cross-cultural communication, viewed from an anthropological perspective . . . Such concepts as ethnocentrism, cultural relativity, accommodation, identification, and so forth, were introduced and discussed, and their implications for Christian mission explored.[21]

The two streams we have cited (the rise of applied anthropology and the expanding horizons of linguistics) came together in the journal and in the shaping of its personality. Apart from its

---

[20]Hiebert, "Mission and Anthropology," xxiv.

[21]Charles Taber, "Change and Continuity," *Missiology* 1 (January 1973): 8.

first editor, Robert B. Taylor (1953–1956), a teacher of anthropology then at Wheaton College, the editors—William A. Smalley (1956–1968) and Charles R. Taber (1968–1972)—were trained linguists. Missionary linguists were prominent among the authors. In 1961, for example, nine of the twenty-two major articles, apart from those written by the editorial staff, were by linguists.[22] In the first decade of its appearance, two authors in particular did a great deal to develop its coverage and personality—Eugene Nida and William Reyburn. From 1953 to 1963, both men accounted for nearly twenty percent of the content.[23] Jacob Loewen (b. 1922) was the third major contributor in these and the following years.[24] All three had doctorates in linguistics.

Yet throughout these years the key question in accepting articles for publication remained closely aligned with that of applied anthropology: "To how large a portion of readership will the article be useful?" Taber, reflecting on the journal's fifteen-year history and its future under his new editorship, wrote in 1968:

> Two basic types of articles are most welcome: those which present useful interpretive insights of general interest to readers of *PA,* and those which present useful procedures and methods. In an article of the first sort, the author should ask himself, once he has described the relevant facts, "What does all this mean? How do these facts throw light on the nature of culture change, or on the dynamics of culture contact, or on the psychological impact of new cultural phenomena, *in general?* How will my missionary colleague halfway around the world be able to apply my insights to his very different situation?" In an article of the second sort, the author must make as clear as possible the problem he was investigating, the hypothesis he was testing, the method he was applying, the results, and an interpretation

[22]William A. Smalley, "Ten Years of 'Practical Anthropology'," *Practical Anthropology* 10 (Jan.–Feb. 1963): 4.

[23]Ibid., 2.

[24]Taber, "Change and Continuity," 8. Many of Loewen's articles are available in the collection of his work edited by William A. Smalley, *Culture and Human Values: Christian Intervention in Anthropological Perspective* (Pasadena: William Carey Library, 1975).

of the results. In other words, authors of all articles should lay equal and heavy emphasis on both words of the title of PRACTICAL ANTHROPOLOGY.[25]

Missionary Anthropology: Its Transition to Consciousness Three

Our concern in this chapter is not with the history of applied missionary anthropology but with the contribution its leaders have made toward the development of Consciousness Three.[26] In two areas especially do we see its contributions to a possible shift.

DYNAMIC EQUIVALENCE

The most significant as yet has been the model of dynamic equivalence, developed particularly by Nida from linguistic and communication theories. The model has been enriched as Nida's own thinking has incorporated elements from transformational grammar, associated with the work of Noam Chomsky, in his earlier structuralist model. But the model's essence, in terms of its place within missionary anthropology, has remained central.

> As Nida developed and popularized it, dynamic equivalence translation captures the meaning and spirit of the original without being bound to its linguistic structure (formal correspondence). The meaning of the text, the purpose of the original writer, and the relationship of the text to its original cultural setting are guarded as much as possible, and are conveyed by new structures as new text in the language of the translation. Dynamic equivalence translation should not be equated with "free translation" because it is rigorous in its insistence that the meaning and purpose of the original is to be

[25]Charles Taber, " 'Practical Anthropology'—A Look Ahead," *Practical Anthropology* 15 (Nov.–Dec. 1968): 243.

[26]An excellent summary of the interaction between linguistics and Bible translation during this period can be found in Karl J. Franklin and Kenneth A. McElhanon, "Bible Translation and Linguistics," *Journal of the American Scientific Affiliation* 31(March 1979): 16–18.

recaptured insofar as possible within the different language patterns of the translation.[27]

Nida's major books in the area of cross-cultural communication have made repeated use of dynamic equivalence as a model or, in his words, as an "elaborate scientific metaphor." Sensitive to the dangers of becoming enamored with or attached to a single model,[28] he has nevertheless used the dynamic equivalency concept widely in his studies of religion as essentially communication. His earliest title in the field, *Customs and Culture* (1954), was drawn from lectures to students at SIL and transposed the model in terms of the anthropological context of communication.

In what some have called his key book in this area, *Message and Mission* (1960), analogies of the model were drawn out in terms of the techniques of missionary communication of the Christian faith. Drawing on studies in symbolics, psychology, social structuring of experiences, and theology, Nida unfolds the structure of evangelization as a process of communication in which the gospel "sender" (S) seeks to reencode the message (M) for the "receptor" (R).[29] The parameters of dynamic equivalency are expanded in terms of these three factors (S, R, M) as essential to communication. How can one avoid restructuring the meaning of the gospel as presented in the original source when communication takes place between sources and receptors who have different cultural backgrounds? What factors are important for the communicator in seeking to insure "the closest natural equivalent" of the gospel, first in meaning and, less importantly, in style? How can insights into language as a cultural communication code of symbols help us in that process? Since effective communication

---

[27]Eric M. North, "Eugene A. Nida: An Appreciation," in *On Language, Culture and Religion: In Honor of Eugene A. Nida,* ed. Matthew Black and William A. Smalley (The Hague: Mouton, 1974), xii.

[28]Note Nida's own remarks on "models" in his collection of essays *Language Structure and Translation* (Stanford: Stanford University Press, 1975), 272.

[29]Heinrich Balz, *Theologische Modelle der Kommunikation. Bastian-Kraemer-Nida* (Gütersloh: Gütersloher Verlagshaus, 1978), 65–72.

within any social context must inevitably follow the social structure, how will the latter effect communication equivalency?

TAGMEMICS

A second contribution to interdisciplinary bridge-building has come from Kenneth Pike and his tagmemic linguistic model. Early in the 1950s, Pike began developing his principles of linguistics into a comprehensive theory of language and behavior, at first termed *grammemics* and later *tagmemics.* In this theory, language is viewed as an integrated part of total human behavior. One of Pike's principal goals was to provide a possible bridge between linguistics and other disciplines, including anthropology.

> I have tried to show analogies between linguistic structure and the structure of society and of nonverbal behavior. . . . We should profit if we can find in theoretical structure some components which will contribute toward binding us into departmental unity—linguists, archaeologists, ethnologists, physical anthropologists, sociologists, and students of personality structure. The fact that we all study man is no longer enough to satisfy all of us—or some of our students.[30]

This tagmemic insistence that language can be adequately studied only as a part of mankind's total behavior has reinforced the ease with which missionary anthropology moves from linguistic modeling to applications in areas as diverse as communications and theology. It has surely been a factor in the call to theologians by linguist-anthropologists like Charles Kraft to listen more carefully to nontheological discussions. "Theologians," he comments, "need to learn to deal more knowledgeably and to communicate to non-theologians much more effectively concerning such vital areas as . . . the closeness of the relationship between

---

[30]Kenneth Pike, *Language in Relation to a Unified Theory of the Structure of Behavior* (The Hague: Mouton, 1977), 166.

language and culture and the implications of this bond for semantic interpretation."[31]

It prompts new questions for theological agendas. What are the implications of linguistic forms, not only for understanding the strengths and limitations of each language, but for understanding the people whose perceptions are shaped by language? What distinctions must be made between cultural (including linguistic) forms and their meanings? How must one "reinculturate" the appropriate meaning of all linguistic and cultural forms employed in Scripture into contemporary forms in their contemporary cultural context? How can we better understand not only the forms and patterns of cultures but also those processes that result in maintenance as well as adaptation and change of that system? The implications for Christian missions are significant.

> Greater anthropological understanding of these and other cultural processes can enable us to work better with them for God. We can also learn to measure and thus to predict more accurately such matters as receptivity, indigeneity, the probable appropriateness of innovations, the behavioral (as opposed to the merely intellectual) impact of Christian teaching, and the like.[32]

Apart from this impetus to bridge-building and more technical applications in the study of linguistics, the impact of tagmemics on the development of missionary anthropology "has been limited for the most part to the popularization of the etic-emic distinction" created by Pike.[33] The emic and etic standpoints are alternative ways of viewing the same reality. "The etic standpoint is a view from outside, either random in its selectivity or with a set of presuppositions that have only a chance relationship to the scene being described. The emic standpoint is a view from within that

[31]Charles H. Kraft, "Can Anthropological Insight Assist Evangelical Theology?" *Christian Scholar's Review* 7, nos. 2–3 (1977), 191.

[32]Ibid., 197–98.

[33]T. Wayne Dye and William R. Merrifield, "Anthropology," *The Summer Institute of Linguistics: Its Works and Contributions,* ed. Ruth M. Brend and Kenneth L. Pike (The Hague: Mouton, 1977), 166.

notices just those features of the scene that are marked as significant by internal criteria."[34] The etic point of view is thus that of an alien, an outsider. The emic point of view is the way the people themselves see their universe and organize it.

How deeply this distinction proper has effected missionary anthropology is difficult to say. The terms are seldom used, even in the literature of the 1970s. Yet the functional distinction is found, particularly in the early recognition of the missionary as an *outside* agent in cultural change. This recognition of "alienness" requires a reexamination of the expatriate's place in the indigenous church. That place is, as Loewen argues, "not nearly as central as has often been assumed."[35] To what degree is the national church indigenous? In the past, that question has by and large been asked and answered by the missionary. But an emic (insider) mentality raises questions about the missionary's ability to make those judgments. Encumbered with one's own cultural assumptions (the etic perspective), the outsider must reexamine his or her role in the church. Out of this, some hope, there will come a healthy movement from a Western self-understanding as leader to a more biblical one as servant of the church. A grasp of the emic-etic distinction can promote a healthier perception of one's role as facilitator, empathizer, mirror, catalyst, source of cultural alternatives.

A NEW AGENDA: ETHNOTHEOLOGY

Out of these emphases in the missionary anthropology of the 1950s and the 1960s has emerged a number of foci that have contributed to the shaping of a new agenda.

[34]Ruth M. Brend, ed., *Advances in Tagmemics* (Amsterdam: North-Holland, 1974), 3.

[35]Jacob A. Loewen, *Culture and Human Values,* 254–55. Compare also David J. Price, "Eliciting the Data for Measuring Indigeneity," *Readings in Dynamic Indigeneity,* ed. Charles H. Kraft and Tom Wisley (Pasadena: William Carey Library, 1979), 154–55.

First, certain attitudinal assumptions flowed from Nida's principles of dynamic equivalence. The effect of these assumptions was to move toward a more open mindset with regard to human cultures and to anthropology as the science that concerned itself with those cultures. The complexity of the communication dynamic suggested that the missionary must be prepared as much to learn as to teach. And the object of learning was not simply the cultural world of "the receptor" but that of "the sender" and "the message" as well. The openness toward the receptor culture that the process demanded called into question any traditional viewpoints that simplistically identified indigenous cultures as merely enemies of the gospel. The indigenous culture was to be "seen and used as a preexisting but essential framework which will give meaning, support and stability both to the individual convert and to the Christian community which will make up the indigenous church."[36]

It was Alan Tippett (b. 1911), Professor of Missionary Anthropology at Fuller Seminary's School of World Mission and for twenty years a Methodist missionary in Melanesia, who played a significant role in reinforcing this openness toward indigenous cultures on the part of the missionary.

His published work provided the evangelical with masterful case histories in the practice of ethnohistory.[37] His concentrated interest in the evangelization of animists did not give him the seminal role in the discussions of ethnotheology that his colleague Charles Kraft was to play. His major contribution lies, to my mind, elsewhere.

His studies in social change under Homer Barnett at the University of Oregon gave him a deep sense of urgency in missions and linked him to the enthusiastic optimism of Donald McGavran. Like McGavran, he saw human cultures as alive with

---

[36]Ibid., xiii.

[37]Compare his *Solomon Islands Christianity* (New York: Friendship, 1967); idem, *People Movements in Southern Polynesia* (Chicago: Moody, 1971).

opportunities. Using his skills in anthropology and ethnohistory, he underlined the themes of McGavran. Christianity and the church can take root and flourish in any and every human culture. The gospel can fit in any imperfect cultural wrapper. Anthropology can be a tool *par excellence* in making the missionary witness relevant, effective, and enduring.

Tippett sought to provide biblical assurances for the evangelical long concerned about the legitimacy of cultural anthropology as an evangelistic instrument. His 1970 book *Church Growth and the Word of God* had by 1978 been translated "into five or six languages" and sold 10,000 copies in English.[38] Neither planned nor rough-drafted, the book grew out of Tippett's devotional studies when the Church Growth movement was under fire from the evangelical side for not being biblical.[39] It was never intended as a critical biblical analysis. And its attempted links between church growth theory and biblical themes were not Tippett's only purpose. The index refers to some twenty-five anthropological concepts.

Whether Tippett deals adequately with the individual pericopes or not is beside the point of our discussion here. Its publishing history is ample evidence that it answered evangelical concerns. It was sufficient to provide the evangelical, always sensitive and open to a devotional use of the Bible, with biblical grounds for a new openness to cultural anthropology. No one before him in the history of missionary anthropology had achieved that end. And in the postcolonial era of missions, when missiologists were crying "Missionary, go home," Tippett's work instead called for a biblical use of old instruments from the behavioral sciences. Tippett's disciplined use of those tools could now be theirs.

---

[38]Alan Tippett, *Church Growth and the Word of God* (Grand Rapids: Eerdmans, 1970).

[39]Personal correspondence of Alan Tippett to the author, dated February 19, 1978.

However, it was not simply in the area of attitudinal assumptions that earlier discussions shaped the new agenda. Nida's communication model formed the basis for one of the most formative attempts at trialogue we have yet seen. We refer to the controversial book by Kraft, *Christianity in Culture* (1979). Kraft's work builds upon Nida, but goes beyond him in significant areas.

In one important area Kraft's work has been perceived by the evangelicals as a setback. Critics have repeatedly expressed concerns about his assertions on revelation and inspiration.[40] Carl F. H. Henry has provided perhaps the fullest such criticism to date. In an eleven-page review entitled "The Cultural Relativizing of Revelation," he accuses Kraft of "a curious and highly ambiguous notion of truth," of a gross understatement of "the amount of objective doctrinal and ethical teaching that the Bible conveys in specific situations." Kraft is said to make "current prejudices of the behavioral sciences normative for Judeo-Christian revelation instead of challenging those very prejudices." Paul's adage, "all things to all men," continues Henry, "is made [by Kraft] to accommodate any and all conflicting beliefs and practices." Henry makes several allusions to the Barthian sources of Kraft's view of revelation as extended by subjective response and to his echoing "the neo-orthodox cliche that 'truth is not informational but personal.' "[41]

This criticism, we argue, misses the point in several significant areas. And because it does, it misses the perspective from which Kraft works. The focus of Kraft's book is not on the question of the authority and infallibility of Scripture. A substantial part of his work does deal with that issue. But it is not as central to the work as Henry's review makes it out to be. It is

[40]For samples of such criticism, consult: William A. Dryness, "Putting the Truth in Human Terms," *Christianity Today* 24 (April 18, 1980): 515–16; Miriam Adeney, "Christianity in Culture," *Radix* 2 (Jan./Feb. 1980): 25–26.

[41]Carl F. H. Henry, "The Cultural Relativizing of Revelation," *Trinity Journal,* 1 (Fall 1980): 153–64.

certainly a view that needs to be subjected to examination—but not for the reasons Henry gives, including the charge of neoorthodox influence.

The center of Kraft's concern is a reexamination of the nature of theologizing done across cultures. And it is not neoorthodox theology that forms the basic model for Kraft's efforts but Nida's model of dynamic equivalence. Henry's review pays no attention at all to the formative influence of this communications/linguistic model. And because it does not, his criticism of Kraft's position on Scripture flows from an improper base.

The heart of Kraft's approach lies in his penetrating understanding of God as being in constant interaction with human culture. It also flows from his angry sensitivity to the fact that this process cannot be adequately described by the evangelical's traditional and simplistic identification of the relation between message and communication. Such a view remains largely, if not totally, oriented to the message (M), with little or no appreciation for questions revolving around the sender (S) and even less the receptor (R).

Kraft's answer to the dilemma comes from an appropriation of the dynamic equivalence model of Nida. Just as revelation from God is said to be receptor-oriented, so too must our communication of the revelation in the process of theologizing be receptor-oriented. "Translation" in Kraft's wider usage becomes "communication of the gospel." It is that equivalency model that forms the background for Kraft's frustrations with the traditional, or what he calls "static," views of revelation functioning among evangelicals.[42] Henry comments rather sarcastically, "Kraft implies that his own principles have the validity of divine absolutes."[43] This judgment is again unfair to Kraft's lengthy discussion of "modeling" in the earlier part of his book. It is the very absoluteness operative in Western theologies that Kraft is protesting. He

[42]Charles H. Kraft, *Christianity in Culture* (Maryknoll: Orbis Books, 1979), 170–73.

[43]Henry, "Cultural Relativizing," 154.

himself warns the reader at the beginning of his study that the models he is about to propose "will suffer from the inadequacies and impreciseness from which all models suffer."[44] An appropriate criticism of Kraft should properly begin with the suitability of the model he proposes, and should not be based on criteria imposed on the argument from outside. We ourselves will raise that very question in the next chapter. Henry's exercise does not raise it at all.

The far-reaching scope of the equivalency model is again underlined in Kraft's work. Part 3 of the book analyzes and modifies the traditional typology of H. Richard Niebuhr's *Christ and Culture* (1951) to lay the foundation for seeing God in relationship to human cultures. Kraft rejects all of Niebuhr's types as inadequate to explain his own position and suggests the phrase "God above but through culture." Unlike the God-in-culture model, it seeks to present God as supracultural (not supercultural, a term that to Kraft implies the existence of some set of absolute cultural forms or structures), God as completely unbound by any culture (except as He chooses to operate within or in terms of culture). Kraft sees the "conversionist" model, often identified with Augustine and Calvin, as too bound by a monolithic concept of human societies. Rather we must see God as above cultures but as employing cultures as the vehicles of His interaction with people. Surely the roots of Nida's model can be seen in this presentation.

Out of this dynamic model, Kraft calls on us as missionaries, linguists, and theologians to carry on the divinely intended pattern in our work. There must be "dynamic equivalence translation" of the Scriptures as God's inspired, classic casebook. There must be "dynamic equivalence transculturation" of the message as we participate in God's communication. There must be "dynamic equivalence theologizing" as we reflect on and communicate God's truth through our culture-bound perceptions. There must be

[44]Kraft, *Christianity in Culture,* 41.

"dynamic equivalence churchness" as each new generation, in its own cultural experience, produces an appropriate church vehicle utilizing its own cultural forms for the transmission of God's meanings.

The links between Nida and Kraft are basic. Nida saw the missionary task as one of communication across languages and cultures. It was a process of translational equivalence, of communicating messages in appropriately reconstructed formal and semantic structures. Kraft has extended the model beyond translation into realms of transculturation and theology. The significance of that broadening cannot be overemphasized. His analysis of the transculturation of the gospel message seeks to make us more sophisticated in our appreciation of the complexities of that process than we have been heretofore. His comparisons of the models of dynamic equivalence and formal correspondence in translation theory provide rich insights into the reason for much evangelical stumbling, not only in the art of translation but also in its wider implications for contextualization. More than even Nida, Kraft moves us to the brink of trialogue.

Kraft has also taken Pike's "etic-emic" distinction and extended it further. He has made use of the model in his understanding of the process of doing theology. And he has done it in tandem with his definition of Western, acculturated theology as "ethnic theology," as a monocultural perspective on the Scriptures that is parochially culture-specific. In this connection, he argues, an emic Christian theology

> would be a specific cultural variety of Christian theology, appropriate for those immersed in it but lacking in comparative perspective (like monocultural Western theologies). *An etic approach to Christian theologizing,* on the other hand, attempts to compare and discover universally applicable theological categories of Christianity on the basis of analyses of many emic varieties.[45]

[45]Ibid., 293–94.

According to Kraft, only the etic approach, since it is broader and cross-culturally valid, may be labeled "theology." It alone is based on comparisons between culture-specific perceptions from a variety of cultures. He admits that the emic approach is important. But it is too specific and narrow to provide theological generalizations based on several single-culture Christian theographies. He concedes, however, that as yet very little etic theologizing is being done.

Behind Kraft's distinction is his understanding of theologizing as a process of human interaction with divine truth perceived and defined according to cultural, contextual settings. His deep concern is not simply with the need to recognize the humanness of theologizing. He wants us to see theologizing and the communication of the results of theologizing as more than simply the passive acceptance of a doctrinal product "once for all delivered." The emic (insider) dimension, the receptor-orientation of theology we often describe as "relevance," is an essential part of the dynamic process that can move toward etic theologizing as an activity and ends in etic theology as a product of that process.

In all of this, Kraft insists, we simply follow the pattern of our Lord Jesus who phrased

> theological truth in terms of whatever emic conceptual framework was appropriate to his hearers. He employed certain kinds of parables with the masses, life involvement (including a variety of verbalization) with the disciples, reserving the overt use of Scripture largely for the Pharisees and Satan. Paul articulated the same approach when he stated that he sought to be a Jew to Jews and a Greek to Greeks (1 Cor. 9:19–23)."[46]

The biblical pattern is said to be one of adopting the linguistic, cultural, and situational frameworks of the evangelists' hearers.

How has the evangelical reacted to this current turn of events? Can Kraft and others avoid the problems raised by past attempts at

[46]Ibid., 300.

dialogue? What new directions should this new focus take? These questions we leave for the chapter following.

Chapter Five

Perilous Currents in the Tide

SUMMARY

Three legitimate concerns make evangelicals reluctant to develop and embrace a biblical ethnotheology. The hesitancy concerning nomenclature that is evident cannot be considered a legitimate danger.

The most crucial problem revolves around an overextension of the category systems drawn from anthropology. Models are ways of viewing reality, and to promote a particular model is to impose limitations on one's perspective. Preconceptions become handicaps when the model is unable to handle new information.

The dynamic-equivalence model first sketched by Nida and expanded by Kraft places an extraordinary emphasis on the human side of understanding divine revelation. Does the nature of the model make this focus on the dynamic-process element in revelation so prominent that it minimizes the divine orientation of revelation? Does the model lead us again into functionism and reductionism?

Another evangelical fear focuses on syncretism. The concern that critical and basic elements of the gospel will be lost in the process of contextualization has its roots especially in the history of the early discussions in the Theological Education Fund of the WCC. More recently, as evangelicals have expanded the horizon of their interest from communications to hermeneutic, the danger of syncretism by omission as well as by commission has been increasingly recognized. The simplistic assumption that confidence in an inerrant Bible would avoid syncretism has been questioned. In the process of hermeneutic, syncretism can enter on several levels. Even the traditional model of "objective, grammatico-historical" exegesis has serious problems.

A third pitfall is that of provincialism—the creation of a theology so localized that it runs the risk of losing its universal "commonness" in a new sort of ethnic parochialism. There is a real danger that speaking of a "gospel core" can lead in this direction. In an ongoing attempt to protect and retain the gospel "core," we may also minimize the broad impact and implications the gospel must have for all of life. There is a similar danger in our use of terms like "supercultural" or "supracultural." We must search for human terms that will adequately express our submission to God's Lordship as the controlling reality in all human cultures.

Chapter Five

Perilous Currents in the Tide

By no means has *ethnotheology* caught on in the evangelical world as an appropriate term to describe the emerging trialogue. The word is absent in the *Willowbank Report on the Gospel and Culture,* a 1978 Consultation sponsored by a subcommittee of the Lausanne Committee for World Evangelization. The concerns of ethnotheology were the object of study at both the Third World Theologians Consultation (August 27–September 5, 1982) and the Sixth Consultation of the Asia Theological Association (August 23–31, 1982). But here too the term did not appear.

Contextualization as a term has fared a bit better. But one also notes a certain reluctance in evangelical circles to use it. It is used only once in the *Seoul Declaration of the Third World Theologies Consultation.* And then it is interpreted as "the New Testament pattern for transposing the Gospel into different historical situations."[1] It would seem that even those evangelicals who have done so much to promote discussion, using a term like *contextualization,*

[1] *The Seoul Declaration. Toward an Evangelical Theology for the Third World* (Taichung, Taiwan: Asia Theological Association, 1982), 3.

are searching for other designations. Support continues to be oriented toward more traditional labels. Kraft recently has suggested "dynamic indigeneity" as a more useful substitute (though he also continues to use "contextualization" freely in connection with theologizing).[2] How shall we explain this terminological reluctance?

We suspect that for some, perhaps many, the reluctance flows from a Consciousness One mentality toward language, which, as we have seen, defines words per se as static, basic units of meaning to be investigated. Fear of the implications of a given meaning associated with a word becomes fear of the word itself. Thus, there are those who avoid terms like *humanism, ecumenical,* and *higher criticism*. In doing so, they seek to place themselves counter to the pejorative connotations they associate with the meanings of the words by avoiding use of the words.

The concerns of others about the current discussions, however, take shapes we see as more sophisticated and legitimate. And these need some preliminary evaluation if we are to make progress.

OVEREXTENSION OF MODELS

Overextension of the category systems we associate with anthropology may be the most crucial concern. Kraft, using the insights of Thomas Kuhn, draws attention to the significance of these category systems. Models and paradigms, he properly contends, affect the way we "see" things in our study. Data are perceived through some combination of models that we construct, "mental maps of reality" as he calls them.

The model scales reality to our preconceived patterns. The model becomes a paradigm, "a normative illustration of proper method, of how to handle new as well as old cases and data. Thus

[2]Charles H. Kraft and Tom N. Wisley, eds., *Readings in Dynamic Indigeneity* (Pasadena: William Carey Library, 1979), xx.

a new world may come into being while the paradigms through which worlds are constructed remains basically the same."[3] The power and advantages of models are significant. They become the eyeglasses through which we observe and interpret reality. They are the principles of hermeneutical order by which we evaluate a cosmos. Models and paradigms offer "ways of ordering experience."[4] Stipe's analysis of the conflict between missionaries and anthropologists, discussed in the previous chapter, flows partly from his criticism of the paradigms used by anthropologists. Tension is created when these overlap with the missionary paradigms.

This need not happen in a Christian construction of theoretical thought. The academic disciplines we call theology, cultural anthropology, and missiology each have their own perspectives on reality, shaped by the paradigms out of which they work. And given the meaningful nature of creation structured by the divine Creator, each has its recognizable limitations of scope (what Abraham Kuyper called "sphere sovereignty"). Each has God-created criteria of assessment, appropriate to its object of study.[5]

But complementarity vanishes when that appropriate paradigm of the category system crosses its established border. The paradigm pushes the new framework into which it has intruded out of kilter. The limitations of the latter model/paradigm, which was developed within a specific context for a particular purpose, cannot handle what now becomes an overload of data for which it is not equipped. This, we suspect, may be the real problem many evangelicals are experiencing with the models of ethnotheology originating in the communication model of Nida and refined by Kraft.

---

[3]Peter L. Berger and Richard J. Neuhaus, eds., *Against the World for the World* (New York: Seabury, 1976), 32–33.

[4]Ian Barbour, *Myths, Models and Paradigms* (London: SCM, 1974), 22, 45.

[5]A full exposition of this from a Christian philosophical position is found in Herman Dooyeweerd, *A New Critique of Theoretical Thought, Vol. 2* (Philadelphia: Presbyterian and Reformed, 1955), 3–54.

Nida's Paradigm

Nida, to reiterate, uses the paradigm of communication and dynamic equivalence as the model for understanding religion (though he warns that this approach "is certainly far from being the whole story"[6]). His goal is simply to find some unifying approach to the complexity of religious phenomena. The link, he says, lies in the paradigm of communication. "In fact, it is in large measure the very essence of religious practice."[7]

Nida's rich insights in the use of this paradigm cannot be underlined enough. Seeing religion first and foremost as the sending of messages to the supernatural allows him to bring to bear all the data, not only those from the techniques of communication but even those psychological and dynamic factors evident in non-Christian religions and in the history of Christendom (the theme of his book *Religion Across Cultures* [1968]).

In fact, almost all of Nida's work concentrates on these human dimensions in gospel communication. His fullest attempt to treat the process from a theological stance comes in the last chapter of his *Message and Missions* (1960). And even here his major concern is structured again around implications for the human process of communication. In doing this, he reaffirms the supernatural source of the divine revelation. And he emphasizes his confidence that this revelation "is absolutely true; but it is not absolute, in the sense that there is nothing more or that we know everything about God."[8] He also draws attention to the affirmation that all divine communication is essentially incarnational, a principle most completely exemplified in Jesus Christ.

With much of this the evangelical can hardly find fault. It is when Nida begins to carry this paradigm over into his understand-

[6]Eugene A. Nida, "New Religions for Old: A Study of Culture Change in Religion," *Church and Culture Change in Africa*, ed. David J. Bosch, (Pretoria: N.G. Kerkboekhandel, 1971), 11–12.

[7]Eugene A. Nida, *Message and Mission* (New York: Harper & Row, 1960), 10.

[8]Ibid., 225.

ing of divine revelation that the ambiguity resulting from overload may occur. Seeing language and communication as "basic presuppositions" for the biblical view of communication, Nida argues for what he calls "dialogue" as a paradigm for understanding the process. In an admittedly brief section of his argument, and in language strongly ambiguous to this writer, he argues that "the entire concept of the covenant of God with men is predicated upon two-way communication, even though it is God who proposes and man who accepts."[9] The focal point of that process is Jesus Christ—"the divine-human conversation is eternal."

Little explanation of the character of this two-way communication is offered in the passage. And it is immediately qualified by Nida's recognition of divine initiation in the process. We are also left to grope for the meaning of his assertion that the conversation is "eternal." Does he simply mean that revelation continues to speak even through the culturally bound limitations of time, space, and language? Or does he mean that revelation is a dynamic, ongoing process that has no canonical *terminus ad quem?*

Kraft's Modifications

Nida's consistent attention to the human dimensions of communication does not allow us to answer these questions fully. But Kraft seeks to draw out these very implications for revelation, using and enriching Nida's "dynamic equivalence" model. Analagous to the receptor-oriented paradigm of human communication is receptor-oriented revelation. God does not speak to people in a vacuum. There are paradigm analogies between the dynamic process of human interaction (the ordinary requirements for effective interpersonal communication) and the divine-human activity that produced the Scriptures. Wary of the model of the Bible as a static, theological textbook of propositional theorems,

[9]Ibid.

he speaks of the text as an "inspired classic casebook." He sees this casebook analogy, drawn from cultural anthropology, as more successful in conveying the personal, dynamic character of revelation. It is an involvement of the reader in a kind of learning by discovery, the same kind of participation with the Holy Spirit that with the original authors resulted in the recording of the events and with the early church resulted in the canonization of these (and only these) records.[10]

Carl Henry has argued for a neoorthodox source behind this argument. And, to be sure, some of the sources Kraft quotes in support of his position might fit more comfortably into that camp than within what most of us would consider the evangelical circle. But the argument misses the real source of Kraft's assertions. That source is his paradigm model of dynamic equivalency.

In the debate he carries on with traditional defenders of inerrancy—Carl F. H. Henry, Francis Schaeffer, Clark Pinnock—Kraft repeatedly notes his strong agreement "with most of their major conclusions concerning the inspiration and normativeness of Scripture. I also agree that it is important to hold and defend a 'high' view of scriptural inspiration and authority."[11] Elsewhere he cries, "I believe strongly that the Scriptures are inspired and that this inspiration may properly be labeled 'verbal' (that is, inspiration attaches to the wording employed) and 'plenary' (that is, the whole Bible is inspired)."[12]

His disagreement flows not from his affirmation of the Bible's "propositional content" as "a very important part of the revelation."[13] Rather, it flows from what he fears is the model that lies behind the affirmations of contemporary defenders of inerrancy. That model he sees as based on static philosophical presuppositions leading to a fear of an overemphasis on revelation as also a

[10]Charles H. Kraft, *Christianity in Culture* (Maryknoll: Orbis, 1979), 198–202.

[11]Ibid., 211.

[12]Ibid., 206.

[13]Ibid., 207.

stimulus to human understanding. In its zeal for the constancy of God's Word (which Kraft also seeks to affirm), it minimizes the humanness of God's revelatory intention. Such a view, he argues, flows from the influence of simplistic views of language, created in a Western culture that concentrates almost exclusively on words. It creates an approach to biblical interpretation that devotes itself almost totally to word-level analyses. And it supposedly models a view of inspiration and revelation that involves what Bernard Ramm calls a "fanatical 'objectivizing' of Scripture."[14]

Kraft's intent is not to minimize or reject what he sees as valuable in this defense. For that reason, he speaks of the Bible as a tether, as yardstick, as the measure of revelation. It is "the in-culture point of reference that provides the set radius within which contemporary revelational encounters may occur and in terms of which all claims of divine revelation are evaluated."[15]

Nevertheless, it is also true that his focus is on the dynamic process element in revelation. And in the light of that focus, he identifies inspiration, not primarily with the content conveyed by the Bible, but with that dynamic process of God's interaction with the biblical authors that produced it. Repeatedly he stresses the continuity of that process with what he sees to be the analogous process of God's interaction with men in various cultures, a process that has copied the process model of the Bible. The uniqueness of the biblical inspiration lies in the fact that "God has led the Church (and Israel before it with respect to the Old Testament) to preserve and employ in a unique way these particular materials in their attempts to discern and follow God's leading."[16]

In keeping with the model of dynamic equivalence, Kraft refuses to restrict "revelation" to some informational product of God's past activity. It cannot be "anything less than the total

---

[14]Ibid., 208, quoting Bernard Ramm, *Special Revelation and the Word of God* (Grand Rapids: Eerdmans, 1961), 99.

[15]Charles H. Kraft, *Christianity in Culture,* 191.

[16]Ibid., 213.

process by means of which God and human beings participate in the actualizing of the potential inherent in either general or special revelational information."[17] The traditional theological distinction between revelation and illumination is rejected by Kraft as implying too static a view of revelation. What others have called illumination, Kraft calls stimulus, the Spirit-guided activation of revelational information within the will of the receptors.

Undoubtedly this kind of argument provides the background to evangelical concerns about Kraft's thesis. His assault on the static linguistic model he sees behind the arguments of many inerrantists will create suspicions. And those anxieties will be reinforced by his strictures upon the use of a technical term like "inerrancy" in an evangelical setting deeply concerned with the problems revolving around this term. It must also be said that his treatment of many of the problem passages that were handled in a harmonistic way in the past leaves me, as well as others, raising questions about what Kraft calls "the dynamic humanity of the Bible."[18]

But the answer to all these concerns cannot be a wholesale

[17]Ibid., 221.

[18]Says Kraft, ". . . to Mark it did not seem important to distinguish the words of Malachi from those of Isaiah (Mk. 1:2–3) or to identify correctly the high priest from whom David received consecrated bread to eat (Mark calls him Abiathar when in fact it was Ahimelech; compare Mk. 2:26 with I Sam. 21:1–6)" (204). Kraft takes a much more controversial position on the larger topic of the salvation of those "pagans" who have not heard of Christ. He asks, "Can people who are chronologically A.D. but knowledgewise B.C. (i.e., have not heard of Christ), or those who are indoctrinated with a wrong understanding of Christ, be saved by committing themselves to faith in God as Abraham and the rest of those who were chronologically B.C. did (Heb. 11)? Could such persons be saved by 'giving as much of themselves as they can give to as much of God as they can understand?' I personally believe that they can and many have" (254). Similarly subject to much concern will be Kraft's suggestion that most of what we have called "heresies" in the history of theological development "can validly be classed as cultural adaptations rather than as theological aberrations" (296). The generalization is probably too broad for evangelicals to swallow.

condemnation of all of Kraft's work because it is regarded as flowing from a "low" view of Scripture. This kind of domino thinking may hurt the critics more than Kraft. There is too much wisdom in his charge that "closed conservatives" display their own frailty in their static views of cultures and language. I take Kraft's criticisms here as a call for evangelical self-appraisal of our traditional methodology in the defense of the integrity of the Bible.

Neither is it necessary to insist that Kraft freeze the meaning of the term *revelation* and limit it to the Bible alone as "the finished product of that activity." Geerhardus Vos does not support that conclusion and neither do we.[19] To do so would demand a Consciousness One mentality toward language.

The question is rather, Does Kraft's paradigm so focus on dynamic process, applied to the theological language field, that it distorts the proper emphasis reflected in that language field? In his extension of the dynamic equivalence model into the theological world of category systems, has Kraft overstepped the boundary, thus making his paradigm less usable? New models, as Kraft has argued, can offer such a radically new way of looking at a given phenomenon or set of phenomena that it creates a paradigm shift, a "scientific revolution." But for a new paradigm to be adopted, it must show that it can solve the problems that led to the crisis of the old paradigm, without creating a larger set of problems to solve.

Kraft's paradigm in the theological category system amplifies richly what Ramm calls the cosmic and anthropic character of revelation. In its cosmic aspect, revelation as the form of the great condescension of God "must truly enter our world and take the forms of our world in order to be comprehended by us."[20] In its

[19]Geerhardus Vos, *Biblical Theology* (Grand Rapids: Eerdmans, 1948), 13.

[20]Bernard Ramm, *Special Revelation and the Word of God* (Grand Rapids: Eerdmans, 1961), 17.

anthropic character it accommodates "to man, his language, his culture, and his powers."[21] Kraft's paradigm works well in the amplification of this latter dimension, the manward perspective.

But this perspective is not the major emphasis of the meaning level of "revelation" within the category system of theology. That emphasis, as Ramm puts it, is on revelation as "the autobiography of God, i.e., it is the story which God narrates about himself. It is that knowledge *about* God which is *from* God."[22] Behind this language is an effort to preserve both the divine origin and the orientation of revelation. Even in recognizing the manward direction of revelation as dialogue between Creator and creature, the theological model underlines

> dialogue which in all its moments has God-given direction and structure and hence in its deepest sense is monologue. . . . The text is that *historical* instance by which the sovereign Lord of history, the one who knows end from beginning, calls forth the interpretative response of man in the interests of accomplishing his determinate purpose and good pleasure.[23]

Kraft's paradigm, we argue, places so much emphasis on the dynamic, anthropic aspect of revelation that it minimizes this key dimension. For the same reason, Kraft argues for no distinction between revelation and the illuminating work of the Spirit. Again, he is motivated here by his concern that evangelical orthodoxy, in making this distinction, "on the one hand, reduces God's dynamic revelational activity to its static informational component and, on the other, diminishes the status of the activating component of all revelation—the Spirit-led stimulus or illumination."[24]

Our concern is the reverse: is Kraft's model in danger of

---

[21]Ibid., 33.

[22]Ibid., 17.

[23]Richard B. Gaffin, Jr., "Contemporary Hermeneutics and the Study of the New Testament," in *Studying the New Testament Today*, ed. John H. Skilton (Nutley, NJ: Presbyterian and Reformed, 1974), 14.

[24]Kraft, *Christianity in Culture*, 225.

minimizing the predominantly Godward dimension of the meaning-level of revelation through a dynamic equivalence paradigm that focuses on the manward side of revelation? And, conversely, does it maximize the human dimensions of illumination to such a degree that again the focus shifts from *illumination* as an ongoing act of the Holy Spirit to *stimulus* as an ongoing response of humanity? Kraft's interest in illumination focuses on the testimony of the Spirit as perception, on that which concretely happens to us, on the testimony as the impartation of saving knowledge and the process by which that impartation takes place on the human level. Again, there is help for all of us in what he says. But what then fades away is the reality focused on in the theological language-field: illumination as a divine action, illumination as a divine persuasion.

Given this strong emphasis on the continuum provided by the divinely initiated interaction between God and culture, the only place for the uniqueness of biblical revelation lies then in its having been inscribed, humanity and all. Does this signal to us that Kraft's preunderstanding of dynamic equivalence begins to override other dimensions of the biblical data not easily discerned in this paradigm? Granted that the evangelical, due to his or her own captivity to a nineteenth-century concept of language and culture, may not have done full justice to the divine interaction of God and culture even in the Bible. But is not the purpose of "inspiration" an effort to communicate the uniqueness of that activity of the divine Spirit in "bearing up" the writers of Scripture (2 Peter 1:21)? Does not Kraft's sensitivity to a static concept of inspiration run into the opposite danger of a view so aware of the "humanity" of the divine object of inspiration that the divine initiative in the interaction is not given full emphasis? Let us take to heart Kraft's legitimate warnings against a theological expertise unaware of its static, monocultural nature as it interprets these concepts to be a mirror image of itself. But may we not also ask whether Kraft's paradigm of dynamic equivalence, forged out of linguistics and anthropology, does not function in his system in the same distorting way with regard to the Godward dimension of these categories that theological expertise functions with regard to the manward dimensions. Does Kraft's model provide sufficient biblical safeguards to keep us from allowing the message of revelation to be made dependent upon the scientific enterprise, either theological or anthropological?

Furthermore, has Kraft's model of dynamic equivalence really escaped the dangers of the functionism we warned against as one of the results of Consciousness Two? Do we face here another variety of the reductionism that minimizes whatever it touches to the level of the useable? Is this why Robert Ramseyer suggests that Kraft has failed to understand the relationship between the Old and New Testaments? According to Ramseyer, Kraft attributes such differences entirely to God's adapting his ways of communication to the culture of the people involved. Thus, there is change as God accommodates his message to changed circumstances in human society, but there is no direction, no fuller, clearer, or higher revelation. Kraft writes, "In many ways tradition ('law'), tribe and ceremony in Hebrew culture were the functional equivalents of grace, freedom, and philosophizing in Greek culture. The latter are not necessarily superior ways of expressing the Gospel, just different culturally."[25] The effect of this, adds Ramseyer, is to attribute our own preference for New Testament revelation to our affinities with the Greek culture of the New Testament world rather than to anything inherently superior in that revelation.[26] Does Kraft's dynamic paradigm misappropriate an important milestone in the history of special revelation and transform it exclusively into one more sample of manward functionism?

---

[25]Ibid., 232.

[26]Robert L. Ramseyer, "Christian Mission and Cultural Anthropology," *Exploring Church Growth,* Wilbert Shenk, ed., (Grand Rapids: Eerdmans, 1983), 111.

Implications

In responding to Kraft as we have done, we do not mean to say that we cannot legitimately use any paradigms from the behavioral sciences in studying Scripture or creating theology. The richness of Kraft's contributions to those very kinds of study must not be minimized by questioning either the propriety of his model or some of its conclusions. There are many legitimate ways to organize the subject matter of Scripture and its cultural contexts for study. There are, after all, many ways of reading a book, just as there are many ways of linguistically describing the color spectrum. Problems arise when the mutuality of the different disciplines is threatened by an overlapping that does injustice to a meaning-dimension discovered by one discipline and distorted through what another sees as "primary" or "secondary."

There is a legitimacy to the concerns of those like J. Robertson McQuilkin who call for a "functional control" of "Biblical priority over contrary non-Biblical opinion." And there is wisdom in his caution that this functional control "will vary in direct proportion to the overlap of that discipline with the substance of Biblical revelation."[27] But the danger in saying this is that we do not mean "biblical priority" so much as "theological priority." Theology, after all, is one more scientific discipline. And, like any other, it too misreads.

The Seoul Declaration, mentioned earlier in this chapter, refers, for example, to the pitfalls into which Western, including evangelical, theology has fallen in the past

> and which we must avoid. . . .We have recognized that if Evangelical theology is to fulfill its task in the Third World it must be released from captivity to individualism and rationalism of Western theology in order to allow the Word of God to work with full power. Many of the problems of our churches

---

[27]J. Robertson McQuilkin, "The Behavioral Sciences Under the Authority of Scripture," *Journal of the Evangelical Theological Society* 20 (March 1977): 31–32.

> are, in part, the result of this type of theology. Consequently, we insist on the need for critical reflection and theological renewal. We urgently need an Evangelical theology which is faithful to Scripture and relevant to the varied situations in the Third World.[28]

Cultural anthropology, as a discipline, serves us best when it serves us in gaining better self-understanding. "Cultural anthropology can help us see how our setting and our experiences have helped to shape our understanding of the gospel."[29] That can be liberating for the task of theology.

SYNCRETISM

Almost from the beginning of the evangelical deliberations on contextualization, a deep fear of syncretism has been evident in the discussions about theologizing. Dr. Byang Kato delivered a major address on these themes at the 1974 Lausanne International Congress on World Evangelization; five of the seven printed pages of the address focused on the dangers of syncretism in the process of "ethnotheologizing."[30] Syncretism was said "to occur when critical and *basic elements* of the Gospel are lost in the process of contextualization and are replaced by religious elements from the receiving culture; there is a synthesis with this partial Gospel."[31]

These concerns have not diminished in the last decade. A 1979 Consultation on Theology and Mission hosted by Trinity Evangelical Divinity School devoted a significant part of its time to "Evangelicals and Contextualized Theology." Their Findings Committee Report warned of the dangers of contextualization:

> (1) It can undermine confidence in the absoluteness of the Word of God. (2) It can undermine confidence in preaching the

---

[28] *The Seoul Declaration*, 2.

[29] Ramseyer, "Christian Mission," 116.

[30] J. D. Douglas, ed., *Let the Earth Hear His Voice* (Minneapolis: World Wide, 1975), 1216–23.

[31] Ibid., 1227.

> truth of the gospel. (3) It can introduce multiple meanings, and thus lead to confusion. (4) It can lead to compromise, syncretistic tendencies, and even Christopaganism.[32]

Most recently, the charges reappear in the *Declaration of the Sixth Theological Consultation* of the Asia Theological Association. This evangelical body saw a tendency to syncretism in an "uncritical affirmative approach" to the evaluation of Asian religions and cultures. "Seldom," the Declaration asserted, "is there any attempt to bring these elements of our Asian cultures which are contrary to God's Word under its judgment. . . . Syncretism as the unjustifiable fusion of irreconcilable tenets and practices is particularly an issue"[33]

There is a legitimacy to these concerns that cannot be minimized. And the particular theorizing that gave birth to the term "contextualization" has underscored that legitimacy for the evangelical. The term received its formal debut in 1972 in the publication *Ministry in Context,* issued by the Theological Education Fund of the World Council of Churches. A study-committee report, the book presented to the churches the third mandate program (1970–1977) of its work and highlighted as "most crucial to this discussion" the idea of "contextualization" as the way towards reform in theological education.[34]

Shoki Coe, the Director of the Fund, notes that "in using the word *contextualization,* we try to convey all that is implied in the familiar term, indigenization, yet seek to press beyond for a more

[32]David J. Hesselgrave, ed., *New Horizons in World Mission* (Grand Rapids: Baker, 1979), 239–40.

[33]*The Bible and Theology in Asia Today. Asian Perspectives No. 30* (Taichung, Taiwan: Asia Theological Association, 1982), 9.

[34]For a full discussion of the background of this theological history, consult Harvie M. Conn, "Contextualization: Where Do We Begin?" *Evangelicals and Liberation,* ed. Carl E. Armerding (Phillipsburg, NJ: Presbyterian and Reformed, 1977), 90–119.

dynamic concept which is open to change and which is also future oriented."[35] At the core of the change are said to be the theological concepts of *Missio Dei* and history as the hermeneutic of God's speaking in the world. Comments Coe, "Contextuality . . . is that critical assessment of what makes the context really significant in the light of the *Missio Dei*. It is the missiological discernment of the signs of the times, seeing where God is at work and calling us to participate in it."[36]

The references to history's dynamic broaden the TEF discussion to take into account "the process of secularity, technology and the struggle for human justice, which characterizes the historical moment of nations in the Third World."[37] Social, political, and economic issues must be added to the church's theological agenda, to the prophetic encounter between "God's Word and His world." And on perhaps the deepest level of concern to the evangelical, there is a call for a new kind of hermeneutic. It must become a dialectical process that moves back and forth between the text and the context—the situational character of all theology. It is a movement of involvement and participation, out of which critical awareness may arise. It is more than simply taking the semantic context seriously. It is even more than taking the social, political and economic context seriously. It is the "conscientization of the contexts in the particular, historical moment, assessing the particularity of the context in the light of the mission of the church as it is called to participate in the *Missio Dei*."[38] Only through the dialectical interaction between the *Missio Dei* and the historical process does the gospel's contextualization take concrete shape. Only through this process do we understand also what is Text

[35]Shoki Coe, "In Search of Renewal in Theological Education," *Theological Education* 9 (1973), 240; Idem, *Ministry in Context* (Bromley, Kent: Theological Education Fund, 1972), 20.

[36]Coe, "Renewal," 241.

[37]Coe, *Ministry in Context,* 20.

[38]Coe, "Renewal," 241.

emerging from texts. The context becomes an essential part of the hermeneutic, not a goal of the hermeneutic.

Evangelical Reactions to Contextualization

Evangelical reaction to this model circled immediately around its concept of text and contexts. Given the dialectical relation of text and context, how does the text of God function in any normative way over context? In this model, the text does not address the context, but functions dialectically in one's hermeneutical participation, involvement, and commitment within one's cultural context. Where in this interplay process does one distinguish between text and context as separate entities? If the traditional model for hermeneutic can be accused of giving priority to text over context, how can this model escape giving priority to context over text? And in this hermeneutical circle, how can it ultimately not avoid destroying both text and context? Further, Coe makes a sharp distinction between "the Text which transcends all, because it is directed to and derived from the transcendent reality of God in Christ" and "interpreted texts" as "mere earthen vessels," having "to be reformed and reinterpreted."[39] The texts are merely derivative pointers to the Text. How does this distinction preserve the once-for-all, the "given" component of the gospel text as Text? For the evangelical, the texts are more than "merely earthen vessels." They are inscripturations, written incarnations of the transcendent Text. The fear is legitimate that the TEF formulation has added one more distancing factor between transcendent Text and context—that of the "interpreted texts." Normativity of the divine Word (Text) over context becomes even more problematic. And where the divine Word does not norm human contexts, syncretism begins or is at least far less controllable. These concerns, we suspect, have

[39]Ibid., 238; Idem, *Training in Context* (Bromley, Kent: Theological Education Fund, 1973), p. 14.

remained within the evangelical camp from the beginning of the discussion.

Surprisingly, evangelical comments on the TEF formulations have often been silent in another area. Does the model see with sufficient clarity the supernatural, demonic manipulation of the contexts in which the missionary task is carried out? The structure of every culture reflects the world as created reality and man as God's image-bearer in that culture. Yet every culture and every theme of culture reflects also the apostasy of sin. Does the TEF mandate for contextualization play so lightly the theme of the pervasive effect of sin on culture that the ministry of the Word of God becomes largely that of a supporting servant to the self-helping process of humanization or to the liberation of mankind in general history? How closely entwined are the roots of the call for contextualization and theology's preoccupation with secularization as a positive process in the 1960s? The literature concedes the need for "decontextualization" and for a prophetic role of the church and its ministry in cultures. But this dimension is not at all prominent. Contextualization within the model of the ministry as participant in the *Missio Dei* gives high potential to the "possibilities for renewal" in an ultimate contribution "to the solidarity of all people in obedience to a common Lord."[40] Is that conception of a "common Lord" too universalistic to give adequate attention to the reasons for the abuse of economic power or the struggle for human justice? It does not appear to see in any explicitly biblical way the kingdoms, whose cultural riches Satan will show to Jesus, beginning to rise like beasts out of the sea.

Since 1972, evangelical reactions to the syncretism question have become more sophisticated and judicious. There is less hesitancy to recognize terminological differences between indigen-

[40]This concern is the critical center for Bruce C. E. Fleming's book *Contextualization of Theology* (Pasadena: William Carey Library, 1980), even to the extent that, given its lack of attention to the later debate, the book simplistically almost turns the question into a single-issue campaign.

ization and contextualization. Byang Kato, in his Lausanne address of 1974, had recognized that "contextualization of the modes of expression is not only right but necessary." But his perception of what he called "modes of expression" never went beyond the cultic forms of Christianity—questions of liturgy, dress, and ecclesiastical service. When he comes closest to the issue and analyzes the value of dynamic equivalence translations, he remains highly skeptical. By 1978, evangelical scholars like James O. Buswell III were using the new term to cover the traditional agenda of indigenization, adding to it questions of ethnotheology.[41] More recently, Kraft and Tom Wisley have proposed a modification of the old term *indigeneity,* a modification that seeks to incorporate sensitivity to ethnotheological questions.[42] What terminology will eventually prevail is difficult to say now. My own general fear is that those evangelicals who work out of a Consciousness One mentality will turn to dictionary definitions to satisfy their structural anxieties,[43] or that they will insist on terminological choices they need not share with others, thinking they have guarded the truth by creating, or reverting to, vocabulary differentiations. With Bruce Nicholls we affirm that "in the end it is not so much the word used as the meaning that grows up around it that is important."[44]

There also seems to be progress toward recognizing contextualization as more than simply the refinement of communication skills. At Lausanne three of the four definitions of contexualization offered in the study group focused on this area. They were (a) the

[41]James O. Buswell III, "Contextualization: Theory, Tradition and Method," *Theology and Mission,* ed. David J. Hesselgrave (Grand Rapids: Baker 1978), 93–99.

[42]Kraft and Wisley, *Readings,* xx.

[43]This seems to be the argument of Krikor Haleblian, "The Problem of Contextualization," *Missiology* 11 (January 1983): 9. He refers to *Webster's New Collegiate Dictionary* for his understanding of "contextualization," which, he says, is clear "but in the literature on contextualization, there is widespread confusion."

[44]Bruce J. Nicholls, *Contextualization: A Theology of Gospel and Culture* (Downers Grove, Ill.: Inter Varsity, 1979), 21.

distinguishing of the gospel from its cultural clothing; (b) the communication of the gospel in pertinent, meaningful cultural forms—both external forms (e.g., liturgical garments) and thought forms (e.g., time-space dimensions); (c) the communication that speaks to the real issues and needs of the person and his society.[45] Though eventually a two-fold definition was arrived at, the hidden agenda was placing normative significance on only one side of the coin: a "meaningful communication in forms that are real to the person." A paper presented at the 1975 Mission Executives Retreat of the Evangelical Foreign Missions Association (EFMA) moves in this same orbit. Dr. Emilio Antonio Nuñez isolates the content of the message of the gospel (theology) from the context (culture), and brings them together by what Nuñez calls "effective communication."[46]

A major shift in understanding is reflected in the 1978 Willowbank (Bermuda) Consultation on "The Gospel and Culture" sponsored by the Lausanne Committee for World Evangelization. One participant suggested that the gathering may well have been "the first church consultation in history to focus exclusively on the role and dynamics of culture in the understanding and communication of the Gospel of Jesus Christ."[47] The gathering had its drawbacks. More than one participant felt that the Consultation dealt more with issues of indigenization than of contexualization. Its links with earlier evangelical perceptions of contextualization as communication were apparent in at least two of the four stated goals of the gathering.

Yet even here the consultation was moving beyond communication as a question of skill or technique. Heavy emphasis was placed on the significance of cultural factors. Two of the most stimulating papers concentrated on the question of hermeneutics.

[45]J. D. Douglas, *Let the Earth,* 1226.

[46]Emilio Antonio Nuñez, "Contextualization—Latin American Theology," *Latin American Pulse* 11 (February 1976): 5.

[47]Robert T. Coote, "The Gospel and Culture," *Gospel in Context* 1 (January 1978): 19.

And beyond all this may have been the legitimation for pushing the discussions further that such an evangelical gathering provided. Western evangelicals could now begin to speak about the "hermeneutical spiral" without looking over their shoulders. That spiral they now saw as formed out of the constant interaction between the contemporary reader's culturally conditioned questions and the original, culturally rooted message of the Scripture.

Once again, this better understanding was cultivated by the contributions of earlier figures like Charles Taber, Alan Tippett, and Jacob Loewen. They had joined a solid contingent of other anthropologists and linguists at the 1978 Consultation to force new questions on the theologians and exegetes trained in a monocultural Anglo-Saxon tradition. Often it seemed that these two groups talked past each other. But in the apparent talking-past a new agenda was being created and a new appreciation for the complexity of gospel communication was being shaped.

For two brief years (1978–1979), the quarterly journal *Gospel in Context,* edited by Charles Taber, placed the Willowbank questions on the world church agenda. Devoted exclusively "to encourage dialogue on the subject of contextualization," it provided a platform and format, similar to that of the journal *Current Anthropology,* and elicited world response to key issues. The topics it covered in that brief span of existence sought to sensitize the world church to "the challenges presented by the new awareness of the Church's inevitable incarnation in particular societies and cultures for a faithful proclamation and demonstration of the Gospel of Jesus Christ."[48] Critical of what it saw as a kind of one-sided captivity of the gospel to North American and European social and cultural interests, it remained also deeply missiological in its emphasis. The dialogue it created was an interdisciplinary one between the social sciences on the one hand and theology and missiology on the other.

Though the lifespan of the periodical was tragically brief, it

[48]Stephen C. Knapp, "Introducing 'Gospel in Context'," *Gospel in Context* 1 (January 1978): 1.

had a broad effect far beyond its years. It typified the trialogue we have spoken of in this book. And to many of those evangelicals who feared that contextualization inevitably meant syncretism, it provided reassurance that this need not be so. It reinforced a growing evangelical sense of the legitimacy of the deeper issues emerging in the debate.

In this ferment of discussion and progress, the concern about syncretism has not diminished. Nor is it entirely accurate to say that "many ignore the factor (or factors) which lead to syncretism."[49] Rather, there is a growing recognition that syncretism is not a simple process of conscious oil-and-water compromise. Earlier evangelical writing tended toward the simplistic assumption that confidence in an inerrant Bible would solve the problem. And there are those, like Bruce Fleming, who even at this stage of the debate seem to fall back on this kind of resolution.

We cannot discard the solid base of an error-free Word of God that this viewpoint is concerned to defend. The Bible remains our guide rope, tied to which we may search for answers. But even this affirmation is no total guarantee against syncretism in the process of theologizing.

Contextualization and Hermeneutic

Evangelical discussions over the last few years have turned to the process of hermeneutic in their concern about the dangers of syncretism. Earlier thinking had recognized that "missions have all too frequently exported with the Gospel an alien culture, and churches have sometimes been in bondage to culture rather than to the Scriptures."[50] This admission has become more refined as the evangelical has incorporated this insight into an increasingly sophisticated understanding of hermeneutic as the process of finding and communicating meaning in cross-cultural contexts.

[49]Haleblian, "Contextualization," 99.
[50]Douglas, *Let the Earth*, 7.

EXEGESIS

In this process of hermeneutic, syncretism can enter on several levels. There can be an insensitivity to the cultural conditioning of Scripture itself, resulting in a slavishly literal obedience or an irresponsible disregard. In discerning the meanings of Scripture, many continue to affirm "the traditional hermeneutical method of grammatico-historical approach to exegesis of the text as our objective reference." But even then it is acknowledged that this method "is not yet full understanding. A fuller understanding is realised only when we are confronted with the Word which has become flesh, that is, when the meaning of the text grasps us in our own situation."[51] The failing of the "traditional" methods of hermeneutics is seen as its propensity for analyzing the text without applying it, for acquiring academic knowledge without obedience.

The evangelical is less sensitive to the problems in this argument concerning the ultimate achievement of "objectivity" through grammatico-historical methods. Exegesis still carries a mythic aura as a final refuge against theological relativism. The standard models for doing exegesis are still drawn from a mentality operating out of a Consciousness One view of linguistics and culture.[52] Often missing in the evangelical trumpeting of "objective" exegesis is an awareness of certain hidden presuppositions, established and reinforced over the centuries. Exegesis has remained essentially a skill exercised by the Westerner, carried on in a basically Western-oriented, monocultural mindset. It moves within a "Constantinian cultural captivity."

Traditionally, "context" in exegesis is usually defined narrowly in terms of the language of the text. As a result of the challenges of the Tübingen school in the nineteenth century and its

---

[51] *The Bible and Theology in Asia Today*, 3.

[52] Harvie M. Conn, "Contextualization: A New Dimension for Cross-Cultural Hermeneutics," *Evangelical Missions Quarterly* 14 (January 1978): 40–42.

attention to the text's *Sitz im Leben,* the traditional definition was broadened. But even so, the classical evangelical model, exemplified by men like J. B. Lightfoot and B. F. Westcott, remained heavily programmed towards lexicography, etymology, and syntax. Thus even today, evangelical commentaries like the *New International Commentary on the New Testament* remain relatively shorn of introductions where questions of context may be fully treated. By and large, evangelical and liberal commentators alike confine themselves to a form of critical interpretation of the text that remains dominated by historical critical methodology.

Forgetting the unique insights into exegetical method provided by John Calvin, the evangelical tradition began to build on the Western Cartesian distinction between truth and its practice, between abstract theoretical cognition and concrete application. Thus, in exegesis and in communicating the results of exegesis, a narrowed view of hermeneutic has been developed that reduces theology to the ideational and application to the practical. In seminaries this view is reflected in departmental compartmentalization: exegesis is defined as the relatively detached judgment on the text by the Old Testament or New Testament Departments, while the study of the text's "application" becomes the reserve of the Practical Theology Department.

The end result of such an exegetical model has been the erection of a methodology for exegesis and communication that leaves the evangelical weak and vulnerable on several levels in the contemporary discussion. The monoculturalism in which Reformation patterns were born has hardened from a backdrop to an ethnocultural blindness that makes the Western interpreter often insensitive to the *de facto* cultural ingredients that play a formative part in exegesis, in church life, and in any efforts at communication. This same blindness creates in the missionary and Western-trained churchman an ecclesiastical parochialism that keeps us from seeing any good coming from the Nazareths of the Third World church's struggle with its own culture. It contributes to the fossilization of the progress of dogma at the seventeenth- or eighteenth-century stage. Syncretism thus enters on the wings of "objectivity."

PERCEPTION

Evangelicals have made better progress in their study of that level of hermeneutic in which the commentator/communicator recognizes his or her own cultural conditioning in the meaning process. Syncretism of an overt sort is more easily recognized on this level, and its recognition is necessary. But it is often not sensitive enough to the deeper temptation of syncretism of a frequently hidden sort, which occurs when we assume that what is meant in the message is precisely what we understand by the words. Words do not always mean what we think they mean. And the greater the unconscious assumptions carried by the communicator as to word "meanings," the greater the likelihood of misperception. This danger is multiplied again when the receptor decodes the message he or she "hears."

A number of factors condition this unconscious process of perception. There is the whole set of presuppositions about language, meaning, worldview, values, and attitudes that shape the reader as he or she comes across words like "poor," "justice," "righteousness," "redemption." Can the Christian raised in a Confucian culture see more in "righteousness" than the Chinese concepts of propriety and middle way of conduct? Will the believer drawn out of a Muslim setting be able to see the full scope of grace in a word like "redemption"? Will a middle-class North American living in the suburbs catch the oppressive note that lurks in the Old Testament concept of "the poor"? What will "justice" say to a black American in the ghetto of Philadelphia?

Then there are the roles we play in our societies. They come with expected attitudes and prescribed behaviors that strongly influence our understanding of the message. Jesus, in His identification with the poor and oppressed, could urge His disciples to "turn the other cheek" (Matt. 5:38–42). Yet Paul in his role as a Roman citizen could protest unjust imprisonment at Philippi and ask, "And now do they want to get rid of us quietly? No! Let them come themselves and escort us out" (Acts 16:37). And what message would "turning the other cheek" convey coming from a white racist and addressed to beleaguered blacks marching for their civil rights in Birmingham, Alabama? Roles often imply someone on top and someone on the bottom, friendship or hostility. And these factors also change our perceptions of the "message."

How do we escape this seemingly endless pattern of covert syncretism? The readers cannot come to the text in a personal vacuum, with a kind of mental *tabula rasa*.

> Instead, they should come with an awareness of concerns stemming from their cultural background, personal situation and responsibility to others. These concerns will influence the questions which are out to the Scriptures. What is received back, however, will not be answers only, but more questions. As we address Scripture, Scripture addresses us. We find that our culturally conditioned presuppositions are being challenged and our questions corrected. In fact we are compelled to reformulate our previous questions and to ask fresh ones. So the living interaction proceeds.[53]

It is not an endless hermeneutical circle but a spiral in which we constantly grow in our conformity to the will of God, in our understanding of that will.

THE "THIRD HORIZON"

There is still a third area in the hermeneutical process where the potential for syncretism exists. It revolves around the receptor of the message and what might be called the "third horizon" of communication. Contemporary theological discussions of the "new hermeneutic" have been generally framed in terms of two

[53]John R. W. Stott and Robert Coote, eds., *Down to Earth: Studies in Christianity and Culture* (Grand Rapids: Eerdmans, 1980), 317.

horizons: that of the first-century text of the New Testament and that of the contemporary reader. The question then becomes, How can we establish a bridge between these two horizons? But there is yet a third horizon, which appears when the reader communicates the message to a receptor. It is the horizon of the receptor, shaped, when the receptor is part of another culture, by still another set of worldviews, values, and role understandings.

In this dimension of hermeneutic, the reader/communicator multiplies his or her liabilities. Kraft notes at least two paths that can lead to syncretism:

> One is by making mistakes when adapting the Christian message to indigenous forms. Often people experiment with using words and customs to express Christian meaning, and it doesn't work well. Sometimes people are even irresponsible about their attempts to contextualize. The risk of making mistakes is always there.[54]

The other way of bringing about syncretism is, however, a much greater threat. It is that of refusing to adapt God's meanings to new cultural forms. Kraft cites that as the failure of the Pharisees and the Judaizers, who sought to preserve expressions of God's message that were foreign to their hearers. Such foreign forms cannot adapt to changing meanings and often become unchristian in the process.

Or again, the receptor may be the major contributor to syncretism at this stage. The dangers for the receptor may parallel those for the reader/communicator: the receptor may be overly dependent on sociohistorically shaped perceptions of the world, values, and general knowledge and thus may not able to "hear" the message. The Sawi of Irian Jaya blocked out their perception of Jesus as the believable center of the gospel because of their value system that saw betrayal as a virtue and not as a vice. When they first listened to the message of Jesus' suffering and death, this

[54]Charles H. Kraft, "The Contextualization of Theology," *Evangelical Missions Quarterly* 14 (January 1978): 35–36.

cultural value system transposed Judas Iscariot into the hero's role and not Jesus.

Other factors also increase the potential for syncretism from the receptor side of the hermeneutical continuum. Charles Taber cites several possibilities, which we need only sketch at this point.[55] The receptor may reject the message simply because it comes under inappropriate circumstances. Or the interpretation of the communication will be affected by what gain the receptor thinks can be obtained from it—the archaic epithet "rice Christian" is a testimony to this danger. Or yet again, the form of the text (poetry or prose, narrative or proverb) will elicit certain cultural expectations on the part of the receptor. Thus, the Muslim spurns the authenticity and authority of the Bible because it is given in some places as history, in others as letters, but not in the consistently psalm-like, poetic structure of the Koran. Or the Western-trained scientist brings the equation of truth with objectivity, precision, and abstraction to a Bible written not in technical language but in ordinary everyday speech; and when the Biblical message is heard, it is perceived as either failing to give right answers or displaying scientific error.

Once more, we see cultural anthropology and the concomitant skills of linguistics and communication as aids in combatting one more pitfall in biblically-shaped theologizing. Syncretism appears when the dictates of Scripture are not allowed to challenge, and then transform, the receptor culture. Anthropology underlines the emic character of syncretism by exploring the three cultural horizons that enter into the communication process. It serves the missionary by helping to strip away the sociocultural presuppositions that are too often carried unbeknownst into the program of understanding, either by the missionary or the receptor. It provides the communicator with what might be called a "hermeneutical tool of suspicion." And with the use of that tool the text speaks with less ambiguity and more cultural clarity.

[55]Charles Taber, "Hermeneutics and Culture—An Anthropological Perspective," in Stott and Coote, *Down to Earth,* 82–88.

PROVINCIALISM

A deep motive that compels Third World churches to try to "indigenize" their brand of Christianity is their hope of de-Westernizing it. Will that motive, reinforced by a Consciousness Two mentality that tends toward a static view of human cultures, swing us in the opposite direction? Will we become so enamored with the particularism of our statically viewed contexts that we descend into theological parochialism? Will we substitute one form of emic Christianity, produced in the West, for another form produced in Korea or Brazil or Uganda? "Will international churches split apart and Christianity become nationalistic too? What happens to the vaunted 'church universal' in all this, and will Jesus be so tied to regional and national differences that we are no longer 'one in Christ' but 'many in Christ'?"[56] No one wants to let Christianity be reduced to a set of racial or national clubs, exclusive and "for members only." How can Christianity remain particular and universal at the same time?

Dr. Sunand Sumithra expresses these fears in his evaluation of the 1982 *Seoul Declaration*. He commends the emphasis of that document on the unity affirmed in the supreme authority of Scripture. But he was "amazed to see how our diverse contexts compelled us to diverse approaches to the same 'basic evangelical convictions.'"[57] Is a Third World evangelical theology necessary? If we confess, using the language of the Declaration, that "our concern is to interpret the Word of God in the light of our own historical context for the sake of Christian obedience," are we not in danger of missing the Bible's privilege and duty to judge the context? In Sumithra's words, is it the self-understanding of the context to which the gospel text must address itself? Or is it not

[56]Frederick Sontag, "A Plea for Common Sense," *Missiology* 7 (July 1979): 366.

[57]Sunand Sumithra, "Third World Theologians Consultation, Seoul, 1982—An Evaluation," *Aim* 13 (November 1982): 11.

rather that that self-understanding must listen to God's interpretation of the text?

I hear the same concerns behind what Haleblian calls "another basic question which remains unresolved. . . .Who shall participate in the quest for local or cultural theology? The foreigner, the national, or both?"[58] Sumithra, in the same spirit, laments the exclusion of non-Third World theologians in the quest for a contextual theology.

Gospel "Core"

Is this also a basic concern behind the search for a supracultural, unchanging "gospel core"? Can that core be identified and separated from the cultural forms in which it is given? What does a noncontextualized gospel look like?

This quest for the core has legitimacy. It is created by an evangelical concern that is a response to a theological history of liberal cutting and paring of the Bible. The result is usually a Jesus remade in terms of the cultural interests of the time; he becomes a rationalist (D. F. Strauss), an idealist (Ernst Renan), an existentialist (R. Bultmann), a revolutionary Marxist. Lost in the shuffle of changing roles is the "givenness" of the gospel, its divine source and preservation. The gospel as both the source and the criterion of our proclamation disappears in the fog of our hermeneutical search for "the gospel within the gospels."

At the same time, this proper anxiety can minimize other equally legitimate considerations. The absoluteness of the divine source of revelation is conveyed through inspired authors who themselves were shaped by cultural worldviews, social values, ethnic behavior patterns. The Bible, though not culturally distorted, is culturally particularized. For that reason we study Hebrew and Greek, spend large sums of money on research into the Dead

[58]Haleblian, "Contextualization," 98.

Sea Scrolls, and analyze ancient Near Eastern attitudes towards women to understand better the radical contribution of the Old Testament on this theme.

And "insofar as the gospel is *news,* there is no gospel apart from concrete correlative acts of proclamation and response. Both of these acts are performed by human beings within the limits of language and culture."[59] And those limitations operate as both binoculars and blinkers. Lacking in sensitivity to this form of communicator/receptor relativity, "we shall be tempted to ascribe to those expressions of the Gospel in the theology, liturgy, and behavior patterns which we know best a finality, fullness, and universality which may only be claimed for the Gospel itself, and for the Christ of whom it speaks."[60]

I have a suspicion that some of the categories with which we have studied the gospel have been thus qualified. From the ancient Greek philosophers comes our description of the gospel "given" as "universal," existing in some absolute form in the ideal mind of God. From Cartesian rationalism comes our idea of the gospel as "essential." A gospel defined in terms of these categories, Taber reminds us, is useless, because as long as it is essential it is by definition unavailable. But as soon as it becomes available it is contextually conditioned. The concept of a universal abstract truth that is valid for all people is a philosophical assumption more at home in Platonic idealism than in the Christian faith. One is deeply suspicious that much Western theology, especially evangelical theology, is built on this concept.[61]

Similar linguistic and cultural problems exist when we speak of a "core" of the pure faith and search for its identifiable boundaries. Haleblian summarizes the recent history of this search

---

[59]Charles Taber, "Contextualization," in Shenk, *Exploring Church Growth,* 122.

[60]J. I. Packer, "The Gospel: Its Content and Communication," in Stott and Coote, *Down to Earth,* 101.

[61]Vinay Samuel and Chris Sugden, "Comments on 'The Contextualization Continuum'," *Gospel in Context* 2 (July 1979): 17.

and concludes in much the same manner we might. It is a misleading quest because

> the biblical accounts are rooted in cultural and historical circumstances, and they cannot easily be disengaged from the forms in which they are given. To separate the content of the gospel from its cultural forms is similar to peeling an onion in order to find its core. What is urgently needed is a method that can sidestep kernel-versus-husk type questions.[62]

Donald McGavran's formulations in this area give us a sample of the difficulties. Anything that damages this core he sees as "forbidden syncretism. Anything which leaves this core intact is permissible adjustment."[63] He defines the core in terms of three affirmations:

(1) belief in and allegiance to the Triune God alone
(2) belief in the Bible as the only inspired Word of God
(3) belief in "those great central facts, commands, ordinances and doctrines which are so clearly set forth in the Bible."[64]

"If," he continues, "a church faithfully transmits the first two parts of the core, a degree of elasticity in regard to part three can be tolerated. Great elasticity in regard to part three cannot be tolerated. No change in a central fact, ordinance or doctrine is acceptable which negates or damages points one or two."[65]

With McGavran, we recognize the dangers of "forbidden syncretism" in connection with the gospel message. And with him, we would allow for "permissible" differences of opinion (we do not like the word "adjustment" in this connection). We are even willing to concede, for the sake of our discussion, that his three affirmations are basic to our understanding of the gospel.

At the same time, has McGavran's distinction helped us in the

[62]Haleblian, "Contextualization," 102.

[63]Tetsunao Yamamori and Charles R. Taber, eds., *Christopaganism or Indigenous Christianity?* (Pasadena: William Carey Library, 1975), 41.

[64]Ibid., 41–42.

[65]Ibid., 42.

task of isolating that is inherent in the word "core"? We think not. Ultimately it does not isolate. McGavran's third point is so broad, so comprehensive, that it is not a limiting factor but an expanding one. The core becomes as broad as the Scripture itself.

We have no difficulties with this expansion. In fact, it merely illustrates the impossibility of the task McGavran sets for himself under the rubric "core." The simple gospel is never that simple. The good news of God's redemption available to us in Christ as Lord and Saviour is always more than "simple core," whether we identify that "core" with some Four Spiritual Laws or the five-point TULIP acronym familiar to the Calvinist tradition out of which I function. The church as the new humanity of the Spirit is part of the good news of Christ. The redemptive healing Christ promises to give to the relationships between husbands and wives and between masters and slaves is part of the good news of Christ. The abandonment of a lifestyle built on laziness, accumulation of wealth, or racism is part of the good news of Christ. Can we allow for any greater measure of elasticity in preaching and living this part of the good news than we can for an infallible Bible or the reality of the triune God in our lives? Even the affirmation of the reality of a realm of life labeled *adiaphora* does not imply the existence of any practice in the Christian life untouched by the demands of God's covenant, whether that be fingernail biting or eating meat from the market place. The demands of the gospel of the kingdom are too comprehensive to allow for a peeled-down core.

May we also say that much of McGavran's argument displays (indeed, presupposes) some of the weaknesses we have outlined as the results of a Consciousness Two mentality? The gospel "core" as McGavran sees it is a functionist set capable of replacing methodologically similar functionist sets within the receptor culture. Cultures, he says elsewhere, are aggregates rather than organisms. While a high degree of interrelatedness is observable, the components are seldom essential to the culture. "Most components can be changed or even abandoned without trauma."[66] In order to penetrate a culture as a functional set or aggregate, we must have a "core" with similar qualities. "Core" as message must also perform as "core" as methodology, again a functional set or aggregate.

Particularization similarly shows itself in a compartmentalizing process of message reduction. The "core" may be dichotomized. Some parts are more functional and fall under the rubric "discipling," the first stage of Christian penetration into the culture, while other parts are more functional and fall under the rubric "perfecting," the advanced stage of Christian expansion within the penetrated culture. The comprehensiveness of the gospel message is compartmentalized by functionism into isolatable bits and pieces. And the transformation process which the gospel carries on as it enters human cultures becomes thereby less achievable.

Gospel "Center"

Ultimately, are we not better served by speaking of the "center" of the gospel than of its core? Even those who, like Charles Taber, speak with such concern about the contextual rootedness of the Bible, are also willing to argue that

> the Bible speaks univocally on one central point: that God intends and in Jesus Christ makes possible the restoration of a lost world to himself and to its true nature; and that it continues to be tragically possible for human beings to reject God's way back and so to forfeit life. The fact that the rule of God is the heart of the gospel in the Synoptics makes it clear that it is impossible to separate salvation from the doing of God's will.[67]

To speak of the gospel center does not require the jettisoning

[66]Donald McGavran, *The Clash Between Christianity and Cultures* (Washington, DC: Canon, 1974), 38.

[67]Charles R. Taber, "Missiology and the Bible," *Missiology* 11 (April 1983): 235.

of the cosmic demands of Jesus as being Himself the gospel for all human cultures. Nor does it require embracing the dilemma of fidelity versus relevance as some sort of eternal paradox we will never escape. The gospel center must always be context-specific. To use Taber's phrase, the good news is never addressed "to whom it may concern." The gospel center of God's redemptive activity in Christ has to be addressed to the specific form the human predicament takes in each given case.

> Thus, if the form of lostness which people experienced was captivity and slavery in an alien land, salvation took the form of an exodus. If, later, lostness took the form of material prosperity, coupled with grievous social injustice and religious idolatry and nominalism, the message was one of judgment with a call to repentance and a promise of restoration.[68]

But the center remains center, whether it be Jesus the Messiah (addressed to a Jewish audience) or Jesus as Lord (addressed to a Gentile audience). The gospel "sameness" is not eroded by the gospel's particularization when presented to Nicodemus in terms of being born again or to a rich young ruler in terms of giving away his wealth. It is simply being made specifically appropriate. If the gospel, in fact, is not big enough, wide enough, enduring enough, to speak to each dimension of the human condition in human cultures, it is not universal enough to take away the sins of the world. Ultimately, "core" language demands that we think in terms of gospel irreducibles. "Center" language demands that we think in terms of gospel expansions.

Supercultural/Supracultural

This expansionism of the gospel makes me reluctant to use other terms currently employed in our discussions. I speak of such categories as "supercultural" and "supracultural" (see p. 156).

---

[68]Ibid., 236.

Behind both these adjectives is a useful and proper intention—to underline the transcendence of God with respect to culture.

> That is, God, being completely unbound by any culture (except as he chooses to operate within or in terms of culture) is "*supra*cultural" (i.e., above and outside culture). Likewise, any absolute principles or functions proceeding from God's nature, attributes or activities may be labeled "supracultural." For they, too, transcend and are not bound by any specific culture, except when they are expressed within a culture.[69]

This same motivation has created the parallel term "supernatural" in the theological past. I have the same concern about both terms. My own reluctance in using either of the terms does not come out of any desire to support the existence of some divine pancultural structure of an absolute sort. Even the divine legislation for the theocracy of the Old Testament cannot be interpreted in that way; it was fulfilled in Christ and we are no longer kept in cultural custody by a tutor (Gal. 3:23–24) but walk in the glorious liberty of the children of God (Rom. 8:21). Nor do I wish to detract from the awesome transcendence of God over the cultural kingdoms of this world.

Rather, I am fearful of the same compartmentalization that is found in the history of the analogous terms "natural" and "supernatural." I see the danger that this history will be repeated in applied missionary anthropology in a compartmentalization of the "cultural" and the "supercultural/supracultural."

The accommodation model proposed by Louis Luzbetak is one example of this. Though Roman Catholic in its theological origin and orientation, the model has been widely commended in evangelical circles. Deeply aware of the dynamic character of cultures, Luzbetak constantly sees the gospel as the perfecter of culture, the fulfillment of culture's aspirations. Using the prior model of Thomas Aquinas, he sees culture as an "adaptive system," one in which culture is that "Nature which Grace

[69]Kraft, *Christianity in Culture*, 120.

presupposes in apostolic work and builds upon." Against this background, applied missionary anthropology becomes the tool through which the missionary "might become the natural instrument of Grace, so that Grace might build upon Nature."[70] Fleshing out the dimensions of his appeal to "reason and prudence" as primary criteria for setting the limits to accommodation and "the expectations of the local people" as secondary criteria in numerous illustrations,[71] his summary statement requires the missionary to adopt in those areas defined as "matters that have a purely culturally defined value" such values and practices himself or herself, "as long as they are in accord with prudence, Faith, Science, the aims of the Missions, and the expectations of the local people."[72]

In this paradigm (which Niebuhr's typology might designate as "Christ above culture"), what Luzbetak calls "the Thomistic view of deprivation" sees the gospel facing culture "as somewhat more sympathetic toward adaptation" than what he terms the Reformed view of distortion.[73] He summarizes the process of accommodation in a paraphrase of Matthew 5:17: "I come to perfect the ideals of my adopted people because I know that they have ideals worth perfecting." This process of adaptation or accommodation requires not merely adjustments to parts of the cultural worldview but to the total organism—the cultural "system of interconnected subsystems . . . in turn made up of interwebbed functionally organized elements."[74]

Luzbetak has modified these earlier judgments. More recently he has found the term "accommodation" to be vague, if not misleading. He now prefers to speak of "incarnational accommodation." The additional element seeks to do justice to the context

---

[70]Louis Luzbetak, *The Church and Cultures* (Pasadena: William Carey Library, 1970), 45.

[71]Ibid., 84–103.

[72]Ibid., 103.

[73]Ibid., 58.

[74]Ibid., 346.

of the specific situation of time and place and to foster interaction in dialogue between the older and younger churches, the younger church respecting the importance of the universal Christian tradition and the older church respecting the local heritage.[75]

As a corrective to the evangelical tendency to operate with a functionist concept of culture that is more modalistic than structural, Luzbetak's emphasis on the unifying configurations of culture's "themes" is useful. At the same time, the accommodation concept can reduce culture (nature, to use the classical term) and the history of culture to the dimensions of "a period of preparation under Law, reason, Gospel and the church for an ultimate communion of the soul with God."[76] Its end result can easily be a "god-endorsing-a-culture perspective"—a charge Kraft makes against the Thomistic model in general.

To be sure, Luzbetak's concept does not seem to be structured overtly and explicitly on the Thomistic theological natural/supernatural paradigm, against whose possible excesses Niebuhr and Kraft warn. The orientation of his model is anthropological and sociological. And it is his intention to stress these disciplines as human tools especially helpful for activities associated with the conversion of groups and of individuals as members of a society or subsociety. He sees accommodation in this context as the human art of preaching Christ by word and deed in a way tailored to the given time and place. No one should quarrel with that insistence.

Nevertheless, we see behind these wholesome admissions an implicit guideline that recognizes accommodation as "the official policy of the Church."[77] And thus it is linked to a tradition of natural law, systematized in theological form by Aquinas. It is a natural/supernatural model in which grace is seen as not destroy-

[75]Louis Luzbetak, "Two Centuries of Cultural Adaptation in American Church Action: Praise, Censure or Challenge?" *Missiology* 5 (January 1977): 63–69.

[76]Luzbetak, *Church and Cultures,* 7.

[77]Ibid.

ing nature but perfecting it, natural reason ministering to faith as the natural inclination of the will ministers to charity. This, we fear, taints Luzbetak's virtues with the defects implicit in the Thomistic compartmentalization of culture as the religiously pseudo-neutral "configurations" of natural law. Thus Luzbetak describes the limits of accommodation to culture repeatedly as "the limits set by Christ—Faith (which includes the nature of the Church), prudence, reason and the goals of the apostolate."[78] Similarly, missionary identification with a culture "is positively willed, discriminating, always in accord with Faith, Science, reason, prudence and the aims of the Missions."[79]

We see operative in this language the Thomistic compartmentalization that divides natural from supernatural. Prudence and reason, as "neutral" tools, can usher a culture to the threshhold of faith. "Matters that have a purely culturally defined value" are matters not tainted by the corruption of the fall, matters that need only a *donum superadditum* provided by faith for their completion, their perfection. Faith becomes an additive, not an essential ingredient.

Protestant theological history has not always escaped this bifurcation either. The older terms *natural* and *supernatural* were coined in apologetic dialogue with the Western Enlightenment mind. Their purpose also was an effort to reinforce the reality of the divine activity in human culture, God as both transcendent and real in the affairs of men. But the practical effect of the distinction, among those wholesome ones, was a miring of the divine activity in the natural, a growing tendency to see God's work as an "exception" to an orderly creation. Miracles became supernatural "interventions" in an otherwise normal process. Out of this came a growing injustice to the integration of the natural and the

[78]Ibid., 348.
[79]Ibid., 99.

supernatural—the creation of a two-realm dualism of mind in the Christian church.[80] This distinction allows culture to be quickly interpreted as a religious neuter in its essential meaning, radically untouchable at its heart by the dimensions of the kingdom of God. Redemption and its results become isolated from its calling to regenerate the creation.

This basic concern continues to leave me reluctant to use even terms like "supracultural." Will it be possible for the models proposed behind this term to make the divine activity once again distant from the process of culture change initiated by the gospel? Can the term be seized by a Consciousness Two mentality and leave us once again with some part of culture in the grip of a determinism that will not allow it to be shaped by the word of grace? Is "transcultural" a better way to express what is intended by "supracultural"? The point, after all, is how to do justice to the culture-boundness of human beings on the one hand and to the freedom from culture-boundness of God and His Word on the other, while recognizing the continuous engagement of that free Word of God as it is contextualized within human cultures. "Supracultural" as a term does justice to the first two elements of the process but minimizes our attention to the third. And it is precisely the third element that can easily be lost in evangelical concerns. "Transcultural" may fare better in acknowledging all three parts of the hermeneutical process. Ultimately we are not "searching for universals or constants, either by probing the deep structures of language or any other aspect of culture (without denying the importance of such studies), or in some timelessly valid truth above and beyond history." We are searching for human language to express our submission to God's Lordship over cultures as the controlling reality in those cultures. "The unique function of the Bible is that it documents by inspiration this

[80]James H. Olthuis, "Must the Church Become Secular?" *Out of Concern for the Church* (Toronto: Wedge Publishing Foundation, 1970), 117.

historically realized lordship and the requisite, historically and culturally qualified submission."[81]

But if the kingdom demands of the gospel "core" are more inclusive than exclusive, and if even this "core" must be contextualized in the variety of human cultures, are we not still left with the danger of cultural particularism descending into theological parochialism?

We are. And there are many Third World theologians today who are not hesitant to point to the Western hermeneutical and theological enterprise as a clear example of that kind of provincialism. The question is not, Can the Third World church avoid provincialism as we have in the West? The question is, Whose ox is being gored?

We are helped here by Kraft's argument concerning the distinction between emic and etic theologizing, reviewed in our last chapter.

Theologizing, argues Kraft, always begins on the emic (insider) level. Through the guidance of the Holy Spirit the message of the Bible is "inculturated" into the human cultural dimension without compromising either the message or the receptor culture. Integrity is preserved on all levels.

Thus, to Africanize Christianity is to promote an African expression of the interpretation of the gospel center. The pastoral dimensions of theology seek to facilitate for Africans the conditions for hearing the gospel. The exegetical dimensions seek to insure that it is heard in terms of the originating message of the biblical documents.

How does this form of theologizing preserve its transcultural form, what many have called its universally applicable shape? Here Kraft reminds us that theologizing must also have its etic dimension. In fact, he contends that it is only this approach, since it is cross-culturally oriented, that may be labeled "theology."

[81]Richard B. Gaffin, Jr., "Comments on: 'Is There More Than One Way to Do Theology?' " *Gospel in Context* 1 (January, 1978): 22.

Emic theologizing (called "theography" by Kraft) is too parochially culture-specific. How is an etic approach to theologizing to appear? Through the comparison and analysis of many emic varieties.

Kraft sees very little of this kind of etic theologizing to date. And in terms of a specific effort at analyzing emic theologizing, with particular attention to the Third World, he is right. At the same time, surely the history of the development of doctrine throughout the life of the church has etic qualities, even though few have approached the problem of the development of doctrine intentionally from that perspective. The problem is at least twofold. Most of the doctrinal developments have been analyzed without sensitivity to the transcultural backgrounds that surely played a role in their shaping. And Western monoculturalism has continued to disregard the increasingly visible agenda of Third World theologies that waits to enrich the doctrinal progress of the world church. Much of this may have happened, if we believe the thesis of Peter Toon, because within the evangelical community of the last hundred years we have operated with a model for the development of doctrine that favored a homogeneous evolution of doctrine. Doctrine, on this model, was seen as merely a continuous, cumulative growth in understanding.[82] With this model went a lack of sensitivity to historic situationalism, to the humanity of doctrinal statements of faith, shaped not only by the Bible but also by historical and cultural conditioning.[83]

When that study begins to be undertaken more earnestly, we sincerely expect that Kraft's skepticism will need altering. Surely the history of the development of doctrine up to this exciting point in time cannot be reduced to merely "theography" (to use Kraft's term). What the church possesses now must have some universal characteristics that can only have come about through transcultural

[82]Peter Toon, *The Development of Doctrine in the Church* (Grand Rapids: Eerdmans, 1979), 81.

[83]Ibid., 86–87.

modifications. Our problem is again a monocultural essentialism that has been blind to this process.

Will the dangers of syncretism in this process be minimized by the participation of non–Third World theologians? Sunand Sumithra speaks for many when he warns against their absence.

Certainly "it is becoming increasingly evident that working within a single intellectual frame of reference . . . makes anyone, willy-nilly, parochial. . . . A hermeneutic worked out exclusively within one civilization and history will have its strong points and its clear insights, but it will also have its inevitable weaknesses, errors and blind spots."[84] The voice of the cultural outsider/missionary, acting as an idea "broker," can under the best of circumstances help to provide "continual cross-fertilization and *mutual* correction."

At the same time, that outsider carries his/her own single intellectual frame of reference, equally liable to parochialism. Tutelage by Western agencies over non-Western churches has not always encouraged the flowering of Third World theologies faithful to the Scripture and to human cultures. Those who imagine that they alone have done truly catholic exegesis and theology do not always make the best tutors in the development of emic theologies. Their presence is not always the best guarantee that we will have a Christianity that is in, but not of, every culture.

---

[84]Taber, "Missiology and the Bible," 240.

Part Three

Reaching for the Future

Chapter Six

Theology and Theologizing: A New Course

SUMMARY

The contemporary world setting calls theology to recover its missiological dimension. The shift in the Christian population from north to south, the vast scale of human poverty, the size of the non-Christian population, the frustration of Third World churches with Western theological hand-me-downs—all demand a reinvestigation of the criteria for doing theology.

Six criteria especially are significant. (1) Biblical theology, the history of special revelation, must seek to retain the dynamic element of revelation-as-process needed by those who fear the static Western character of present-day systematic theology. (2) A covenantal dimension will underline that divine truth is radically transforming faithfulness in word and deed to God's faithfulness. It rejects theologizing as an "objective" task, isolated from the lifestyle of a discipline. In this process, what the anthropologist calls "meaning" becomes what the theologian calls "application." (3) Theology must be culture-specific in recognition of the receptor-oriented character of divine revelation. Paul's discussions of "Christian liberty" and of "offense" make these demands on us. (4) In the process of doing theology, we seek to recapture the evangelistic task of theology as confession before men. The creedal formulations of the church in the West have largely become tests of the orthodoxy of the members. The original role as evangelistic response to a contextual crisis must be recovered. (5) As communal statements of faith, theologies and theologizing cannot simply be borrowed or imposed. Neither can the process of creating theology isolate one part of the church from another. The Third World acceptance of Western creedal formulations can be healthy if certain conditions are carefully kept. Furthermore, how will theology as a communal statement include poor as well as rich and address a cultural agenda crucial to the marginalized? (6) Related to this question is theology's calling to be prophetic. How can it function to confront the agendas of human cultures and challenge the sociocultural ideologies of the world's societies? How can it also carry out this prophetic ministry in hope and joyfulness?

Chapter Six

Theology and Theologizing: A New Course

WINDS OF CHANGE

In a sense, asking for a new collaboration between theology, missions, and anthropology is misleading: It can imply that there was no interaction before. Our previous chapters have indicated that this is not true. But there is a newness of background that now shapes or prepares to shape the discussions. The agenda is no longer largely a metaphysical one supplied by Western philosophy. We are no longer primarily interested in purely ontological or epistemological topics, in questions of formal theological encyclopedia. These questions need to be faced, and the answers provided will have a deep effect on what we do in missions and in theologizing. But rightly or wrongly, the background is more urgent and pressing.

There is the *shift in the Christian axis.* By the end of the twentieth century, the new center of ecclesiastical gravity will have moved from the northern to the southern regions of the world.

This is not a threat to the North American church but rather the fruit of 150 years of gospel endeavor. "The old centers of theological influence in Europe and North America are becoming the new peripheries, while the new centers of vitality and importance in church growth and theological construction are in Asia, Africa and Latin America—where the majority of Christians will be living in the year 2000."[1]

There are the *political dimensions* of the missionary task that increasingly demand our attention. Nearly every Third World nation today is under an authoritarian government. How will we prepare the church for that awesome reality? How do we live and witness to our faith under conditions of oppression and authoritarianism? What is the mission of the church in the People's Republic of China and in the Philippines, in North and South Korea? How should Christian discipleship face the suppression of human rights, the torture of dissidents, the strictures against baptism and church building?

The vast scale of *human poverty* in traditional "mission fields" presses us.

> The numbers of the poor are increasing in the world today. . . . It is generally accepted that up to two billion people—one half of the world's population of four billion—are now poor. The World Bank describes one billion of these people as "individuals (who) subsist on incomes of less than $75 a year in an environment of squalor, hunger and hopelessness. They are the absolute poor, living in situations so deprived as to be below any rational definition of human decency. . . . It is a life at the margin of existence." For the other billion who are living slightly above this absolute poverty level, life is nearly as

[1]Gerald H. Anderson, "Facing the Realities of the Contemporary World in Mission," *Educating for Christian Missions,* ed. Arthur L. Walker, Jr. (Nashville: Broadman, 1981), 50–51.

> joyless and has improved little if at all through decades of "development" efforts.[2]

Should missions alone address the intolerable fact that two-thirds of the human family go to bed hungry every night? What will our theology say about, and to, fifteen thousand people who starve to death every day? What portion of our theological curriculum will we devote to the twenty percent of the human family who control eighty percent of the world's resources?

There is the awesome *size of the world's non-Christian population*. In Jesus' time it numbered 250 million. Today, it is estimated that out of a total population of 4.2 billion, 2.8 billion are non-Christians—eleven times as many non-Christians as when Jesus preached the Sermon on the Mount. By the year 2000 the world population will have increased by fifty percent and Christians will constitute only fifteen percent of that vast multitude. Is this only a missiological concern?

There seem also to be signs that the evangelical theological community is beginning to engage in serious *self-evaluation*. It is asking itself harder questions than it has in many decades. And in this process of inquiry, the questions traditionally labeled "theological" or "missiological" frequently converge.

The current debate over the Bible grows. And as it does, the complexities of the question grow. Theologians ask about the metaphysical presuppositions that have gone into shaping our paradigms. Scholars like John Vander Stelt[3] and Jack Rogers[4] raise angry questions about the distorting influence of Scottish Common Sense Realism on a view of Scripture long associated with the

[2]John G. Sommers, *Beyond Charity: US Voluntary Aid for a Changing Third World* (Washington, DC: Overseas Development Council, 1977), 2.

[3]John Vander Stelt, *Philosophy and Scripture: A Study in Old Princeton and Westminster Theology* (Marlton, NJ: Mack Publishing, 1978).

[4]Jack Rogers and Donald McKim, *The Authority and Interpretation of the Bible: An Historical Approach* (New York: Harper & Row, 1979).

evangelical cause. Solid scholarship has responded to these charges with much wisdom.[5] But at this point I draw attention not to the correctness of the exposition but to the fact that questions are being raised.

Similarly, the recent report of the Reformed Churches in the Netherlands on the nature of the authority of Scripture begins with a philosophical discussion of "Changes in the concept of truth." With many others, I am concerned about the "relational" idea of truth with which the report leaves us.[6] What is meant when we are told that our conceptions of Scripture must attempt to transcend the traditional dilemma between the objective and the subjective? Will all of this really accomplish the avowed purpose of promoting a better listening to Scripture? It is not my purpose to answer that question now. I only note the significance of a Reformed church asking again about metaphysical presuppositions. As Herman Ridderbos notes regarding the discussion, "All Reformed theology, wherever it is done, . . . ought to be more critical than it is of its own position."[7]

As we noted earlier, Kraft challenges us on the same issue from another direction. He demands that we rethink the question of inspiration in terms of anthropological models and see the Bible as an inspired, classic casebook, as "ongoing dynamic revelation." He refuses to allow the debate over the Bible to become simply a question of scriptural justification. The missiological dimension is put in the foreground as an essential key to progress. Authority, he insists, must be defined in terms of that which is addressed by authority—namely, human cultures.

Out of this community of interests come new questions.

---

[5]For helpful critiques, consult John D. Woodbridge, *Biblical Authority: A Critique of the Rogers/McKim Proposal* (Grand Rapids: Zondervan, 1982); Richard B. Gaffin, Jr., "Old Amsterdam and Inerrancy?" *Westminster Theological Journal* 44 (Fall 1982): 250–89.

[6]Al Wolters, "Truth as Relational," *RES Theological Forum* 9 (January 1982): 7.

[7]Herman N. Ridderbos, "Evaluation," *RES Theological Forum* 9 (January 1982): 56.

Have we propositionalized revelation into an acultural vacuum? Can our confidence in the "bearing along" work of the Spirit (2 Peter 1:21) lift the Bible up, over, and around human cultures without ever going through those cultures? What do we mean by anthropomorphism in revelation? Is this theological category ultimately a missionary method of God Himself? There is always the danger that the gospel truth will be lost in cultures. And many have fears that Kraft's views could lead us, either wittingly or unwittingly, in that direction. At the same time, is there not also the danger that cultures will be lost in the gospel truth?

In the last chapter, we drew attention to the new questions raised by both theologians and missiologists in the area of hermeneutic. In the evangelical-theology camp, Anthony Thiselton presses upon us the urgency of the concerns of "the new heremeneutic." How may the New Testament text speak to us anew? How must we understand understanding? If a text is to be understood there must occur an engagement between at least two sets of horizons, namely that of the ancient text and that of the modern hearer or reader. How does this happen?[8]

In an evangelical atmosphere traditionally hostile to the methods of Heidegger and Bultmann, Thiselton has forced us to look at the seriousness of their questions. Some evangelicals are already entering the debate,[9] a sure sign of more yet to come.

In this discussion, missiology reminds us that Bultmann's motivations behind his demythologization paradigm arose out of a concern for a non-Christian, shattered Europe. Evangelical theology has labored to critique Bultmann's method correctly. But have we labored with equal concern to see how much deeper our own grasp must become of the problems he and others force us to face?

[8]Anthony Thiselton, *The Two Horizons: New Testament Hermeneutics and Philosophical Description* (Grand Rapids: Eerdmans, 1980), 10–17.

[9]See the reactions of Walter Kaiser, Jr., in "Meanings From God's Message: Matters for Interpretation," *Christianity Today* 22 (October 5, 1979): 30–33; and *Toward an Exegetical Theology* (Grand Rapids: Baker, 1981), 29–40.

How distant are these concerns from the liberation theologians who struggle with this same question of the two horizons and end up defining theology as "reflection on praxis"? Third World evangelicals like René Padilla and Samuel Escobar are not at all satisfied with the answers of either Bultmann or Gustavo Gutiérrez. But they are also angry about the cultural interference from Western evangelical theology that has distorted the airwaves between the two horizons. They criticize past hermeneutical methods and remind us that "neither our understanding of the text nor our understanding of our concrete situation is adequate unless both constantly interact and are mutually corrected."[10]

There are other indications of change in our midst. But these should be enough to allow us the liberty of suggesting a new collaboration between cultural anthropology, missiology, and theology and, through this, some new dimensions for theology and its task.

THE MISSIOLOGICAL CALL FOR NEW DIRECTIONS IN THEOLOGY

Theology and Missions in the Past

In its times of greatest glory, theology was more than reflection *in* mission—in pilgrimage on the road among the time-bound cultures of the world. It was also reflection *on* mission—on Jesus as the good news for the world, on the church as salt and light and leaven for human cultures.

John Calvin's theological methodology exemplifies much of that combination for us. His battle cry of *sola Scriptura* was not simply the demand that we approach the Bible with an empty slate. As a pastor, he approached the Bible from his contemporary situation, as we approach it from ours. His work had an

[10]René Padilla, "Hermeneutics and Culture—A Theological Perspective," in *Down to Earth, Studies in Christianity and Culture,* ed. John R. W. Stott and Robert Coote (Grand Rapids: Eerdmans, 1980), 76–77.

evangelistic dimension and he tried to apply the gospel to his own time and place. As a "physician of memory" he reached back into another time and place through the Scriptures and sought to transform the present through the insights thus gained. He "translated" the gospel without benefit of morphology or phonemics and recovered for the church the covenant dimension of theologizing. Across the infinite gap between Creator and creature, God baby-talked to His creation and we responded in covenant responsibility. That response was missionary theology. "Calvin, having first established what stands in the text, sets himself to re-think the whole material and to wrestle with it, till the walls which separate the sixteenth century from the first become transparent! Paul speaks, and the man of the sixteenth century hears."[11]

The uniqueness of Calvin's missionary theologizing is particularly awesome when we remember the scholastic origins of theology as an academic discipline. Theology as a scholarly study had gone hand in hand with the slow development of the twelfth-century schools into the first universities. G. R. Evans cites three ingredients in that development.

The first of these was *the study of the Bible.* But with it also came increasingly a perception of *theology as a metaphysical science of speculation,* dependent to a considerable extent upon the secular concepts of *philosophia.* Thus theology saw its task as a universal one of ontology. And as a result of that ontological self-understanding, it spent its time on abstracted definitions, affirming God as Being with a capital *B.* It transmuted the Aristotelian distinction between an object's "essence" and its "accidents" into the

---

[11]Karl Barth, *The Epistle to the Romans* (London: Oxford University Press, 1953), 7. For a fuller exposition of this view of Calvin, consult Jim O'Brien, "Ford Lewis Battles: 1915–1979, Calvin Scholar and Church Historian Extraordinary," *Calvin Theological Journal* 15 (1980): 163–83.

assumption that subjects can gain "objective knowledge" of given objects, in this case God.[12]

The danger of this abstractionist thinking has always been that things are viewed as existing in themselves without taking into consideration the relationships in which they stand to other things. It thus asks, What is God in Himself? No movement can be applied to God; therefore we confess that He is immutable and eternal. No limitations can be applied to God; therefore we hold that he is infinite, almighty, and invisible. No composition can be ascribed to God; therefore he is simple and good. Finally, no essential multiplicity can be ascribed to God; therefore God is one.[13]

A third ingredient was part of this scholastic approach to theology. Evans calls it "a missionary theology."[14] But that designation seems inaccurate to me. *Polemical theology* would be more appropriate. The "polemical" approach betrays the danger of ontologizing thought. In this case, its concern is with truth as it exists in itself. It minimizes truth in relationship to its hearers. Unbelievers are transformed from covenant creatures needing covenant renewal that only Christ can bring into *infideles, haeretici, increduli,* those who dispute the true knowledge. In the twelfth century, the church had begun again its dialogue with the Jews. But the dialogue was polemical, not missionary. The goal of the church was not simply conversion but elimination by the pen or by the sword. The scholastic polemicist pursued the truth, not sinners. And that pursuit was not intended simply to woo hearts to Christ but to do battle with the irrational *philosophi* in the defense of truth.

Calvin's contextualization of the gospel confronted that

---

[12]Alfred Krass, "Contextualization for Today," *Gospel in Context* 2 (July 1979): 27.

[13]John Timmer, "G. C. Berkouwer: Theologian of Confrontation and Co-relation," *Reformed Journal* 9 (December 1967): 17.

[14]G. R. Evans, *Old Arts and New Theology: The Beginnings of Theology as an Academic Discipline* (New York: Oxford University Press, 1980), 38, 137–66.

approach in a radical way. His covenant theology admitted no realm of "objective," outsider knowledge of God as object. The path of knowledge always began with the Creator and ended with self-understanding as creature. As a result of this recognition, Calvin's polemical training in the law was modified by the evangel intent of the pastor. His use of the rhetorical discipline was transmuted by the pastoral calling of the theologian.[15]

The Present Demand for Change

Evangelical theology in the years following Calvin lost those insights. And the contemporary discussions over the nature of theology and of missiology may be traced in large part to this failure. It is a delayed symptom of a disease that has been endemic to evangelical theologizing.

In keeping with the scholastic shape of our past, one can find this quest for pure essentials in many theological traditions. The Reformed theology I embrace is one of these. Thus, divine election in the approach of a Louis Berkhof may be seen as a logically inferred corollary of the doctrine of the divine decrees.[16] It resembles an "accident" of grace logically consequent to the "essence" of divine sovereignty. Against this view has risen what some now call the "functionalism" of G. C. Berkouwer. He has no desire to leave any believer in the dark as to the ultimate and prior question of his or her election. And this pastoral concern of his theology may be much more than simply pastoral in the academic sense of "practical." Is it the setting free of theology from the bondage of deduction that is linked to an essentialist approach to theology? "He does not seek to arrive at theological

[15]Ford Lewis Battles, "God was Accommodating Himself to Human Capacity," *Interpretation* 31 (1977): 20.

[16]Louis Berkhof, *Systematic Theology* (Grand Rapids: Eerdmans, 1949), 109.

definition. . . . Rather he seeks to arrive at an understanding of problems by viewing them in the context of their relationships."[17] Is Berkouwer's method signaling a new way to do theology, one that is missiological in a good sense and not simply essentialist?[18] Can we sense his struggle with the question of methodology behind what appears to many of us to be a fuzziness with regard to distinctions ?

Do I sense a similar struggle with method, albeit with far more useful formulations, in John Frame's definition of theology as "simply the application of Scripture to all areas of human life"?[19] Frame says, "We do not know what Scripture says until we know how it relates to our world. The question of interpretation and the question of application are the same. To ask what Scripture says, or what it means, is always to ask a question about interpretation."[20]

Surely we can all identify the missiological concerns of contextualization in this kind of language. Questions about the meaning of Scripture do not arise simply out of essentializing concerns. This is not to ignore or minimize the definitional characteristic of all theologizing that is done by covenant. It is simply to recognize that such questions are also missiological—our calling to relate the words of Scripture to our worldviews, our cultures, our homogeneous units of world "peoples."

Related to this struggle is the evangelical's perception of theology as some sort of comprehensively universal science. Theology becomes functionally the queen of the sciences, the watchdog of the academic world, the ultimate universal. Combined with Western ethnocentrism, it produces the tacit assump-

---

[17]Timmer, "Berkouwer," 20.

[18]A full discussion of Berkouwer's hermeneutic methodology will be found in J. C. DeMoor, *Towards a Biblically Theo-logical Method* (Kampen: Kok, 1980).

[19]John M. Frame, *Van Til: the Theologian* (Phillipsburg, NJ: Pilgrim, 1976), 25.

[20]Ibid.

tion "that the Christian faith is already fully and properly indigenized in the West."[21] Our creedal formulations, structured to respond to a sixteenth-century cultural setting and its problems, lose their historical character as contextual confessions of faith and become cultural universals, having comprehensive validity in all times and settings. The possibility of new doctrinal developments for the Reformed churches of Japan or Mexico is frozen into a time warp that gnosticizes the particularity of time and culture. The Reformation is completed, and we in the West wait for the churches of the Third World to accept as their statements of faith those shaped in a *corpus Christianum* by a Western church three centuries ago.

In all this, there is no desire to diminish the place of a creed as the expression of the progressive understanding of truth conveyed by the Holy Spirit. Nor do we want to minimize or question the system of doctrine found in the Reformed creeds of these past centuries. What we are concerned with is how we have diminished their historical, contextual character. The creed as a missionary document framed in the uniqueness of a historical moment has too often been remythologized by white paternalism into a universal essence for all times. Contextualization, as a missionary demand of theologizing, is relegated to the non-Western "mission field."

Herman Bavinck objected to this process of universalization in 1894. In the strongest language, he commented:

> All the misery of the Presbyterian Churches is owing to their striving to consider the Reformation as completed, and to allow no further development of what has been begun by the labor of the Reformers. . . . Calvinism wishes no cessation of progress and promotes multi-formity. It feels the impulse to penetrate ever more deeply into the mysteries of salvation and in feeling this honors every gift and different calling of the Churches. It does not demand for itself the same development in America and England [and the author of this volume adds, Africa, Asia and Latin America] which it has found in Holland.

---

[21]David J. Bosch, "Theological Education in Missionary Perspective," *Missiology* 10 (January 1982): 16–17.

> This only must be insisted upon, that in each country and in every Reformed Church it should develop itself in accordance with its own nature, and should not permit itself to be supplanted or corrupted by foreign ideas.[22]

Today the Bavincks of the Third World churches speak even more stridently. Borrowed Western creeds have been accepted by them as testimonials to the catholicity of the gospel, as fraternal symbols of a new relationship with the Western churches that have sometimes "mothered" them. They make them their own confessions in order to affirm their place in the historical, theological continuum. But in doing so, they also find themselves saddled with sixteenth-century definitions of the church concerned with what happened inside the church: on preaching, the sacraments, and discipline. "In these historic creeds, the church was a place where something was being done (passive voice), and not a people who did something."[23] Stephen Neill says that the Reformation pronouncements in England on the church

> call up a vision of a typical English village . . . where all are baptized Christians, compelled to live more or less Christian lives under the brooding eye of parson and squire. In such a context "evangelization" has hardly any meaning, since all are in some sense already Christian, and need no more than to be safeguarded against error in religion and viciousness in life.[24]

The objections of Third World church leaders are not to theology per se but to the Western nature of their borrowed systems. Does the gospel require them to become Western Louis Berkhofs and John Murrays before they can be themselves? Their agony is not usually so much over theology as over the construction of a logically coherent system, organized around a

---

[22]Herman Bavinck, "The Future of Calvinism," *The Presbyterian and Reformed Review* 5 (1894): 23.

[23]Bosch, "Theological Education," 17. Compare also Lesslie Newbigin, "Theological Education in a World Perspective," *Ministerial Formation* 4 (1978): 5–6.

[24]Stephen Neill, *The Church and Christian Union* (London: Oxford University Press, 1968), 75.

Western historical agenda insisted upon as universal by the Western church. They cry out for the missiological dimension to creed making. The mission of the gospel to their cultural worlds demands creedal attention to ancestor worship, polygyny, the Islamic state, to group movement conversions, and how to shepherd them. How will the Three Standards of Unity and the Westminster Confession, Luther's Catechism or the Augsburg Confession help them? Intuitively the Third World church is making a discovery. Systematic theology is not simply a coherent arrangement of supracultural universals. It is a compilation of the Western white history of dogma. And that history, in the process of compilation, has lost its missiological thrust.

The effect of this process on the Western churches is similarly destructive of mission. Seeing theology as an essentializing science and the creeds as the product of that kind of theological reflection inhibits us as well from facing up to our own contemporary missiological task and its risk. We assign all the problems of contextualization to distant, exotic places and worry about how others will avoid syncretism with this view of theology. We assume that such risks and such challenges are absent, or at least less pressing, in the West. We let our theologizing slip into a naive sort of idealistic pride in "our" model. We become less aware of the rosy presuppositional glasses with which we look at our rosy theological world. And our theology loses its evangelistic edge.

Will this missiological thrust destroy the uniqueness of such a confessional system as the Reformed faith? Not when we are willing to see that uniqueness, as Fred Klooster does, in the Reformation slogan *sola Scriptura et tota Scriptura* (Scripture alone and all the Scripture).[25] Rather, missiology's task then becomes that of a gadfly in the house of theology:

---

[25]Fred H. Klooster, "The Uniqueness of Reformed Theology," *Calvin Theological Journal* 14 (1979): 32–54. I find it intriguing that Klooster sees this principle as needing elaboration in at least two major areas to which we have devoted so much time in this book—the nature of theological science and the problem of hermeneutic.

> It must exert itself in and out of season to help theology—especially Western theology—find its way back down from the upper regions of the towers of academia to the ground floor of human reality. . . . By the same token missiology also has a mission to the church. The church, too, must ever be reminded that its *raison d'être* lies in the gospel of the kingdom. The fellowship of the new covenant must be urgently summoned to obedient covenant response, to live its covenant life. The congregation must be called to become what it is in Pentecost, to reaffirm its being and existence by living in mission.[26]

Reformed theological orthodoxy is no guarantee that the world perspective of the Scriptures will receive the attention it is due. Missiology stands by to interrupt at every significant moment in theological conversation with the words "among the nations."

CRITERIA FOR DOING THEOLOGY

With Charles Taber, I prefer to speak of "criteria for Christian theologizing" rather than of "rigid limits" of theologizing.[27] Our attention is thus focused on central norms rather than peripheral frontiers. And our question becomes, Where are the centers from which we proceed? At the same time, we are concerned legitimately with how far we can go. Too often, questions as to outer boundaries may hide the assumption that the Western world has already discovered the central norms and that we may leave the periphery to Third World church discoveries. In addition, to talk of centers allows for more freedom, more openness to biblical discoveries still to be made as the Bible and human cultures interact.

---

[26]Jerald D. Gort, "The Contours of the Reformed Understanding of Christian Mission: An Attempt at Definition," *Calvin Theological Journal* 15 (1980): 46.

[27]Charles R. Taber, "The Limits of Indigenization in Theology," *Missiology* 6 (January 1978): 29–30.

Biblical-theological

To speak of "biblical theology" is to speak of far more than simply the recognition that our theology must be biblical. We refer to a relatively young discipline, to "that branch of exegetical theology which deals with the process of the self-revelation of God deposited in the Bible,"[28] more easily called the history of special revelation. Like systematic theology, it is exegetically based and aims at synthesis or coordination. But unlike systematic theology, whose structure is logical, biblical theology is historical. It deals with revelation as an activity or process, not primarily as a finished product. It approaches the Bible not as a dogmatic handbook but as a historical book.

All of this we see as opening new dimensions in the interaction between anthropology, missions, and theology. Biblical theology's focus on revelation as a historical activity underlines the dynamic, rather than static, character of revealed truth. John Murray speaks of the "tendency to abstraction" on the part of systematic theology, the tendency to dehistoricize, to arrive at "timeless" formulations in the sense of topically oriented universals.[29] This danger becomes even more real for Third World theologians whose agendas of concern do not fit easily into the traditional Western loci of theology. Biblical theology provides a model that, by its very nature, reminds us of the historico-contextual character of our theologizing.

At the same time, that history of special revelation is organic in character. The Bible is not merely a heterogeneous collection of oods and ends, nor a symposium of biblical theologies. Biblical theology seeks to do justice both to the diversity of the divine testimony within the diversity of human settings and to the

---

[28]Geerhardus Vos, *Biblical Theology* (Grand Rapids: Eerdmans, 1948), 13.

[29]John Murray, "Systematic Theology," in *The New Testament Student and Theology*, John H. Skilton, ed. (Presbyterian and Reformed, 1976), 25.

underlying unity of that testimony. It studies the data of revelation given in each period of cultural history in terms of the stage to which God's self-revelation progressed at that particular time and place. But its unifying element is always the end point of the process, not the process itself. Its wisdom is always defined in terms of the administration of the mystery hidden in ages past, revealed in Christ, made known among all the world's cultures, and consummated at his return (Eph. 3:8–10; Rom. 16:25–26; Col. 1:25–27).

Biblical theology reminds us of the Christ-centered heart of the Scriptures, of its history as the history of redemption. Theologizing, as the application of that redemptive history, then becomes eschatological in a deeper sense than we usually think. It is an eschatology defined not only with reference to the second coming of Christ but inclusive of His first coming and the present existence of the church in the world (Heb. 1:1–2, 1 John 2:19). We are those "on whom the fulfillment of the ages has come" (1 Cor 10:11). We are part of the eschatological history of redemption, living as we do in the tension between the beginning of the end and its consummation at Christ's return. Contextualization then is covenant activity taking place between the "already" of redemption accomplished in Christ and the "not yet" of redemption to be consummated in Christ.

The realization of that place of tension should create humility and patience with ourselves and with one another in the work of theologizing in context. It reminds us of the ease with which our perceptions of the gospel can be deeply influenced by unconscious impositions of cultural and socio-structural perspectives on the biblical data. Contrary to Alfred Krass's opinion, biblical theology does not pride itself on its "objectivity," its "presuppositionlessness," its "value-neutrality."[30] The "not yet" of biblical theology should make us "pervasively suspicious" about our ideas, our ideologies, our value judgments.

---

[30]Alfred C. Krass, *Evangelizing Neopagan North America* (Scottdale, Pa.: Herald, 1982), 95.

This eschatological dimension also provides the biblical structure for our place in the divine hermeneutic with culture. Kraft's argument places great stress on our work of theologizing as a contemporary continuation of the same dialogue between God and man that we see exhibited in the Scriptures. As stated, our problems with that formulation revolve around the difficulty of preserving the distinctiveness of the Scriptures as part of that process while recognizing some element of continuity.

We now suggest that eschatology, oriented toward the central significance of the coming of Christ in the history of redemption, provides us with more than a static theological formulation. It has deep and dynamic implications for the methodological significance of contextualization. It reminds us, to quote Vos, that "we ourselves live just as much in the New Testament as did Peter and Paul and John."[31] Putting it in terms we have used in this volume, it means that hermeneutic in the context of the church stands closer to the teaching of Paul or the preaching of Peter than the latter stand to the prophecy of Isaiah or the Psalms of David.[32] The contextualization provided by Scripture and our task of contextualizing theology are both concerned with the same subject and done with the same methodology. Both are oriented toward and derived from the history of redemption. In other words, we share a common contextual, hermeneutic interest. With the Bible itself, we engage in interpretation of interpretation.

Yet, at the same time, there are important differences between our contextual theologizing and the theologizing furnished by the biblical writers. Our method and procedure are dependent on and derive from theirs. Their theologizing is God-breathed and inerrant; ours is always tentative and in need of correction.

Is it possible that biblical theology can provide a way of escape from the inherited dangers of "systematic theology"? Can

---

[31]Vos, *Biblical Theology*, 325.

[32]Richard B. Gaffin, Jr., "Contemporary Hermeneutics and the Study of the New Testament," in *Studying the New Testament Today*, ed. John H. Skilton (Presbyterian and Reformed, 1974), 17.

we find here that sense of freedom, of openness to new approaches to the Bible as the Scriptures are brought into contact and confrontation with the world's diverse cultural and social contexts? Is "systematic theology" so captive to the encumbrances of Western categories and methodologies that we must now, for the sake of a truly emic theology, discontinue its use or look to biblical theology to reinforce its strengths and minimize its weaknesses? Can we use "biblical theology" "to designate the comprehensive statement of what Scripture teaches (dogmatics), always insuring that its topical divisions remain sufficiently broad and flexible to accommodate the results of the redemptive-historically regulated exegesis on which it is based"[33] and, we would add, to reflect the varieties of the world's contextual agendas? Is it possible that biblical theology can return us to a methodology more in keeping with the organic, historical character of special revelation itself? And in doing so, will we come closer to what Kraft calls for: an understanding of the original situation in the original frame of reference?

Such a biblical theology will not demand formulations expressed only in the categories and images of the Bible itself; as we have said, it clearly affirms the place and role of the contemporary communicator. From a redemptive-historical perspective the interpreter affirms not only that he or she stands in the same continuum of the presence of the kingdom as, for example, the apostle Paul; the interpreter also affirms that, just as biblical theology demands fullest justice to the cultural context of redemptive history, so the commentator too must look at his or her own situational context with care. Our contemporary setting is part of that flow of redemptive history that is addressed by the Scriptures.

Finally, will the biblical theological method also reaffirm the "communication situation" in which all theologizing must be

[33]Richard B. Gaffin, Jr., "Systematic Theology and Biblical Theology," *The New Testament Student and Theology*, John H. Skilton, ed. (Presbyterian and Reformed, 1976), 49.

done? Such a setting centers neither around the original frame of reference nor around that of the communicator—rather, it focuses on the hearer, the receptor. Its purpose is to reencode the original message within the hearer's frame of reference. And it is done in such a way that both communication and response are dynamically equivalent to those of the original situation. Here biblical theology shifts our focus again to the continuity of experience between Paul and ourselves, drawing on the dynamic equivalence of our common existence in the overlapping tension between this age and the age to come. We are called on to grasp with heart and life that we are all members of God's eschatological kingdom, the kingdom that is not only at hand but also present in Christ the king.

We do not pretend in all this that biblical theology will escape forever the stigma of "purely empirical, deductive research." But our place in the process forbids us to go in that direction. Let him who is without ideology cast the first stone. As interpreters of the text we read by faith. But that faith is wrapped in our presuppositions about society, cultures, and history. For that reason, our approach to the Bible is not a once-a-lifetime reading but an all-our-lifetime "being-read-by."

Covenantal

Theology as a process should be radically transforming reflection, the discipled reflection/action of "knowing God." It is the encounter of truth with context.

Truth conveyed in revelation is not simply an objective word, verified propositionally by God. It is a covenant knowledge, the call of the covenant Suzerain for the expression of our covenant faithfulness in a God-centered way of living (Titus 1:6–9, 2:1ff). There is a distinction between sound teaching and godly living (Titus 1:9). But there is also a necessary relation—and theology must reflect that relation.

This is seen in the Scripture when it speaks of God as Truth and of His revelation as true. The thought is not primarily that of accurate doctrinal assertions or rationally exact declarations, which can then finally be fed by us into human creedal formulations. Assuredly, they can be and they are. But that is not the point. God as Truth is God in covenant faithfulness to Himself.

Philip Holtrop has argued that we must define truth in terms of faithfulness (*emet*), the enactment by word and deed of God's faithfulness to Himself and to humanity, the constancy of God in covenant with His creation.[34] "Your word, O LORD , is eternal; it stands firm in the heavens. Your faithfulness continues through all generations" (Psalm 119:89–90). In keeping with this merger of truth with faithfulness, the Septuagint renders the Hebrew word *emet* as *aletheia* (truth) 119 times and as *pistis* (faith) 26 times. *Emet* becomes a comprehensive term in the Old Testament for true religion (Ps. 25:5, 26:3, 86:11, Dan. 8:12, 9:13, 10:21). So God is the "rock" of Israel: "He is the Rock, his works are perfect, and all his ways are just. A faithful God who does no wrong, upright and just is he" (Deut. 32:4). The name symbolizes his unchangeable fidelity, the truth of His words, the solidity of His covenant promises. His words will not pass away (Isa. 40:8). His promises will be kept, for God does not lie or retract (Num. 23:19). His plan is carried out by the power of His word, a word that does not return without fulfilling its mission (Isa. 55:11). God does not change (Mal. 3:6). He unites with Himself the spouse He has chosen by a bond of perfect fidelity (Hosea 2:20). Without that faithfulness there is no knowledge of God in the land (Hosea 4:1).

Again, this character of knowledge and truth reinforces the receptor-oriented character of the revelation of God and our modeling of that orientation in the task of theologizing. Truth consists in an actualizing of *emet* in our lifestyle, in "maintaining covenant" (Exod. 34:6–8; Ps. 31:6). The opposite of truth in Scripture, therefore, is not simply error but disobedience,

---

[34]Philip Holtrop, "A Strange Language," *Reformed Journal* 27 (February 1977): 9–13.

infidelity, forsaking the covenant. In that light we understand the commendation of Rahab in Hebrews 11:31. In that light the references to "sound doctrine" in the Pastoral Epistles take on covenant dimensions.

The focal point of the concept, says Holtrop, is imbedded in the context of living, acting, or doing the truth within a covenantal setting (1 Tim. 1:8–11; 4:6ff.; 2 Tim. 1:13; 4:1ff.; Titus 1:9; 2:1–5). Thus, those who "teach sound doctrine" must be spiritually mature, for their teaching will be in their lives and not merely in the words they utter. The "teaching" must be entrusted to "faithful men who will be able to teach others also," those willing to take their "share of suffering as a good soldier" (2 Tim. 2:1; cf. 1 Tim. 6:3–5).

This emphasis is particularly strong in the Johannine materials. There the truth that sets us free is not a Greek ontological or essentialist category. It is Jesus, the concrete expression of the Father's covenantal fidelity to His covenant promise (John 8:31–36; 15:10–11). He sends forth "the Spirit of truth" which leads us "into all the truth." But again, the truth into which He leads us is the truth of faithfulness and reliability, of steadfastness to His own given word, of the trustworthiness of his covenant, of His redemptive promise. Faithfulness and truth are very much the same in John. *Aletheia* in the fourth gospel has sometimes a meaning very close to Paul's *pistis* (faith).

Recent discussions of contextualization have begun to incorporate this understanding. Under its impact theologizing becomes more than the effective communication of the content of the gospel to the cultural context; it becomes the process of the covenant conscientization of the whole people of God to the hermeneutical obligations of the gospel. We can no longer simply ask, How are the demands of the gospel of the kingdom communicated in cultural thought forms meaningful to the real issues and needs of the culture at that time? We ask, How shall the child of God, as a member of the body of Christ and the fellowship of the Spirit, respond with integrity to the Scriptures in his or her culture in order to be able to live a full-orbed kingdom lifestyle in covenant obedience with the covenant community?

Contextual theology merges the two questions of proclamation and presence into one: "doing the will of God" (Matt. 6:10; 7:21) in "doing the truth" (1 John 1:6). Doctrine and Christian living, faith and life, "orthodoxy" and "orthopraxis" cannot be separated, held in balance, or even considered apart from each other. If I tell the truth apart from love and piety, I am not "doing the truth" at all—and consequently I am not telling the truth, according to Scripture.

At the heart of this process will be what we might call praxis. Liberation theology locates that praxis in the dialectic interaction of reflection and action in the concreteness of history. It defines that concreteness by reducing its motivations ultimately to the economic factor, using the concepts of Karl Marx. God-centered praxis cannot be content with that explanation of history. Humanity is not *homo laborans* but *imago dei,* covenant creature called to live by covenant before the Great King (Gen. 1:26).

The most important contribution of liberation theology is its emphasis on the significance of doing (in its societal form) for correct understanding or hermeneutic. Its failure is its emphasis on the autonomy of practice (following the modern inversion of the relation between theory and practice).

> A theologically appropriate understanding of the relation between theory and practice must take into consideration the *already–not yet* structure of Christian existence. Because of the *not yet* aspect of Christian existence, theology cannot accept the self-sufficiency of theory disinterested in practice. And because of the particular historical *already* in Christ, theology cannot accept practice freed from independent normative theory.[35]

Praxis, then, as we understand it, is not isolated from theologizing as some "second step" (Gustavo Gutiérrez). "It is

[35]Miroslav Volf, "Doing and Interpreting: an Examination of the Relationship Between Theory and Practice in Latin American Liberation Theology," *Themelios* 8 (April 1983): 19.

rather a reflection that takes place in the concrete missionary situation, as part of the church's missionary obedience to and participation in God's mission, and is itself actualized in that situation."[36]

Theologizing, in this sense, can never be "objective." It is created out of covenant commitment to the covenant God. Sovereign grace bestowed creates reciprocal responses of faith, love, and obedience. In creating a response, grace testifies to divine initiative. That the response created is reciprocal testifies to the human obligation involved. In faithfulness to His covenant, Jehovah liberated His people from Egypt (Exod. 6:7). And in faithfulness to the covenant the people of God must express their nature as "a kingdom of priests and a holy nation" (Exod. 19:6; 1 Peter 2:9). Keeping covenant is not a call to reflection on praxis but to reflective commitment in praxis.

As we have said elsewhere, too often theology has lost this praxeological dimension. It has become known as an abstract discipline, not as a "conscientizing" instrument. Brevard Childs reminds us that the eschatological "now" of our stance between the *already* of Christ's first coming and the *not yet* of His second coming can be manipulated to separate the history of redemption from our place with Peter, Paul, and John in that history.[37] If theology is to be biblical theology, its focus is not simply the self-reassurance of an exegetical job well done. It calls for the reappraisal of those demands and solutions we originally brought to it at the initiation of our participation in the "hermeneutical spiral." Theologizing is the task of each new generation standing in its particular moment of history. It searches the Scriptures in order to discern the will of God and strives to receive guidance on its way toward the obedient life that must be pursued within the concrete issues of the world's concrete cultures.

---

[36]Orlando Costas, *Theology of the Crossroads in Contemporary Latin America* (Amsterdam: Rodopi, 1976), 8.

[37]Brevard Childs, *Biblical Theology in Crisis* (Philadelphia: Westminster, 1970), 123–28.

"Praxis" then is not just a matter of semantic manipulation, creating one more faddish word for "practice" or "application." The latter terms come from a traditional distinction between "meaning" and "application," between "theory" and "practice," a bifurcation that needs radical reexamination. The distinction is still maintained even by those willing to recognize the legitimacy of "contextualization."[38] In the light of our discussion of "sound doctrine," we suggest that "application" as an English verbal symbol comes close to "teaching" (*didache, didaskalia*) in the New Testament sense. Teaching in the New Testament, as my colleague John Frame has argued, is the *use* of God's revelation to meet the spiritual needs of people, to promote godliness and spiritual health. It is not a mere description of human religious feelings (Schleiermacher) nor is it an attempt to formulate truth in some merely "objective" sense.

Every request for "meaning" becomes a request for an "application." To borrow again the language of John Frame,

> whenever we ask for the "meaning" of a passage we are expressing a lack in ourselves, an ignorance, an inability to *use* the passage. Asking for "meaning" is asking for an application of Scripture to that need: we are asking Scripture to remedy that lack, that ignorance, that inability. Similarly, every request for an "application" is a request for meaning: the one who asks doesn't *understand* the passage well enough to use it himself.[39]

One does not understand Scripture unless one can apply it to new situations, to situations not even envisaged in the original text (Matt. 16:3; 22:29; Luke 24:25; John 20:31). So the whole process from exegesis/translation to application-in-cultural-life could be called "interpretation" or "finding the meaning"; or it could be called "application." And the results of this dynamic process we

[38]For an example of this sustained usage, consult Richard W. Engle, "Contextualization in Missions: A Biblical and Theological Appraisal," *Grace Theological Journal* 4 (1983): 135.

[39]John Frame, "Doctrine of the Knowledge of God." Mimeographed lecture notes, Westminster Theological Seminary (1980), 58.

designate "theology." Otherwise, how could truth be suppressed by unrighteousness (Rom. 1:18)? How else could he who does the truth come to light that his deeds might be manifested as having been done in God (John 3:20–21; cf. 17:6–8; 1 John 4:8)?

At this point we see converging the anthropologist's discussion of "meaning" and this theological usage of "application." Kraft uses the word "meaning" as a receptor-oriented category to describe "the structuring of information in the minds of persons."[40] It is a structuring that moves within the hermeneutical spiral between the text and the interpreter's obedience-in-love. In the process, what has traditionally been called correct practice becomes the preinvolvement for correct theory (to use the old language). And equally, correct theory becomes the preunderstanding for correct practice. And throughout this covenant dialectic, Scripture alone functions as the criterion for the whole of the process.

Culture-specific

The missiological dimension of theology requires people to step outside their setting and look at theologizing as intrusion into a human culture by an outside force that aims at directional change. Endemic to the missiological dimension is its cross-cultural character. Thus the pastoral intention of all theologizing adds to the obligation to be relevant the complexities of being relevant in a cross-cultural setting.

Recent models of Christian exegesis are dealing with this question of relevance through the insights of redaction criticism. Scholarship increasingly recognizes, even within evangelical circles,[41] the pastoral motivations of authors like Luke and Matthew,

[40]Charles Kraft, *Christianity in Culture* (Maryknoll: Orbis, 1979), 135.

[41]Stephen S. Smalley, "Redaction Criticism," *New Testament Interpretation: Essays on Principles and Methods,* ed. I. Howard Marshall (Grand Rapids: Eerdmans, 1977), 181–95; compare also Grant R. Osborne, "The Evangelical and Redaction Criticism: Critique and

who selected and used historical materials to suit a didactic purpose aimed at a particular readership. What were those purposes? How are they displayed in the choice of materials, in the arrangement of those materials? In this quest for author intention, differences are studied in the search for, e.g., the individual character of Lukan theology; harmonization efforts are minimized though not forgotten. At this stage of our argument, we see the value of redaction criticism in its recognition of the receptor-oriented character of divine revelation, making it a tool that affirms the culture-specific intention of the biblical writers. The Scriptures again provide us with a model that calls for contextual rootedness in addressing the Word of God to human cultures.

Are there biblical guidelines, flowing out of the church's realization of its eschatological place in the history of redemption, that may help us in extending this model into our own time and settings? To my mind, there are. Evangelicals have usually considered them under the limited rubric of Christian liberty. But in doing so, they have been reduced to limited Western topics like theatre attendance, smoking, and the use of alcoholic beverages, and thus their larger dimension has been obscured.

In the Pauline context, the question of the participation of believers in life in the world's cultures flows out of the eschatological tension we have touched on before: "On the one hand, in virtue of their communion with Christ believers belong to the new creation, they have been redeemed from the present aeon and have gone over into the kingdom of Christ (2 Cor. 5:17, Gal. 1:4, Col. 1:13); on the other, they are still in the flesh, and consequently with all their present mode of existence they still belong to the present world (Gal. 2:20, 1 Cor. 5:10)."[42] Paul structures his

Methodology," *Journal of the Evangelical Theological Society* 22 (December 1979): 305–22. The fullest attempt at use of it will be found in: Robert H. Gundry, *Matthew: A Commentary on His Literary and Theological Art* (Grand Rapids: Eerdmans, 1982).

[42]Herman Ridderbos, *Paul: An Outline of His Theology* (Grand Rapids: Eerdmans, 1975), 301.

sensitivity to that twofold relationship of the church to the world around the biblical idea of "offense" (*skandalon*). For Paul and the New Testament, the term is broad enough to include a whole range of questions, from an intellectual repugnance at the idea of a cross (1 Cor. 1:17) to ethical stumbling at the idea of eating meat (1 Cor. 8:13), from personal questions (Matt. 5:29–30) to social issues (Mark 4:17).

The core of the idea of offense is never a matter of hurt feelings or even individual sensitivity. It is always a matter of some hindrance to one's faith in Jesus Christ. It is the conflict over anything that hinders the free and open expression of our faith in Christ—whether a right hand, a left eye, Greek wisdom, or a Roman cross. It may concern meat offered to idols or not offered—or even the receiving of little children (Matt. 18:5).

Dr. Harvey Smit outlines two features of this approach to the idea of offense that have relevance for our questions. He calls them "two lines which are in tension": [43] (1) All unnecessary offense must be avoided as something that endangers another's faith; (2) there is an essential offense that must never be avoided, for it is only by overcoming this *skandalon* that a person comes to faith.

Paul's handling of the question of the weak and the strong in Corinth (1 Cor. 8:1ff; 10:23ff.) and in Rome (Rom. 14:1–15:7) underlines Smit's first point. The question revolves around different issues in the two contexts. In Corinth, the problem is that of meat offered to idols, in Rome it is the tendency to totally abstain from certain articles of food on religious grounds. But in both churches the collision of divergent views causes a *skandalon* for those whom Paul designates "the weak." In Corinth the *skandalon* can lead to division in, or to the separation of the weak from, the community (1 Cor. 8:10–11). In Rome the *skandalon* is

[43]Harvey Smit, "An Approach to Practical Apologetics, with Specific Reference to the Japanese Scene," *The Christian Faith in the Modern World*, ed. Paul C. Schrotenboer (Grand Rapids: Reformed Ecumenical Synod, 1970), 6.

that the weak will act with wavering faith and against their culturally framed conscience (Rom. 14:20, 23).

Paul does not underestimate the danger of this "offense." It has eschatological seriousness. The strong with his freedom destroys the brother whom Christ has saved (Rom. 14:15). He wounds the conscience of his brother (1 Cor. 8:12). The weak, by acting against conscience and against faith, "has (already) fallen under the condemnation of the judge" (Rom. 14:23). In all of this, Paul shares the faith of the strong (Rom 15:1, "we then that are strong. . ."). But he takes the side of the weak (". . .ought to bear the infirmities of the weak").

In both of these contexts Paul is primarily focusing on the need for placing liberty under the discipline of Christian love for the sake of the building up of the body of Christ. But at the same time he is not unaware of the relation of these questions and their solution to "those who are without." Sanctification and mission merge these questions into one cultural center of concern.

In none of his discussions does Paul accede to a religious neutrality with regard to the significance of cultural practices. To him or her who lives by faith in Christ, no food or gift is wrong in itself. But neither is it neutral with respect to religious roots. The Colossian heresy, which seems to have been associated with a legalistic-ascetic list of prohibitions and slavish prescriptions, leads to "worldly" scrupulousness and timidity with regard to foods. The church has been redeemed from this religious bondage to handle-not-and-taste-not levels of meaning. Our bondage is to Christ (Col. 2:18–23). Eating and drinking and marriage are rituals with religious meaning in this context. But "what in faith and with thanksgiving is received from the hand of God is not to be rejected. It gets its holiness through the Word of God that speaks of the redemption of the whole of life, and through prayer in which it is received believingly (1 Tim. 4:1ff)."[44]

"All things are yours . . . whether the world, or life, or death,

---

[44]Ridderbos, *Paul,* 302.

or things present, or things to come, all are yours; but you are Christ's; and Christ is God's" (1 Cor. 3:22–23). Perhaps "equivocacy" is a better word than "neutrality" to describe the character of cultural forms in their relationship to function and meaning.

The same is true with regard to those cultural matters that more directly involve the service of other gods. Paul calls for response by the church. Here too one could reason that if an idol is nothing there is no objection to sitting down to a heathen sacrificial meal out of social considerations. At this point, however, Paul draws a distinction between the nothingness of idols and the demonic character of the service of idols.

> On this account the ordinary daily association of the church among the heathen must also compel it to caution . . . For even though an idol is nothing, that does not mean that the demonic powers who incite men to the service of idols may be said to be imaginary. Rather, those who have communion with the worship of idols enter into communion with the demons to whom the heathen sacrifice, whether they know it or not . . . Here every man who appeals to his "knowledge" or to the fact that he is "strong" must ask himself whether he thinks he is "stronger" than God Himself, that is, by willing and doing what God does not will (1 Cor. 10:22).[45]

This is simply to confirm also the second of Smit's theses. The true rock of offense is Jesus Christ (Rom. 9:33). Through the overcoming by faith of this one and only inevitable *skandalon,* the natural mind is brought into obedience to Christ. Christ is the pivotal point in the basic approach to cultures. And this simply means that "the way in which this offense is presented must vary with the listener and must be given maximum force at the essential point where it clashes with his own deepest attitudes."[46] Thus, for the Jews, the death of the cross was accursed by God. For the Greeks the offense lay in the idea that by dying a man could save others. A Buddhist will not be offended by the idea of Jesus'

[45]Ibid., 303–4.
[46]Smit, "Practical Apologetics," 8.

suffering, but only by the idea of Jesus' cross as the *only* way of suffering to salvation. The Sawi of Irian Jaya will find the offense of the cross in the idea of Jesus' betrayal. The theological apologetic of contextualization must be oriented toward this kind of offense. It must be ready to remove all unnecessary stumbling blocks that do not lie on the level of faith. And it must always insist on that particular element of Christianity that stands in direct conflict with the nonbeliever's mindset.

The Jerusalem council of Acts 15, in my judgment, illustrates the operation of these principles. The decree issued by the apostles "did not constitute a definition of what was necessary for the salvation of the Gentile Christians, but was an attempt to solve the problem of a limited group of mixed communities where Jews and Gentiles were living together."[47] The force of James's remarks on the substance of the decree (Acts 15:21)

> seem to mean that since there are Jews in the cities, and since they are devoted to the Law of Moses, the Gentile Christians, in order to avoid offending them, ought to refrain from certain of those features of the Gentile manner of life which the Jews would regard as most repulsive. . . . Such a respectful attitude toward the Jewish way of life would contribute not only to the peace of the Church but also to the winning of the non-Christian Jews.[48]

None of this is meant to suggest that such discriminative, culture-oriented theologizing is done with ease. If we coordinate Galatians 2:1–10 with the report of the Jerusalem council, we find evidence that Peter, though agreeing with the judgment, was not always consistent in its exercise. And his withdrawal from Gentile Christians caused other Jewish Christians to follow his example. Even Barnabus was carried away.

In all of this we merely reaffirm the dialogical character of theologizing, a dialogue not only within the community of

[47]J. Gresham Machen, *The Origin of Paul's Religion* (Grand Rapids: Eerdmans, 1947), 92.

[48]Ibid.

believers but "dialog with the world in which it is being evolved—the culture, the religion, the politics, the economics, the social system."[49] Only in this way may theology preserve the open-ended character it needs to do its work. As society and culture evolve and change, issues change. The hermeneutical spiral changes its shape as some issues disappear and others take their place. A Consciousness Two mentality that assumes a static view of cultures and of theology hinders all this. It chips away at the modesty required in our perception of theology as an end product of the process and drives the possibility of reforming our theology farther from us.

Confessional

Theologizing is an elaboration of confession, an affirmation of loyalty to Jesus Christ (1 Cor. 12:3). Its celebrants proclaim to God, "Lord, this we believe." And they affirm to their fellow believers, "Come and hear, all you who fear God, and I will tell you what God has done for my soul" (Ps. 66:16).

But if theologizing remains on merely these levels, it will drift into abstraction. Its concrete timeliness demands that it also utter its words to the world. And here it becomes evangelistic testimony to all mankind. "In this sense the church is for the world. It is the messenger of the Lord to all mankind, not to give imperial directives but to issue humble and firm testimony to the believers' united faith. We must confess Christ before men where the temptation to deny him is great."[50]

Here is both the glory and the graveyard of most written creeds and confessions. Their richest service lies in their function of translating the gospel to address the needs of their own day and cultural context. Thus, the Westminster Confession of Faith of the seventeenth century, for example, is more than simply a gleaning

---

[49]Taber, "Limits of Indigenization," 75.

[50]Paul G. Schrotenboer, "On Creeds and Making New Ones," *International Reformed Bulletin*, 42 (Summer, 1970): 16.

from the Scriptures of what its authors believed to be faithful teaching on a wide variety of topics: it addresses those words of Scripture to its historical setting, to a world in apologetic conflict with Rome and with Anglican high-church principles. In the process, it affirms truth to its own world. And the need for correction becomes eventually apparent. The Westminster Confession, for example, spoke originally of the relation of church and state in a way that is now foreign to the large majority of Reformed Christians. With some notable exceptions, such as the Heidelberg Catechism, the Reformation-century creeds are not strong on life-relatedness. They stress Scripture doctrine but are short on explaining the Christian's task. Nowhere in these creeds is anything resembling appropriate attention paid to a topic like the kingdom of God, a center of intense debate in recent decades.

All this is not meant to judge but simply to affirm the topical, contextual character of the creeds and to reaffirm their proud heritage. Creeds, as an expression of the confessional character of all theologizing, are "historically situational." They are human acts of confession of God's unchanging good news, addressed to specific human cultural settings. Insofar as they reflect divine teaching they demand binding commitment from those who have made them theirs. They are the fruit of struggle in the hermeneutical spiral, the crystallization of the dialogue the church carries on between the word and its world.

In the West, however, that contextual character is frequently forgotten under the pressure of essentialism. The creeds can take on a universalistic dimension that reduces their confessional character to an in-house, defensive posture. They become documents to exclude people from the church, not to include them.

A confessional statement, as John Kromminga asserts, may be any or all of three things: (1) a witness to the world concerning the beliefs held by the church; (2) an instrument to instruct church members in those beliefs; (3) a test of the orthodoxy of the members, particularly of those entrusted with propagating and defending these truths.

The element of witness to the world, he continues, usually seems to enjoy its greatest prominence when a confession is first written and adopted. This is related to the contextual character of the confession as it responds to some crisis on which the church must take a stand. But as time goes by and the contextual crisis fades into the past, the accent tends to fall more and more on the second and third functions of a confession.[51] The evangelistic focus is lost with the passage of time, and the function of the confession more closely resembles the protection of the church against heresy from within. Those who have bound themselves to the creeds as to human expressions most closely approximating biblical truth minimize this process of change and the contextual character of the confession and maximize what to them is their universalistic character as a transcultural statement of faith.

None of this is meant to deny the continued validity of any biblical truth the confessions seek to convey. Neither do we question the right of churches or theological institutions to demand adherence to them as the confession of one's faith or as a "summary and just exhibition of that system of doctrine and religious belief, which is contained in Holy Scripture, and therein revealed by God to man for his salvation" (the language of the vow I am required to take as an instructor at Westminster Theological Seminary). Nor do we question the propriety of their doing so.

We are simply calling for the reaffirmation of such statements of faith as evangelistic declarations, as invitations to faith, reflecting the biblical concern for "those who are without" (Mark 4:11; Col. 4:5; 1 Thess. 4:12). Paul developed his theological action/reflection with his eye on the unbelievers. They were before him as he uttered his theological malediction of "shame" on Christians who institute lawsuits against other Christians (1 Cor. 6:1–5). He commends to the believer a life of quietness, of minding one's own business and work—"so that your daily life

[51]John H. Kromminga, "The Shape of a New Confession," *Calvin Theological Journal* 7 (November 1972): 149.

may win the respect of outsiders" (1 Thess. 4:12). It is the presence of the unbeliever that prompts Paul's cautions about the use of tongues in the assembly (1 Cor. 14:23–24). And are we wrong in assuming that Paul's admonition to the women to keep silent in the churches may flow from his perception of the cultural stigma of "shame" that Corinthian society in general will attribute to women speaking in assembly? The church in the manifestation of its life in the world's cultures ("in the present world") is always to be conscious of the fact that "the grace of God bringing salvation has appeared to all men" (Titus 2:11, 12). Donald McGavran expresses it well:

> All creeds and confessions, if they would be fully Christian, should express the overriding intention of God that men, in answer to God's choice of them, believe on Christ, repent, and live in him. Every doctrine, if it is true to God's revelation in the Bible, should be colored with this dimension of God's will. . . . A *missionary* confession of faith for today will *in every doctrine* similarly *spell out at great length* the will of God as revealed in the Scriptures that all men of every economic stratum, every tongue, every tribe, every religion, and every ideology be given the opportunity to say "yes" to Jesus Christ.[52]

Third World churches of a confessional character have long made use of the sixteenth-century Reformation creeds, primarily as a communal link with their Western maternal forebears. (Those purposes have an ecumenical legitimacy we will touch on shortly.) But in doing so they have adopted confessions framed in a mentality that falls within the borders of Western, historical Christianity.

Theologians like Anthony Hoekema may seek to justify the "missionary theology" of the Canons of Dort.[53] Other theologians may testify to the "home missionary" intentions of the

[52]Donald A. McGavran, "A Missionary Confession of Faith," *Calvin Theological Journal* 7 (November 1972): 133,144.

[53]Anthony Hoekema, "The Missionary Focus of the Canons of Dort," *Calvin Theological Journal* 7 (November 1972): 211, 220.

Heidelberg Catechism and call on the contemporary church to "emphasize what is explicit in this Catechism and amplify what is implicit."[54] But it is the missiologist, such as Robert Recker, who examines the Belgic Confession and agonizes:

> The Belgic Confession projects an image, in the main, of a church talking with itself rather than a church before the world. It reveals a church concerned with certain doctrinal points rather than a church burdened to proclaim Christ to the multitudes in the valley of decision. But the marks of the church make one ask, Who is the Church for? Is it for the Church or for the World? At one point the Confession rightly says: For God and mankind! Oh, that this insight could have penetrated the entire document from beginning to end.[55]

Recker's judgment seems to me to come closest to the truth.[56] But if his judgment is true, it also offers a theological clue to the confessional indifference toward transcultural evangelism among the Western churches adhering to these creeds. It maximizes as well the tragic effect time has on the evangelistic focus. What is already faded becomes more fading still.

And beyond all this, these Western creeds emasculate confessionally what is existentially the great task of Third World minority churches in non-Christian cultures: a missionary passion to disciple and heal the world's *ethnē*. The church in Asia, observes one writer, has tended toward a ghetto mentality. The Christian community has been more like glue than leaven. The churches are preoccupied with their own existence and organization. What will break the evangelical churches free from their minority con-

---

[54]Fred H. Klooster, "Missions: the Heidelberg Catechism and Calvin," *Calvin Theological Journal* 7 (November 1972): 206.

[55]Robert Recker, "An Analysis of the Belgic Confession As To Its Mission Focus," *Calvin Theological Journal* 7 (November 1972): 1979–80.

[56]For supplementary support of these judgments, consult John H. Piet, *The Road Ahead* (Grand Rapids: Eerdmans, 1970), 21–29; Richard R. DeRidder, *The Dispersion of the People of God* (Kampen: Kok, 1971), 212–14; David J. Bosch, *Witness to the World* (Atlanta: John Knox, 1980), 120–30.

sciousness in Muslim and Hindu lands to pursue vigorously the evangelistic mandate of the gospel?

Part of the answer may lie in a second problem hindering the Asian churches in their theological development. Christianity, someone has said, has been largely a "potted plant" in Asia. It was transported without being transplanted. "It is still viewed by Asians as a foreign importation and imposition."[57] The adoption of Western creeds by the Asian church affirms that misperception. The fact that Christianity began in Asia does not matter. It has traveled to Asia for the most part in confessional carts and wagons made in the West for a Western context. The challenge remains for the churches to relate themselves more fully to the soil of Asia, to get down to the rice-roots level of Asia's diverse cultures. Creeds and confessions fashioned in a Western *corpus Christianum* and minimizing the evangelistic dimension of theologizing cannot dig deeply enough to do the job.

Communal

As confession, theologizing is communal, a "saying along with others of the same thing" (from *homologein,* the Greek term we translate as "confess"). Thus we affirm the ecclesiastical character of the process.

> To make confession is not a matter for one person alone but for the entire congregation of Christ. To the church has been given the words of God, the entrusted charge and the oversight of doctrine. Built on the foundation of the apostles and prophets, the church of the living God is the pillar and bulwark of the truth (Eph. 2:20; I Tim. 3:15).[58]

Theologizing in Western and Third World churches must struggle with the reality of this communal dimension in at least

[57]Gerald H. Anderson, ed., *Asian Voices in Christian Theology* (Maryknoll: Orbis, 1976), 5–6.

[58]A.D.R. Polman, "The Confession in Crisis," *International Reformed Bulletin* 60 (1975): 26.

two areas: (1) in their attitude toward past and future formulations of theology done in both settings; and (2) in their perception of those for whom theologizing is done. Both questions involve the problem of the universalization of theology. The first asks, How may we work out our theologies without isolating them from the church universal? The second asks, How may we work them out without isolating them from any segments of human society?

Too often we in the white West ask the first question in deep suspicion of the efforts to create an African theology (or theologies) or a black theology (or theologies). Fearful of syncretism from "their side," we minimize that possibility in us. "Too often it seems to be expected that such theologies will merely substitute African/Asian categories as counters in the same Western-style word game."[59] Behind such expectations are the racist assumption of the automatic superiority, even normativeness, of our Western approaches, and our perpetual tutelage over Christian thinkers of other societies.

These feelings are reciprocated in a correlative way by the Third World church. Long under the covert domination of Western theological colonialism, the non-Western church accepts the psychodynamics of colonialism's division of the world into "settlers" and "natives." "The natives," long accustomed to withdrawing "theology" from the "educational bank" (the language of Paulo Freire), come to believe the self-image imposed by the missionary "settlers." They become spectators without a theology of their own, robbed of any free relationship with the Word and the world. They accept the identity created for them by missionary language. They are "younger churches," passively dependent on the "mother church." So, Third World church leaders like René Padilla can speak of the Latin American church as "a church without a theology of its own."

Often it is that same spirit that leads these churches to embrace Western creedal formulations without thought of refor-

[59]Charles R. Taber, "Is There More Than One Way to Do Theology?" *Gospel in Context* 1 (January 1978): 9.

mulation; the fear of misunderstanding by the Western "mother" church becomes too strong. I recall the time in the 1960s when one of Korea's Presbyterian Churches formally adopted the Westminster Confession of Faith and the Larger Catechism as part of its creeds. Since 1907, the church had used the Shorter Catechism and a simpler twelve-point Creed first in use in the Presbyterian Church of India. One of the leaders of the church had been raising funds in the United States among a sister denomination. He had been queried at the Synod of that American church as to why his body had not yet adopted the Confession and the Larger Catechism as well. He perceived this as a suspicion on the part of the American denomination that his Korean church was not fully Presbyterian. In a phone call to the General Assembly of the Korean body, he urged their adoption. And within twenty minutes that group had acted to receive them as a full part of their system of doctrine. At that time, no translation of the Larger Catechism was in print and no official translation of either document had ever been made. But within twenty minutes they had been adopted.

I say none of this as a pejorative judgment on the Korean church. If anything, it is a display of the "settler/native" mentality that is a heritage imposed by the West.

At the same time, there may be other motivations behind the Third World acceptance of Western creedal formulations, motivations that can be perceived as healthy. As the product of the theologizing process, creeds and confessions can only come into being as a deposit of theological reflection, only after a certain crystallization has taken place. They are, after all, fashioned out of experience but they should not have an experimental character.[60] Raden Soedarmo of Indonesia sees the legitimate function of Western creeds as an interim function, helping the church in its self-understanding till it can form its own affirmations.

[60]J. L. Helberg, "The Place of the Creeds in a Young Christian Church," *International Reformed Bulletin* 42 (Summer, 1970): 19.

Speaking of the Indonesian church's history, he remarks,

> It is easy to understand that the mission churches did not possess a written or unwritten creed. Their creed was that of the Dutch or German sending church. All problems concerning the faith were solved according to the conviction of the church of the missionaries, though of course with regard for the situation. This fact is not mentioned in criticism. It could not have been otherwise. And it was very fortunate that the young Indonesian churches then were not "wise in their own eyes," but rather were aware of their own inexperience, and were willing to follow the older churches. They would else have gone astray because these churches stood very near to their past with its mysticism, tradition and a heathen religion. God saved His churches from all these.[61]

Obviously there is danger even in such admissions. Interim periods of missionary tutelage can extend into endless periods of missionary captivity. Patterns of theological response constructed and then taught to a young church by missionary "outsiders" can, with the best of intentions, create covert paradigms of theologizing. And these can continue, in subtle ways, to form and control indigenous responsiveness to indigenous cultures long after the missionary and the missionary's creed have overtly stepped aside. Theology, the final product of theologizing, can be mistaken for theologizing itself. And the self-perceptions of the "young" church as still confessionally immature and theologically unsophisticated may make it unable to perceive and reflect on the theologizing already at work and displayed in its sermons and hymnody—often the first place where theologizing begins to be apparent on the verbal level. The "young" church may wait too long for its "theological teachers" to return with their earned doctorates from Europe and North America to construct a theology sophisticated enough to write dissertations about in Western theological institutions. And always, over everything, looms the sociocultural prestige of the formulations of the

[61]Raden Soedarmo, "The Place of the Creed in a Young Church," *International Reformed Bulletin* 42 (Summer, 1970): 25.

"mother church." Shame-oriented societies, sensitive to the feelings of the communicator as much as of the receptor, may reinforce hostility to abandoning (or even altering) what the parent institution obviously regards with such favor and love.

A second positive function of the Western creed in the Third World is its perceived ecumenical character. Through the Western confessions, the churches of Indonesia or Korea express their unity with others around the world. To affirm that they belong together, the Ugandan church and its Western counterpart may hold hands through a common creed.

Even here the dangers loom. The Western church may be saying through this act, "You are our sons and daughters," while the Third World church intends to say, "We are brothers and sisters." How may such subtle forms of theological racism be avoided in this act of intended confessional unity? How can this desire for biblical ecumenicity be kept from transforming the intent of the Third World church into what Taber calls "tagging along at the tail end of the long history of Western embroidery"?

Let the Third World church not take this step of confessional unity without study or without the conviction that the creed fashioned in the West, which they now seek to affirm as their bond with a sister institution, is one they may honestly live with as their own. The Reformed Church in Japan has apparently done just that. Writes Ryuzo Hashimoto, one of their pastors:

> Thus the adoption of the Westminster Standard by the Reformed Church in Japan was the second case of adopting a Historic Creed in our church history. But the manner in which we adopted this Standard was quite different from the case of the Church of Christ in Japan. First, the Reformed Church in Japan adopted the Westminster Confession of Faith voluntarily. The Reformed Church in Japan was organized before the missionaries returned to Japan after the war. Second, the founders of the Reformed Church in Japan have long studied

> these historic creeds, and they hold strong conviction that the Westminster Standard is the best among the historic creeds.[62]

Further, let the Third World church not take this step without initiating, along with it, the conscious process by which it will also address its own unique context and cultural setting. In that spirit, the Reformed Church in Japan expressed in 1969, over two decades after its founding, their conviction that "the time has come to step forward in order to make a definite schedule for formulating our new confession of faith."[63] And as a step toward that formulation the church issued in 1973 a "Declaration of Faith Concerning Church and State." It plans to complete the new confession by 1986. The context of their Declaration is the government effort to nationalize the Shinto shrine at Yasukuni, perceived by the church as part of the Japanese militaristic and nationalistic tendencies increasingly evident in state policy. The failures of the Japanese church to resist this state encroachment in the past also are a motivating factor.

Dr. R. J. Poerwowidagdo, a teacher of theology at the Theological College ("Duta Wacana"), Yogjakarta, Indonesia, reflects the same concerns in his plea for reformulation of the historic creeds.

> The churches in Asia today cannot fully commit their being to Jesus Christ if they are complacent with parroting the response of the Western churches to the gospel message many generations ago. The churches in Asia should be capable of responding to the gospel in their own way in their own language and in their own style. The churches in Asia today must be capable of *doing theology* on their own, and they should be able to say what they believe to be the gospel for the world in this day and age.[64]

---

[62]Ryuzo Hashimoto, "Reformulating the Historic Creed," *International Reformed Bulletin* 60 (1975): 3–4.

[63]Ibid., 6.

[64]R.J. Poerwowidagdo, "Reformulating the Historic Creed," *International Reformed Bulletin* 60 (1975): 17.

A third warning is also appropriate at this stage. Let the Third World church not take this step without also some expression of willingness on the part of its Western sister institution to sharpen its own insight and self-understanding through the mutual correction such a Third World confession might provide. Let the formation of a Third World creed be seen by the Western church as an opportunity for etic theologizing, for the initiation of cross-fertilization. It is not only the Western churches that can function as theological "brokers" in stimulating new understanding of the Scriptures. Let the Third World churches help the West in its flight from the temptation of theological parochialism. Interdependence and mutuality, even in creed-making, are not truly ecumenical until they flow in both directions—the West helping the Third World, the Third World helping the West. Every church must learn to be both learner and teacher in theologizing. The Third World church will find its greatest struggle in learning to be a teacher of the West. The Western church will finds its agony in being taught to be a learner.

How can the struggle of a church in a Muslim context, seeking to communicate the biblical doctrine of the Trinity to a society that radically misunderstands it, help the Western church in a reformulation of the Athanasian Creed that might communicate more effectively in a world that has forgotten its Greek? Can Western concepts of ecclesiology take on a more dynamic and functional shape after they have been assisted by the formulations of a minority church in an ideological state opposed to Christianity? Eschatology in the Western church has been bogged down for over a hundred years in a never-ending argument over the sequence of events surrounding the second coming of Christ. In the process, the center of eschatology appears to be more the millennium than Jesus Christ's coming. Can there be help from an African church as it seeks to frame its biblical eschatology against a cultural view of time that, scholars like John Mbiti tell us, has no real concept of the future or the distant present?

So important is this third element to us that we can caution the Third World church against any adoption of a Western creed unless this mutuality is guaranteed. Otherwise, the church may assume that it is traveling down a two-lane highway when in fact it is moving down a one-way street in the wrong direction. It courts self-destruction.

The communal task of theologizing, however, needs to face still other questions before its work is done. Its mutuality should include not only Western and "non-Western." A truly universal orientation must speak for the nearly two-thirds of the world's population that is deprived of the essentials of life. How shall theology and theologizing identify with the poor and oppressed? How shall we reorient our doing of theology so as to demonstrate the identification of Jesus with the poor? How can we correct the way in which our Western, white theology has ideologically translated "Gentile" into "nonwhites in and outside North America"?

The current discussions of contextualization began with reminders from the Theological Education Fund that the human context addressed by the gospel also includes social, political, and economic questions: wealth and power, power and powerlessness, privilege and oppression, white and nonwhite. How will theology be done from "the underside"? Is there a place for justice in the good news of the gospel? Black theologies in the northern hemisphere and liberation theologies originating in the southern hemisphere have loudly underlined the force of these questions. Theologizing must ask again, In whose interests are we doing theology? With whom are we already siding and with whom ought we to be siding? And how?

White, Western evangelicals generally have not responded quickly or positively to this set of questions. Our pietist tradition segregates "spirituality" from "the world."[65] And our fear of the

[65]For a fuller discussion of these problems of "spirituality," consult Harvie M. Conn, *Evangelism: Doing Justice and Preaching Grace* (Grand Rapids: Zondervan, 1982), 57–71.

"social gospel" spectre haunts our ability to formulate theology for the marginalized, the people on the periphery.

Yet there are evidences of a new wind blowing among the Third World's evangelicals. The 1982 *Seoul Declaration* we have referred to earlier draws up a theological agenda for the future that has not omitted questions of this sort. It declares:

> Those of us in *Asia,* will have to grapple with such questions as the resurgence of indigenous religions, the struggle for justice in the face of oppression, totalitarian ideologies and regimes, the tensions between traditional values, corruption, and modern consumerism. To this end we need to develop our hermeneutical tools.[66]

The African theological agenda calls for taking seriously such expected items as the traditional African worldview, the reality of the spirit world, and the resurgence of Islam. But at the same time it does not forget "the competing ideologies, . . . the contemporary cultural, religious and political struggles."

Latin American concerns particularly reflect these lacunae.

> Those of us in *Latin America* will have to forge theology from within a context in which the social, economic and political structures are in a state of disarray, unable to close the gap between the rich and the poor and to solve the problems created by economic and technological dependence. Theology will have to give priority to problems related to justice and peace, the control of the arms race, the evangelistic implications of demographic and urban growth, the pathetic conditions of aboriginal peoples and other ethnic groups.[67]

Why, by contrast, do we read so seldom and so late of a similar agenda for the doing of theology in the West? One reason is that our hermeneutic for understanding is shaped by our sociological presuppositions concerning knowledge. The sociology of knowledge

[66]*The Seoul Declaration. Toward an Evangelical Theology for the Third World* (Taichung, Taiwan: Asia Theological Association, 1982), 2–3.

[67]Ibid., 4.

> insists that even within one cultural tradition, persons are further conditioned in their outlook by their particular locus in the overall structure of society. That is, there are aspects of the world view of persons who occupy dominant positions in society that reflect and legitimate that dominance. . . . Similarly, persons who are oppressed in all societies tend to develop some similar mental constructs, images, and processes.[68]

Cornelius Van Til has spent a lifetime in the study of apologetics, arguing for the influence of presuppositions on our view of the world and the Scriptures. We add to his list of philosophical and theological preunderstandings those that underlie social structures. Personal, class, and social agendas tend to reshape the world we see and the way we see it. Aspects of reality that are uncongenial to those social interests are filtered out in the interest of self-serving alternative interpretations. Thus, when theologizing is done by Western experts who by their very training (if not background) have become part of the "professional" middle- or upper-class white society, can one really expect that Western theology will see the poor and sinned-against? Theology, if it is to become truly and comprehensively communal, must emerge from a praxis of commitment to God's peace for the poor (1 Cor. 1:27–28). To become revolutionary and not resolutionary, our theologizing will have to validate itself and its claims in the same way Jesus validated His. His allegiance to the poor marked His preaching and was a sign of the coming of the kingdom (Luke 4:18–21). His healing of the sick and the blind and his preaching to the poor became a validation to a doubting John the Baptist of his messianic theologizing (Matt. 11:2–6). It must become an integral part of ours as well.

Where shall we begin this identification? By sitting where the poor and disenfranchised sit, in the ghettos of our cities, in the waiting rooms of public health clinics, in the unemployment lines and welfare offices. By bringing to life in our inner cities those

[68]Charles R. Taber, "Missiology and the Bible," *Missiology* 11 (April 1983): 241.

features of the Base Ecclesial Communities that have been an important part of the Roman Catholic renewal movement in Latin America—Bible study with the poor and not simply for the poor, Bible study in communities seeking to understand the injustice and racial animosity that has desacralized their lives, and commitment to hope together.

Especially here we must be dependent on Third World and black contributions to our theologizing. Orlando Costas outlines this aid program in terms of four specifics.

(1) Third World churches can serve as a mirror for the critical self-understanding of American white Christians. The writings, lectures, and leadership of theologians and church leaders from the Third World and the American black community need to help us see ourselves and the limitations of our communal understanding.

(2) These voices can offer models of authentic contextualization.

> To be sure, after almost two hundred years of Anglo-Saxon-culture Christianity, the American church and theology need desperately a process of deculturation. Michaelson's assertion that mission in America "must begin by de-Americanizing the Gospel" cannot be treated lightly. Yet the process of de-Americanization must go along with an inverse process of incarnation in the present American reality. Otherwise the Christian faith in the United States will succumb further to an otherworldly, escapist faith, which in the end will be no more and no less than a silent supporter of the same system.[69]

Here the marginalized can provide models of a critical insertion in their cultures and societies that has given prophetic depth to their life, witness, and theology.

---

[69]Orlando Costas, *Christ Outside the Gate. Mission Beyond Christendom* (Maryknoll: Orbis, 1982), 82.

(3) They can provide meaningful paradigms of dynamic, liberating church leadership. In contrast to the highly clericalized white church life of the United States, the churches of the marginalized are strongly lay-oriented. Training is begun in the heat and sweat of everyday-life Christian service. Their patterns of ministerial training and theological formation are not bound by the formal, academically abstract structures of American theological education.

(4) They offer a partnership for radical discipleship. In this partnership the poor are no longer hidden from the eyes of theology. Nor do they become merely the objects of our action and reflection. The communal demands of the process of theologizing see the weak and downtrodden as also subjects, doers, in our action and reflection. For a long time, theology in the West has been formulated from the perspective of the powerful and mighty; radical discipleship says it is time that it be done from the standpoint of the black, the Korean, the Hispanic. The category of the meek and the needy must be rescued as a fundamental category of the communal character of the gospel and of the gospel reflection we call theology.

Prophetic

For theology to fully exhibit the communal dimension we have mentioned, it will have to do more than merely baptize the agendas of human cultures. There is also that inevitable confrontation between gospel and culture, the clash over the rock of ultimate offense. Contextualization as part of the process of doing theology must go hand in hand with prophetic decontextualization.

Our hermeneutical quest must challenge the values and standards of the culture in which it is being done that mirror the demonic and dehumanizing forces of sin and rebellion against God. The agenda for theologizing

> is not content with transforming political, economic, social and cultural spheres of life until those spheres and their presuppositional framework has been subjected to the judgment of the Word of God. In that sense, the demand for de-contextualization, ignored largely by both liberation theologian and evangelical, becomes as important as contextualization. It does not take up the questions of culture without evaluating the legitimacy of the questions themselves. Neither is it content with the oversimplification that defines the self-understanding of the church either in terms of participation in politicization or in terms of participation in spiritualization. It cannot be content with defining contextualization as a theological process wholly in terms of "critical reflection on the pastoral action of the Church" or in terms of "a spirituality without discipleship in the daily, social, economic, and political aspects of life." The one leads to a religionization of the revolution, the other to a Christianization of the status quo. How may the people of God be the fellowship of the Spirit in politics, in economics, in the home, in the bush? How does the *colonia* of the kingdom of God emerge in the *barrios* of Latin America?[70]

Juan Luis Segundo, a liberation theologian, offers some useful terminology for doing this in what he calls a "hermeneutic of suspicion." We see it as a tool seeking to uproot from our selective viewing of Scripture those unnamed, transplanted ideologies with which we rationalize self-interest. It assaults those ideals that support the oppressive status quo and resist turning the eschatological hope of heaven into a revolutionary transformation of cultures. "The idea of Christian brotherly love, for instance, in a society founded on serfdom remains an unrealizable and, in this sense, ideological idea," says Segundo, "even when the intended

[70]Harvie M. Conn, "Contextualization: Where Do We Begin?" *Evangelicals and Liberation,* Carl E. Armerding, ed. (Phillipsburg, NJ: Presbyterian and Reformed, 1977), 104–5.

meaning is, in good faith, a motive in the conduct of the individual."[71] All of us are captive to ideologies. The task of "hermeneutical" suspicion is to confront those hidden ideologies and to wrestle with the inhibitions against change they leave with us.

> Since the God of the Bible is on the side of the poor, why are we undisturbed by the fact that we are among the nonpoor? Since the God of the Bible calls out for justice, why are we such complacent participants in economic or racial injustices? How does our white ideology inhibit us from identification with the humiliation of the Black? And does not the same ideology become an equal danger for persons in the oppressed community who achieve social and economic prosperity?[72]

The scholarly reflection that is a part of theologizing is not exempt from these dangers. Even in the exegetical task we build up our little principalities where God cannot rule. The prophetic side of theologizing seeks to uncover those concealments. Our missionary commitment to evangelistic engagement for change raises suspicions about the innocence of our ideas and methods as we approach the Scriptures.

There is also a positive side to this prophetic shaping of the theological process. After all, the prophetic office in Israel was not simply one of divine judgment. And the message was not always one of doom. There was also the word of hope and grace from God through the prophet. So too with the doing of theology. Our prophetic responsibility does not end with the raising of suspicions about our ideas and methods as we approach the Scriptures. Our heremeneutic is also one of hope. In the language of Beatriz Melano Couch, "it hopes to let the text itself rephrase our own questions and rephrase our own conceptions about life and death,

[71]Juan Luis Segundo, *The Liberation of Theology* (Maryknoll: Orbis, 1976), 100.

[72]Harvie M. Conn, "Theologies of Liberation: Toward a Common View," *Tensions in Contemporary Theology*, 3rd rev. ed., Stanley N. Gundry and Alan F. Johnson, eds. (Chicago: Moody, 1979), 403.

our own epistemology, our own knowledge of society, our ethics, politics, etc."[73] Even our prophetic dimension is qualified by our missionary intention: not immobilizing despair but liberating hope. We are not brought to frustration by the knowledge of our past mistakes in theologizing. Hope sees the future, not the stained past; it is God's no to the old and His yes to the new. To theologize prophetically is to theologize redemptively. Doing theology must never be without the fun of joyful creativity in hope.

---

[73]Sergio Torres and John Eagleson, eds. *Theology in the Americas* (Maryknoll: Orbis, c. 1976), 306.

Chapter Seven

Theological Education: Looking for New Models

SUMMARY

Current discussions of contextualization are rooted in current worldwide frustration with historical models of theological education. These models are being questioned more and more, both outside and inside the evangelical community.

Behind this ferment lie the different concepts of the ministry after which we model our educational goals. Two especially have been prominent in the history of the Western church—the minister as pedagogue and the minister as indispensable professional. Out of these models comes a definition of "adequate" preparation for ministry that equates learning with schooling and a highly trained ministry with an institution-processed ministry. Coupled with the traditional distinction between clergy and laity and the professionalized model of one-paid-pastor-per-congregation, churches of the Third World are left with patterns for ministry more functional in the West than in their own cultural settings. How can this be avoided?

The focal points for educational renewal must answer three questions: (1) Who are the people of God and how does their vocational calling to serve in the world affect their views of ministry? (2) How do we teach the practice of theology in distinction from theology as the result of that process? How can theology, using the tools of scholarship, edify without surrendering to abstraction? (3) How can we change the process of education so that truth becomes not simply something that is memorized or cognitively processed but also something that is done? How can theological education become a process of conscience awakening and life-changing liberation?

Chapter Seven

Theological Education: Looking for New Models

Increasingly the Christian world community is recognizing that a key place for changing the way we do theology is the theological seminary. At the Tambaram meeting of the International Missionary Council in 1938, theological education was described as "the weakest element in the entire enterprise of Christian Missions." But the diagnosis could not yet be acted on. The language still couched the problem in an outlook that assumed that missionaries and not national churches must deal with it. And it left untouched the preconceptions behind the categories "weak elements" and "strong elements." World War II would hinder further exploration of the theme.

HISTORY OF THE CURRENT DISCUSSIONS

With the end of the war, the Council was free to undertake the mandate it was given at Tambaram: "The preparation of detailed studies of the situation, where these have not already been made, to visit the main centres of theological education, and to work out a policy and programme for the training of the ministry in the younger churches."[1] Several such surveys were carried out and published from 1950 to 1962. And, stimulated by their findings, the Council meeting in Ghana in 1957–58 established the Theological Education Fund. The Fund went through three Mandate periods until its ministry was terminated in 1977, its concerns to be carried on and strengthened through the formation of the Programme on Theological Education that same year.[2]

The history of those Mandates forms an excellent historical commentary on the church's growing sensitivity to the question of "excellence" and the widening search for its identity. The First Mandate, extending to 1964, "showed a deep concern for better trained and better educated ministry to meet the new day; its undisguised thrust was towards the raising of the level of scholarship and striving for academic excellence."[3] Major grants, totaling more than $2,800,000, went to twenty or so schools "which offered the greatest possibility for qualitative growth in the future," and over $1,000,000 was eventually spent towards the development of school libraries and the publication of theological textbooks. All this mirrored the wide consensus that excellence was to be defined in terms of academic standards and, more specifically, of the patterns of the Western theological institution.

With the second Mandate period (1965–69) the theme became "Rethink" and deeper questions about excellence began to be asked: What is an authentic ministry for which theological training exists to serve? How could theological education reflect a growing consciousness of Third World churches as the subject in mission and not simply objects of missions? How was the ministry to respond to the increasing pressures of nation-building, the resur-

[1]Douglas Webster, *Survey of the Training of the Ministry in the Middle East* (Geneva: Commission on World Mission and Evangelism, 1962), 4.

[2]"Programme on Theological Education: An On-going Concern of the Churches Now an Integral Part of the WCC," *Ministerial Formation* 1 (January 1978): 3–5.

[3]*Ministry in Context* (Bromley, Kent: Theological Education Fund, 1972), 12.

gence of non-Christian religions, the renascence of ancient cultures, rapid social change, the emergence of new ideologies?

A pastoral concern had begun to emerge from the struggles for definition within the Fund, one that was continued and heightened by the emphasis of the Third Mandate period (1970–77) on contextualization and on what its then director, Shoki Coe, called "double wrestle": "wrestling with the Text from which all texts are derived and to which they point, in order to be faithful to it in the context; and wrestling with the context in which the reality of the Text is at work, in order to be relevant to it."[4]

In all of this a conscious shift was and is taking place, away from earlier satisfaction with academic concepts of excellence revolving around "sound scholarship" and toward excellence in terms of a threefold search—"for quality, authenticity, and creativity in theological education in the Third World."[5] Quality in this process is to be found "through the praxis of wrestling with one's own religious, cultural, social and political realities." The *what* of theological education only comes through taking the *how, where,* and *when* questions seriously. The stage has now been set, predicted Coe, for the church's search for creativity, discovering its *own* problems and dealing with them in its *own* ways.

The worldwide dimensions of this fundamental discontent about Christian ministry and mission cannot be denied. Everywhere "the key question has become: how can Third World theological education discover and develop forms of theological

[4]Shoki Coe, "In Search of Renewal in Theological Education," *Theological Education* 9 (Summer 1973): 238. For a theological analysis of what contextualization means in these documents consult Harvie M. Conn, "Contextualization: Where Do We Begin?" *Evangelicals and Liberation,* ed. Carl E. Armerding (Nutley, NJ: Presbyterian and Reformed, 1977), 90–119.

[5]Shoki Coe, "Reflections," *Northeast Asia Journal of Theology* 18/19 (March/Sept. 1977): 72.

training and ministry authentic to particular cultural contexts within Asia, Africa, and Latin America?"[6] Page after page in the 1969 report of the Theological Faculty Conference for Africa speaks of the church and its ministry as "still alien institutions (in Africa),"[7] and shouts, "Training for ministry in contemporary Africa must be indigenous."[8] Theology must become the translator and reinterpreter of the gospel into African culture.

In Latin America the struggle for excellence has spawned the now worldwide movement known as Theological Education by Extension. Its phenomenal growth from a single seminary in 1966 to 760 institutions in 57 countries by 1974 represents far more than just a pragmatic effort to prepare more pastors than can be trained in a residential seminary. F. Ross Kinsler, a founder of the movement, perceived it as an alternative to the perennial "struggle to 'upgrade' the seminaries and Bible institutes in the Third World," as a rejection of the elitist pattern of training for a professional ministry in which "the minister (servant) actually becomes the ruler; the concept of the ministry (service) is inverted to mean privilege; and the members maintain their dependence upon an 'imported' clergy to direct the life of the churches."[9] In the background of the traditional system's argument for "adequate" preparation he sees the perpetual tendencies toward hierarchization, legalism, traditionalism, dead orthodoxy, and unfaith. Extension provides a recuperative method of subversion of these trends by challenging the traditional patterns in several

---

[6]James A. Bergquist, "The TEF and the Uncertain Future of Third World Theological Education," *Theological Education* 9 (Summer 1973): 246.

[7]Paul E. Hoffman, ed., *Theological Education in Today's Africa* (Geneva: Lutheran World Federation, 1969), 2.

[8]Ibid., 3.

[9]F. Ross Kinsler, "Extension: An Alternative Model for Theological Education," *Learning in Context* (Bromley, Kent: Theological Education Fund, 1973), 30–31.

areas—the nature of the ministry, the nature of the church, and the mission of the church.[10]

Offering less concrete models but equally strident in their questions, Asian voices over the last decade have raised the same issues. The concluding statement of the First Consultation on Theological Education and Ministry defined the aim and purpose of the theological school in terms of a "community that exists in encounter with the world, a witnessing community in the forefront of Christ's loving involvement and prophetic confrontation with society . . ."[11] Among the eight questions it addressed to the theological institutions of North East Asia were these:

> Do courses of study consistently contain the dimension of mission? For that mission do teaching methods encourage the students personal articulation of the Christian message in a manner that reveals a comprehension of his own society and culture? Is the hermeneutical effort a serious wrestling with the word of God in such a way that the will of God for 20th century North East Asia is disclosed and made known?[12]

From a 1970 Consultation on Theology of the Indonesian Council of Churches came a denunciation of

> a form and system of education inherited from the West which lays too heavy emphasis on historical-theological analyses of a highly academic character whose aim is to transmit the logical knowledge and tradition as a complete whole which is not sufficiently open to new developments. This system does not take account of the rapid social change experienced by the people. The system is not sufficiently directed toward or rooted

[10]F. Ross Kinsler, "Theological Education by Extension: Service or Subversion?" *Missiology* 6 (April 1978): 183–94. Compare also: Peter Savage, "Four Crises in Third World Theological Education," *Evangelical Missions Quarterly* 9 (Fall 1972): 28–34.

[11]*Theological Education and Ministry. Reports from the North East Asia Theological Education Consultation. Seoul, Korea* (Tainan: The Presbyterian Bookroom, 1967), 297.

[12]Ibid., 297–98.

> in the reality of the Indonesian world and is not sufficiently concerned with the concrete problems of the people.[13]

By 1975, Emerito P. Nacpil, executive director of the Association of Theological Schools in South East Asia, saw those desired changes taking place. "I detect in the current situation," he wrote, ". . . a shift of emphasis in the pursuit of excellence—from the narrower understanding of it as academic excellence to one that is broader and more adequate to the needs of theological education in the region today."[14] Utilizing "the critical Asian principle" as a method in that search, theological education becomes

> a way of saying where our area of responsibility and concern, is namely the varieties and dynamics of Asian realities. . . . For another thing, it is a way of saying that we will approach and interpret the Gospel in relation to the needs and issues peculiar to the Asian situation. It functions therefore partly as a hermeneutical principle. Thirdly, it is a way of saying that a theology worth its salt at this time in Asia must be capable, not only of illuminating Asian realities with the Light of the Gospel, but also of helping manage and direct the changes now taking place along lines more consonant with the Gospel and its vision for human life.[15]

At the same time, we must recognize that these voices do not speak for all the world church. In fact, the frequent stridency of their tone may indicate their minority position. The majority still clings to the traditional model defined by the Western past. And this is preeminently true of those institutions that reflect the nonconciliar voices of the evangelical tradition.

As late as 1972, Dr. Bong-rin Ro, administrator of what has

[13]"Our Hope for Theological Education in the Future," *South East Asia Journal of Theology* 13 (1971): 25.

[14]Emerito Nacpil, "The Question of Excellence in Theological Education," *Mission Trends No. 3. Third World Theologies*, ed. Gerald H. Anderson and Thomas F. Stransky (Grand Rapids: Eerdmans; New York: Paulist, 1976), 25–26.

[15]Ibid., 28.

since come to be called the Asia Theological Association, after a month long visit of eight African countries, commented,

> Some far seeing evangelicals in Africa are acutely aware that we are not interpreting the biblical faith in an African context. One person put it to me this way: "The liberals are asking the right questions but do not have the right answers, whereas we evangelicals have the right answers but are not asking the right questions." One case which was pointed out to me was that of an African who was not willing to think out the questions of polygamy. Another person, a teacher, asked some students what questions were troubling them. They answered 'life after death and witchcraft.' He found that in his library he had only 10 pages on these subjects.[16]

The picture in Latin America, though the seedbed of the extension movement, often seems no better. Hugo Zorrilla speaks of the crisis in theological education there: "The seminaries go in one direction while the church wrestles in another. Non-contextualized churches carry out a ministry not suited to their reality while seminaries perpetuate theologies, methods, and strategies best suited to churches in an opulent and wealthy society."[17] Zorrilla traces much of this to the importation of borrowed theological content, "an implantation of academic and theological systems by the mission boards" that results in a "people of God passive in the education of their leaders and helping to perpetuate the dependency of the local church," maintaining "forms of worship, stereotyped theological categories, and 'prepackaged' models of irrelevant ministries."[18] Copied curriculums, translated textbooks of translated theology, teachers (the majority still missionaries) who treat their students as a captive audience to be "domesticated"—all these militate against contextual education.

Even the potential of the Latin American extension movement

---

[16]Bong-rin Ro "TAP Administrator Reports on Visit to Africa," *Theological News* 4 (October 1972): 5–6.

[17]Hugo Zorillo, "Crucial Issues in Theological Education in Latin America," *Mission-Focus* 5 (March 1977 Supplement) C.

[18]Ibid.

for finding new dimensions has not always been actualized. William J. Kornfield, reflecting on six years of experimentation in Bolivia, judges that "the cultural overhang so frequently characteristic of residence seminaries is also applicable to extension education."[19] Most programmed texts/workbooks are still written by missionaries,[20] and continue to reflect a cultural transplant at times foreign to the thought patterns and norms of the recipient culture. The extension teacher too often begins with a concept of what is needed, based on Western experience, and then implements a strategy in the name of what is called "felt needs" (but which are frequently the instructor's own appraisal of the "real" needs). No in-depth evaluative criteria have yet been developed to determine to what extent extension education is filling the needs of the church. And the end result can be that foreseen by Ross Kinsler: "It is true that some extension programs have simply extended the old system of theological education in a way that imposes itself upon the people."[21] Thus, the pattern seen in the Spanish "culture of conquest" of the indigenous peoples of Latin America is repeated through the "donor" model of extension.

There are no doubt many reasons behind the time lag between conciliar and clearly evangelical discussions of training models. Evangelicals have been much later in establishing associations for theological education and thus for a time lacked the stimulation these associations have obviously provided in these areas. A proportionate lack of financial resources has delayed consultation and joint action. Legitimate concerns about the various theological

[19]William J. Kornfield, "The Challenge to Make Extension Education Culturally Relevant," *Evangelical Missions Quarterly* 12 (January 1976): 16.

[20]The need to avoid cultural overhang and to tie in educational procedures with the felt needs of the local cultures is indirectly touched on in Edward Brainerd's evaluation of programmed instructional materials, "The 'Myth' of Programmed Texts," *Evangelical Missions Quarterly* 10 (July 1974): 219–23. Note the responses to Brainerd's thesis in *Evangelical Missions Quarterly* 11 (January 1975): 48–56.

[21]Quoted in Kornfield, "Extension Education," 17.

perspectives participating in much of the current discussion of training may make evangelicals wary of proceeding too quickly. And it must be remembered that the conciliar discussions in their initial stage focused on these same concerns.

Like the conciliar discussions, however, there is growing evidence that current evangelical thinking in the Third World is moving beyond the seedbed stage. Within the circles orbiting the World Evangelical Fellowship, debate heightens on the question of contextualization and how it may be understood in a way consistent with biblical givens accepted by the evangelical.[22] While the tendency remains to view the question negatively[23] or to confuse it with indigenization-level issues, other indications point to more sophisticated directions. Increasingly, priority needs are recognized for research "into the need for human development and social justice in the context of the dehumanizing political, economic and social structures of society, . . . into theological educational methodology in the context of changing educational structures and methods, curriculum design and evaluation."[24] The 1982 *Seoul Declaration,* referred to in earlier chapters, offers new trails that theological education may explore in the next decade. Samples of the papers appearing at the 1982 Consultation that prepared the Declaration indicate that the discussion among evangelicals has moved to increasingly deeper levels of questioning.[25]

At the same time, the evangelical faces hindrances to rapid

---

[22]For a recent sampling of attitudes that reflect on the role of contextualization in the area of theological education, consult Paul Bowers, "Accreditation as a Catalyst for Renewal in Theological Education," *East Africa Journal of Evangelical Theology* 1(1982): 11–21.

[23]*Theological News* 5 (October 1973): 6–8.

[24]Bruce J. Nicholls, ed., *Defending and Confirming the Gospel. The Report of the 1975 Consultation of the Theological Commission of the World Evangelical Fellowship* (New Delhi: WEF Theological Commission, n.d.), 17.

[25]Consult the special issue of *Asia Theological News* 9 (January-March 1983). The theme of the issue is "Is Asian Evangelical Theology Possible?"

progress in these discussions. Conciliar debates began in the midst of a deep sensitivity to the need to put an end to the colonialist missions mentality of "sending/receiving church" so prevalent in missions. The continued presence of missionary teaching majorities in Third World institutions and the continued insensitivity on the part of too many to the depths of the cultural questions may not allow institutions the leeway to experiment and ask. Theological fears of contextualization as another form of syncretism may be a restraining factor in more ideologically conservative cultures. Cultural conservatism, often unidentified by the evangelical or identified falsely with a Bible-centered conservatism, as well as different and uncritically assumed purposes, values, customs, and traditions brought by both missionary and national to the question of training, may hinder cooperation in change.

WESTERN CONCEPTS OF MINISTRY

Ultimately, however, the current search, no matter who carries it on, will not be resolved until we recognize that behind our divergent viewpoints lie divergent culturally and historically formed concepts of the ministry after which we model our educational goals. Our conceptions of excellence are rooted in and strongly committed to our preunderstanding of the ministry and the church in mission. This I interpret to be the conundrum expressed at the 1976 Seminar of the Commission on Non-Traditional Study of the Association of Theological Schools, Southeast Asia.

> Somehow, every major discussion, particularly at plenary meetings, returned to this question: 'What do we mean by excellence?' Our difficulty in arriving at a consensus in answering that question is probably not so much a failure on our part as it is the facing of the inescapable fact that in a many-faceted Christendom we probably have to allow for different

> definitions of what constitutes excellence, each determined largely by a different context.[26]

What are the elements that enter into our models and what impact do they have on our conceptions of education?

One feature of the traditional model is that it sees the minister as pedagogue. This model has been deeply influenced by the Greek regard for the primacy of the intellect and by a concept of education that views the whole life of man as integrated by his cognitive center. Under its influence, the biblical model of "edification" soon began to shift away from the God-centered call to build up others (Rom. 15:2), not through the service of cognitive abstraction, but through love (1 Cor. 8:1). The formulations of the Alexandrian theologians in the second and third centuries of the church's history made this shift even more permanent. Clement of Alexandria (d. c.215) combined the concepts of a priestly hierarchy and of the pastor as gnostic, placing cognitive knowledge at the pinnacle of the ecclesiastical ladder. Origen (d. 253) solidified this by transforming the catechetical schools for new converts into advanced theological schools. The long road toward identification of theological education with schooling, and of schooling with the intellectual defense of the gospel, had begun.[27]

Through the intervening centuries, this identification was confirmed directly and indirectly. The barbarian invasions began the process of the degeneration of the Roman Empire's culture, and the monastery model, in the face of learning's low ebb, reinforced the role of the ministry as pedagogue to the world. By the end of the Middle Ages, Thomas Aquinas had synthesized this

---

[26]Dr. Manfred Berndt, Chairman, *Commission on Non-Traditional Study of the Association of Theological Schools, Southeast Asia Triennium April, 1974–March, 1977. Reports and Recommendations* (Hong Kong: Association of Theological Schools, Southeast Asia, n.d.), Y–1. The Report includes three helpful appendices on the question of "excellence."

[27]H. Richard Niebuhr and Daniel D. Williams, eds., *The Ministry in Historical Perspectives* (New York: Harper and Brothers, 1956), 42–46.

emphasis on reason with his own ideas of Christianity, and the schooling model for ministerial preparation was arguing that

> in the realm of nature, philosophy, natural science and the like, man could think and act independently of God, attaining to truth by reason alone. He could discover the "universal" pattern which determines the nature of each individual fact. Indeed, man could even reach certain divine truths by speculation, but he could not by this means alone press very far into the supernatural realm.[28]

In a real sense, the Protestant Reformation constituted a break with that mentality. Scholasticism's increasing isolation from the pastoral ministry and preoccupation with the stereotypes of academic scholarship were shattered by the Reformers' emphasis on the pastoral nature of scholarship, on theology as a tool of pastoral edification. Progress, however, was mixed. Within the Lutheran camp, Philip Melanchthon (1497–1560) became the constructor of educational philosophy; his high esteem for humanistic learning as the rational man's struggle to know nature and self led him back to the scholastic standpoint.[29] John Calvin (1509–64), with his concept of the reason and its place in the "piety of learning," made much more progress,[30] though he too, even after his conversion, retained much of his humanist background in his approach to education.[31] These tendencies, coupled with the Reformation focus on teaching and "pure doctrine," reinforced the call for excellence in terms of educational standards for the ministry. "The gown of the secular scholar, commonly worn by the men of learning among the burghers . . . , became the outward

[28]W. Stanford Reid, "Calvin and the Founding of the Academy of Geneva," *Westminster Theological Journal* 18 (November 1955): 1–2.

[29]Bernard Ramm, *The Christian College in the Twentieth Century* (Grand Rapids: Eerdmans, 1963), 31–51.

[30]Harvie M. Conn, "The Concept of the Reason in the Theology of John Calvin" (Th.M. thesis, Westminster Theological Seminary, 1958), 114–28.

[31]Reid, "Calvin," 4.

sign of ministerial vocation and social status," the garment of the Protestant minister.[32]

Prior to the middle of the seventeenth century

> there was little disposition on the part of anyone . . . to minimize the importance of education as a qualification for the ministerial office. Indeed, the emphasis was in quite the contrary direction, for there was a strong insistence upon the necessity for a learned ministry. The person who would teach the mysteries of God, Richard Baxter was to declare, 'must not be himself a babe in knowledge.' "[33]

Widespread ignorance among the clergy formed the concrete basis of this emphasis.

In the latter half of the seventeenth century the ideal of an "educated ministry" began to be questioned. But the predominant pattern for England and the fledgling colonies of America remained the university as the seedbed of the clergy. It became increasingly the normal expectation that a minister should possess a university degree. In fact, "the primary purpose in the establishment of all the colonial colleges, with the possible exception of the College of Philadelphia and King's College, had been to train ministers. This purpose . . . they fulfilled satisfactorily until past the middle of the eighteenth century" when religious decline decimated the ranks of ministerial students going to colleges.[34]

With the secularization of the universities in England and the colonies, and with the impact of the growing evangelical movement, new experiments in ministerial training began. But the academic model was not discarded, only modified. In the Anglo-Saxon world, the theological college or seminary came into being. Its growth rate was especially accelerated in the United States where the war of independence had shut off the ministerial supply from the old world, and the great revivals increased the demand

[32]Niebuhr and Williams, *Ministry,* 147.

[33]Ibid., 203.

[34]William Warren Sweet, "The Rise of Theological Schools in America," *Church History* 6 (1937): 264.

for ministers beyond the already taxed inadequacies of private instruction. Between 1807 and 1827 no fewer than seventeen permanent institutions arose to train a professional clergy in a professional way.

This reinforcement of institutional preparation for the ministry served to underline the role of the minister as pedagogue. Schooling, by its very nature, evaluates students' progress in terms of a certain quota of adequately digested knowledge. Its approach is content-oriented rather than student-oriented. And, if Peter Savage is accurate, it leads to an obsessive interest in abstract reality on the part of professor and student, a reveling in the delights of conceptual debate withdrawn from the daily life of the culture and the church's response to that culture. Curriculum offered a model for the ministry "where emphasis has been placed on the digestion of packets of knowledge rather than on bringing each student to spiritual maturity and effective ministry."[35] Within this network, the teacher-student relationship moved from that between brothers to that of father and son, from fraternal to paternalistic. Measurements were taken in terms of cognitive input rather than ministerial gifts.

This was the pattern the missionary of the nineteenth century was trained under, a model developed in the exigencies of Western history but assumed by the missionary to be usable anywhere in the world. It was the model, for example, that the Board of Education of the Presbyterian Church in the U.S.A. held up to its church in 1847: "The basis of all operations of the Board of Education is that a pious and well-qualified ministry is the great instrumentality appointed by the Head of the Church for the conversion of the world." The model was questionable, even back then. The Presbyterians had five hundred churches without pastors in the United States. Yet, a few years later the first Presbyterian missionaries carried the gospel, along with the educational model, to Brazil. According to one commentator, the model there

[35]Savage, "Four Crises," 31.

produced rigid institutional structures and seriously hampered the church's ability to respond to the Brazilian situation.[36] To the Presbyterian, schooling was the equivalent of a highly trained ministry. But in "most of Latin American and much of the Third World [it] is primarily a vehicle of escape from poverty, and it alienates people from their own families, communities and cultures."[37] In other contexts, the cognitive abstractionism that has been part of the model from its origins may result in other cultural distortions.

Few critics of the traditional pedagogue element, if any, disparage the need for a "highly trained ministry." The source of frustration does not lie in the need for scholarship or adequate preparation. It is rather the hidden assumption behind the terminology, which too often equates schooling with education, Western patterns of learning with patterns appropriate to distinct cultures, cognitive orientation with contextual response. In this area the radical criticisms of Ivan Illich and Paulo Friere are worth listening to. Both demand, among other things, that living, learning, and working be interconnected and contextual. They flatly reject the thesis that learning is a direct result of teaching and that learning and schooling are synonymous.[38] Education, they cry, must start with the needs of the student, with the student in his unique context. An educated ministry is not of necessity an institution-processed ministry. The judgments of these critics need assessment and modification.[39] But even on a simple level, their warnings need heeding. Seminary teachers tend to reproduce their

[36]Ronald G. Frase, "A Sociological Analysis of Brazilian Protestantism: A Study of Social Change" (Th.D. diss., Princeton Theological Seminary, 1975).

[37]Kinsler, " Extension," 184.

[38]Ivan Illich, *Deschooling Society* (New York: Harper & Row, 1970); Paulo Freire, *Pedagogy of the Oppressed* (New York: Seabury, 1968).

[39]Some helpful criticisms may be found in John L. Elias, *Conscientization and Deschooling* (Philadelphia: Westminster, 1976). A more pertinent analysis in terms of our topic is found in Stephen C. Knapp, "Ivan Illich and the Evangelical Missionary Enterprise." Unpublished paper available through Partnership in Mission, Abington, Pa., 1974.

own kind—the one who revels in research in the library or disparages the gifted ministry of another who does not have the same learning. The student becomes one whose knowledge of the church and the world comes mainly through the careful phrases of the academic tutor and who copies that pattern in a future ministry.

Reinforcing this feature is the perception of the minister as indispensable professional. Apart even from the pejorative sense in which the term "professional" can be used,[40] the sociocultural characteristics of the pattern as it has developed in history display major weaknesses. Professionalization of an occupation depends on several factors: (1) full-time work with full financial support; (2) a quasi-unique function with some social significance; (3) relative absence of extraprofessional criteria for evaluation (the more specialized the profession, the more the profession itself is needed to evaluate its own capabilities); (4) the discouragement of amateurism and the assumption that aspects of a vocation are best done by one person, the specialist; (5) specialist functions as interchangeable, capable of being performed by any professional, wherever you find one, and no matter who he may be.[41] The history of the development of "the professional ministry" contains these elements and all too frequently magnifies their worst features.

This professional aspect of the model gained ascendancy in the church especially from the fourth century on. As congregations grew in number, the administrative role of a bishop began to take on more prominence, and spiritual guidance became transmuted into ruling, into administrative authority. With the accession of Constantine in 312 A.D. and the eventual marriage of the church

[40]John Howard Yoder, "The Fullness of Christ: Perspectives on Ministries in Renewal," *Concern* 17:73, offers a full list of what this word, used in a pejorative sense, implies.

[41]Most of my list comes from Yoder, "Fullness of Christ," 75–80. Note also Samuel Rowen, "The Future of Theological Education," *Issues for Christian Leaders: Briefs from Westminster Theological Seminary* (November/December 1977): 2–3.

and society, the temptations of magisterial indispensability began to be codified. A hierarchy of clerical orders capped by the bishopric made a specialized profession of the ministry, the bishops acting in consort with the state as the accrediting agents. The dichotomy between the cleric-specialists and the lay-amateurs became even more prominent. Celibacy as a mark of the ministry underlined the division between clergy and laity. And with the greater wealth that came to the church after the conversion of Constantine, the church moved from its freer attitude towards providing a fixed stipend or salary into increasing and more regular support of the clergy as a whole.[42] The effect, then as now, was to isolate the ministry even further from the laity. The lay-amateur found his gifts being evaluated (or devaluated) financially. Ordination began to shift from its biblical function as the church's affirmation of gifts of the Spirit to the institutionalized imprimatur of salaried status, rank, and authority.

As these concurrent trends were amplified in the course of the Middle Ages, the biblical integration of gifts and office, of ecclesiastical order and charismatic ardor, receded more deeply into the background of the emerging model. The interchangeable features of professionalization weakened the place of gifts in the criteria for evaluating qualifications for ministerial service. The priesthood took on more and more of an innate authority, carrying its own magisterial power apart from the authenticity of gifts recognized by the body. In this process, the body's own authenticity began to be measured by the clerical office, rather than the opposite.

With the Reformation came a rediscovery of the nature of the church and the abolition, in principle, of the distinction between clergy and laity. But even this rediscovery did not totally escape professionalization. The restitutionists' advocacy of universal ministry was modified by the failure of Luther and Calvin to question radically the centuries old equation of "baptized Chris-

[42]W.G.B. Ream, "The Support of the Clergy in the First Five Centuries A.D." *International Review of Missions* 45 (October 1956): 428.

tian" with a truly believing Christian, and by a membership whose spiritual maturity was on such a low level that they could not yet suddenly function as Reformational adults rather than children.

> These factors, coupled with the reformation stress on the preeminence of the preaching office, and an emphasis on "adequate" training for that office (largely defined by inherited classical patterns) "encouraged the practical recognition of a secondary status of the laity in comparison with the ministry, the breeding of an attitude of passivity in the laity as a whole, the accentuation of the significance of office and its leadership."[43] Addressing itself to the Roman Catholic definition of the church as clerical, the Reformation focused its attention of necessity on the reformation of the clergy with a proportionate lack of attention to the laity. The result was practically to define the clergy as "spiritual persons" by profession, and to reduce the laity to secondary status. If Kraemer's evaluation is correct, even Calvin, more successful than Luther in realizing a relative independence of church from state, through his high conception of the excellence, indispensability and authority of the clergy, "implied however involuntarily a neglect of the real significance and relevance of the laity".[44]

The years between the Reformation and the beginnings of the world missionary movement offered no real correctives to the seamy side of professionalization. The cultural identification of the work of evangelism with the work of the clergy grew stronger, a more consistent working out of the expert-amateur bifurcation. The pattern flowing from the professionalized model of one-paid-pastor-per-congregation began to be transported with the gospel to the Third World. Missionary financial policies did not escape this pattern, whether one defended subsidization of the national pastor by the mission or the self-support ideology of the indigenous church formulations of Henry Venn and Rufus

[43]Hendrik Kraemer, *A Theology of the Laity* (Philadelphia: Westminster, 1958), 66.

[44]Harvie M. Conn, "Training the Layman for Witness," *Training For Missions,* Paul G. Schrotenboer, ed. (Grand Rapids: Reformed Ecumenical Synod, 1977), 77–78.

Anderson. Both assumed a professional clergy and both identified that with full-time, salaried employment. There were early warnings of the effects of this idea of ministry on the growing Third World church. Bruno Gutmann spoke of his fears that a group of specially trained pastors would tend to form a dangerous isolationist body, to the detriment of the ministry of the congregation as a whole.[45] But his warnings went relatively unheeded. Even the prophetic voice in the wilderness of Roland Allen did not fully escape the weaknesses of the indispensable-professional ideology. Operating as an Anglican with such a high view of orders that it takes a fully ordained priest to ensure the church's valid presence, Allen retained the quasi-unique feature of the minister as specialist. That theological commitment led him to plead, in the face of stout opposition, for a rapid multiplication of national clergy, faster ordination in recognition of an individual's ministry, and a tent-making method of clergy support.[46] The effect of the sociological dimensions of the ministry as a profession were missed.

The results are being felt today and are increasingly recognized in the discussions of educational excellence. Western patterns, adopted wholesale, have left the world church with no resistance to their own indigenous hierarchical patterns of leadership. Western overhang has only reinforced the hierarchical authority patterns in the Third World. Those ethnic tendencies toward all-powerful, authoritative leadership models combine with the Western missionary model to produce a clericalism more rigid than even the imported kind. The prophet-oriented communities of many of the African churches, the Indian guru's authority as the criterion of truth, the Confucian respect for the teacher now imposed without thinking on the Asian model of pastor-leader—all underscore the elitist function of the ministry.

Even the retreat of the missionary from an overt leadership

---

[45]Neal Braun, *Laity Mobilized* (Grand Rapids: Eerdmans, 1971), 29–30.

[46]Yoder, "Fullness of Christ," 53–54.

role in the church has not helped. The ordained national cleric has simply taken over the professionalized role. And, in order to meet the needs of a growing church financially unable to support a full-time, fully-paid clergy under any method, a hierarchy of unordained, academically ill-trained, poorly paid workers has arisen. Thus, in statistics prepared by Bengt Sundkler in 1957, among all the traditional Protestant churches in sub-Saharan Africa, just over 88,000 Africans were employed in pastoral work. Slightly fewer than 83,000 of these people were unordained cathechists and teachers with pastoral responsibilities, while only 5,760 were ordained pastors. These statistics show a situation almost identical to that in India: only 6.5% of pastoral responsibilities are in the hands of ordained pastors and priests, while 93.5% are the responsibility of unordained people.[47]

The problem cannot be solved simply by ordaining those presently functioning as unordained pastors. Ross Kinsler speaks of the strong opposition on the part of the clergy in Latin America to such a possibility, even to the possibility of ordaining those trained in extension (regarded as inadequate and "mediocre" by older men).[48] I have heard this same resistance in Korea and Japan. Deeper questions must be asked: What are the real roots of our conception of ordination? Must there be a "pedagogical conversion" of our functional definition—from the inherited professional pattern to a biblical one? Is our understanding of the ministry pseudo-sacramentalized by a specialization motif that isolates it in some hierarchical way from the body of Christ? Has the inherited pattern of one-fully-paid-pastor-per-congregation, borrowed from the parish system of the West, overpowered our appreciation for the relation of spiritual gifts to ecclesiastical office? Does the specialization model of ministry inhibit us from a fully biblical exploration of excellence in ministerial preparation?

The major alternative to these features of the traditional

[47]James A. Bergquist and P. K. Manickam, *The Crisis of Dependency in Third World Ministries* (Madras: Christian Literature Society, 1974), 13.

[48]Kinsler, "Extension," 186–87.

model being offered today would seem to revolve around the issue of contextualization, introduced by the TEF in their search for the renewal and reform of theological training. Regarded as a missiological necessity, the process expressed in the cumbersome term revolves around "the capacity in theological education to respond to the context."[49]

Initially, the term seemed to function as a rallying point for the polarities of the past—the academic versus the situational approach to theology; the Western versus the Third World setting for advanced studies; degree- versus non-degree-oriented study; the elitist versus the proletarian understanding of leadership; theological versus nontheological types of study.[50] And in some of the written reflections that have appeared since the discussions began in 1972, one or more of those polarities remain very close to the center of understanding.

At the same time, one cannot do justice to the discussion by seeing it simply as a gathering place for negative responses to history or even as a continuation of past discussions of indigenization or of the functional ministry. It extends and corrects indigenization in several directions:

1. Indigenization, even in its most refined usage, focuses on the cultic accoutrements of the church—the acculturation of patterns of worship, forms of organization, and leadership. Contextualization adds to this list the macrocosms of our culture—the social, political, and economic questions: wealth and poverty, power and powerlessness, privilege and oppression.

2. Indigenization "tends to be used in the sense of responding to the Gospel in terms of a traditional culture," a culture thought to be static and relatively unchangeable. Contextualization sees cultures in an era of explosive, rapid social change. It "takes into account the process of secularity, technology, and the struggle for

[49]"Focal Points of Authentic Renewal," *WCC Education Newsletter* 4 (December 1972): 5.

[50]"Faculty Development in Third World Theological Education," *WCC Education Newsletter* 3 (June 1972): 2.

human justice, which characterizes the historical moment of nations in the Third World."[51]

3. Indigenization presumes a concept of the church still identified with "the mission field," understood in a colonial sense—the mission church "there" and not "here." Contextualization functions with a vision of the church as "the church in six continents," the issues it faces no more "exotically foreign" than those faced by any of the world's people of God. It calls on all the church everywhere to speak to "the more radically politicized situation in Asia, Africa and Latin America"[52] in the same way that it must prophetically address the situation in Europe and North America.

4. Indigenization as a formula was originally "intended to place responsibility, authority, and initiative in the hands of national Christians. It usually did so in only a part of the total missionary enterprise. . . . As a result, extremely Western patterns were perpetuated and Westerners remained in charge, leading to frustration and resentment on the local scene."[53] Contextualization flows out of a functional moratorium on the missionary as subject and the church-as-object. It recalls the church to its place as subject in the missiological discernment of the signs of the times, the church "seeing where God is at work and calling us to participate in it."[54]

5. Indigenization operated with something resembling the classical view of hermeneutic. It saw the task of theology as the construction of a bridge between the culture/interpreter and the biblical author by means of what has been popularly called the grammatico-historical methodology. Influenced by a monocultural, idealistic perspective of communication, it saw hermeneutic as a

---

[51]*Ministry in Context,* 20.

[52]James A. Bergquist, "Third World Theological Education," 246.

[53]Charles R. Taber, "Contextualization: Indigenization and/or Transformation" *The Gospel and Islam: A 1978 Compendium,* Don McCurry, ed. (Monrovia: MARC, 1979), 145.

[54]Coe, "In Search of Renewal," 241.

linear process of transposition of the gospel from one world to another, with interference largely of a linguistic sort.[55] Contextualization within the conciliar movement sees hermeneutic as a dialectical process that moves back and forth between the text and the context—the situational character of all theology. It emerges as a process of "involvement and participation, out of which critical awareness may arise."[56] It is more than simply taking the semantic context seriously. And it is even more than taking the social, political, and economic context seriously. It is the "conscientization of the contexts in the particular, historical moment, assessing the peculiarity of the context in the light of the mission of the church as it is called to participate in the *Missio Dei*."[57] Only through the dialectical interaction of the *Missio Dei* and the historical process does the gospel's contextualization take concrete shape.

6. Indigenization, within its colonialist mold, created a concept of the ministry with a "middle class ideology"[58] that directed us largely to the church and not the world, a mentality more ameliorative than prophetic. The ethnic ministry, modeling on the reluctance of the missionary to participate in social, political, or economic questions, cultivated a mentality reluctant to deal with social responsibilities. Like the missionary, the minister approached the poor as objects of service, not as subjects with the evangelist. The standard of excellence in this pattern was determined by the level of participation in the institutional church. That involvement was to be spiritual, not secular. Contextualization, by way of contrast, calls for a ministry not simply involved *in* the world but deriving its agenda *from* the world, for a mission that, as

---

[55]For a fuller picture of how this hermeneutic developed, consult Harvie M. Conn, "Contextualization: A New Dimension for Cross-Cultural Hermeneutic," *Evangelical Missions Quarterly* 14 (January 1978): 39–46.

[56]Coe, "In Search of Renewal," 241.

[57]Ibid.

[58]Samuel Escobar, "The Social Responsibility of the Church in Latin America," *Evangelical Missions Quarterly* 6 (Spring 1970): 136–38.

defined by the formulations of Uppsala 1968, removes the line between the history of salvation and the salvation of history, between the church and the world. In this restructuring, ministerial calling extends beyond even the functional one of secular involvement promoted frequently in the 1960's.[59] The standard of excellence becomes commitment

> to a lifestyle of solidarity with the poor and the oppressed and involvement in action with them. Theology is not neutral. In a sense all theology is committed, conditioned notably by the socio-cultural context in which it is developed. The Christian theological task in our countries is to be self-critical of the theologian's being conditioned by the value system of his environment. It has to be seen in relation to the need to live and work with those who cannot help themselves, and to be with them in their struggle for liberation.[60]

An adequate response to this new model will have to wait as we see how it will be unfolded in the myriad cultural colors it demands for its self-exposition. Ethnic worldviews, where they have features of the traditional model we have already surveyed, can be expected to modify and correct it. Scanning the various theological periodicals discussing its implications, one already senses much regional shaping taking place. The strident tones of the statement from twenty-two Third World theologians gathered at Dar-es-Salaam in 1976 (quoted in the previous paragraph) are much more muted in the tentative judgments of Dr. Chung-choon Kim as he evaluates the significance of "the contextualization questions" for his Korean setting.[61] The search of Mennonite Albert Widjaja from Central Java for a theology willing to be

[59]For samples of this focus on "Functionalism," see Steven G. Mackie, *Patterns of Ministry* (London: Collins, 1969), 103–6; " 'Functionalism' in Ministerial Training," *Study Encounter* 3 (1967): 180–85.

[60]"Theology From the Third World," *JSAC Grapevine* 8 (February 1977): 7.

[61]Chung-choon Kim, "The Contextualization of Theological Education," *Northeast Asia Journal of Theology*, 12 (March, 1974): 1–9.

called "beggarly" in its identification with cultural experiences too long considered as "inferior garbage by the missionary" shows great sensitivity to the macro issues of missions. But his willingness to live deeply with the agony of the world does not obliterate the church in the world. Contextualized theology for him remains "a search for an authentic path of a mature church."[62]

Still, some judgments must be made, even if on a preliminary basis, and many of these may be positive in comparison with the evaluation of the pedagogical, professional model. The core of the participation model, in opposition to the abstractionist tendencies of the classical pattern, aims at the deepest level of integration between the gospel and the concrete situation in which the church is called. Thus, it seeks to shift from training *for* ministry to not merely training *in* ministry but to ministry that is itself training. The concreteness of the situation in which the church is called holds promise for encompassing more than merely a recognition of philosophical or linguistic preconceptions in gospel communication; this model demands that attention be paid also to the shaping influences of political and sociological ideologies on our conceptions of the ministry. Its aversion to the monolithic concept of culture out of which the old model arose and its sensitivity to the rapid social changes of culture's many faces today cannot but help retard the imposition of any ethnocentric pattern for ministry on others. It remains to be seen whether its focus on context and the implementation of that focus will allow the model to escape the dangers of professionalism we saw in the traditional pattern remain to be seen. We see more severe problems plaguing the new pattern.

Compare Kim's earlier remarks in "Seeking Relevance in Methods of Theological Education," *Northeast Asia Journal of Theology* 7 (September 1971): 29–41.

[62]Albert Widjaja, "Beggarly Theology: A Search for a Perspective Toward Indigenous Theology," *South East Asia Journal of Theology* 14, no. 2 (1973): 39.

Some of these problems we have already outlined in our consideration of the problem of syncretism. We expressed our concern about the fact that this model minimizes the sweeping effects of sin's touch on humanity's cultural building. And we stated our fear that this will lead to a severe weakening of the normativity of Scripture over context in the process.

There are still other dangers that might be added at this point: How shall this model of the minister as participant-in-context avoid the cultural impact of Westernization? The call to participation is a call to involvement in a global village already linked together by the vast penetration of Western secularization. The mandate for contextualization, for example, was said to arise out of the need for a gospel response "to the issues of social justice and human development." But are these issues themselves not symptomatic of a hidden agenda influenced by the thrust of Western technocracy and industrialism? Similarly, the mandate calls for an awareness of the dialectic between the cultures and religions of the Third World and a universal technological civilization. But is technology not ultimately a Western product used by the Western world, all too often for the benefit of the Western world?[63] Just as the traditional model capitulated to Western concepts of professionalism and epistemology, is not the participation model in the framing of its concerns in danger of capitulating to Western concepts of technology and social development?

Finally, the participation model seeks the closest possible integration of the task of the ministry and the *Missio Dei*. Does that missiological thrust do full justice to the profoundly God-centered emphasis of the New Testament, an emphasis explicit in the Latin

[63]Victor Nazario, in the volume, *Learning in Context,* 18–25, raises these same questions from the perspective of liberation theology. His skepticism, however, is not over the intrinsic problems of contextualization as modeled by the TEF formulations but over the "weakness of the principles which lead to it." We see the formulary and its three main concerns as more intimately related than he appears to do and are suspicious of the Marxist preconceptions from which Nazario may be judging the state of affairs.

phrase but used in the literature to focus on humanity's participation in the general historical process of humanization? Does the diminishing of the distinction between the church and the world not reinforce a diminishing of the Godward side of the process of humanization, of God's accomplishing His mission of justification, reconciliation, and liberation through the redemptive atonement of His Son?

> Sociopolitical liberation is certainly an integral part of this biblical pattern of mission, both as an eschatological reality foreshadowed in the inner life of the church as a community practicing radical discipleship and an extrachurch reality towards which Christians contribute through their prophetic/evangelistic proclamation and service. At the same time, participation in the general historical process, and even in its liberating and humanizing aspects, is not what gives the church its identity, nor can the reality of the process of humanization function as the church's hermeneutical baseline.[64]

Will the evangelical commitment to missions, rooted in the centrality of proclamation and its calling out a people from the world to be sent back in again, be dimmed as the emphasis on participation blurs the obligations of the church to cross frontiers that are no longer recognized as existent? Can a ministry be adequately prepared by the promotion of a concept of excellence that, through its insistence on solidarity with the world, blurs the reality of the church as the arena for that ministry?

BIBLICAL FOCAL POINTS OF RENEWAL

Against this background of inherited and proposed patterns, we suggest that deeper questions still wait to be answered. And only in responding to them from a more radically biblical

[64]Stephen C. Knapp, "Contextualization and Its Implications for U.S. Evangelical Churches and Missions" (Paper available through Partnership in Mission, Abington, Pa., n.d.), 13.

perspective, alert to the filtering and retarding impact of sociocultural dynamics, will we begin to come to our answers.

1. Who are the laity, the people of God, and what is the integrating point that unites people to ministry, even to ministry in a specialized sense? How should our calling as "an elect race, a royal priesthood, a holy nation, a people for God's own possession" (1 Peter 2:9–10) affect our view of ministry? What cumulative cultural processes have inhibited that biblical vision? Are there models seeking breakthroughs or at least modifications?

2. How can the doing of theology be taught to the people of God? How can theology edify, using the tools of scholarship, without abstraction, without surrendering to the tools of scholarship?

3. What is education? Must it be reduced to schooling or magnified into the secularization of church and world in solidarity? Is there a biblically orbed conscientization that can escape both the Western individualism that defines the object of ministry largely in terms of souls saved and a socializing universalism that reduces evangelism to largely political action of a structural sort?

Who Are the Laity?

Emancipated from a duality in Graeco-Roman society, where *laos* (the people) was only one of two sectors of municipal administration (the other being *kleros,* the magistrate), the New Testament transformed the *laos* into the unifying covenant category of the whole people of God, the "new man" formed by Gentiles and Jews (Acts 15:14), reconciled "in one body to God through the cross" (Eph. 4:16, Col. 3:15). Battered since then by cultural accommodations to sacred and secular categories, the "laity" are constantly tempted to function as an ingredient rather than the salt of the earth. Its pilgrim nature threatened by the fleshly lusts of materialism and success-orientation, the *laos* still defines its existence in terms of the dwelling of God with His assembled children. Constituted a people in redemptive assembly at Sinai (Exod. 5:1, Deut. 4:10), her future outlined in terms of the gathering of the Gentiles at the great festival assembly of God (Isa. 2:2–4; 56:6–8; Ps. 87), a future made present by the coming of Christ (Heb. 12:18–24), the church still gathers in assembly (1 Cor. 11:18; 14:26–28) till the final gathering at the coming of Christ (2 Thess. 2:1).

But integral also to that biblical portrayal of the people of God as gathered is the imagery of the *laos* as the gatherers, a traveling, scattered community now unencumbered by temples of stone (Acts 7:44–47). They themselves are "living stones, being built up as a spiritual house for a holy priesthood" (1 Peter 2:4–5). Called at Sinai to "fulfill a priestly role as a people in the midst of the peoples," to represent God in the world of nations (Exod. 19:6),[65] that calling is renewed in the redemptive authority of Christ (Matt. 28:18–20).

As "the twelve tribes who are dispersed abroad" (James 1:1; 1 Pet. 1:1), the new dispersed people of God is committed again "to proclaim His name among all the nation" (Luke 24:47). God in Christ gathers His new Israel at Jerusalem to scatter them from Jerusalem "and in all Judea and Samaria and even to the remotest part of the earth" (Acts 1:8). In the last days, inaugurated by Christ's kingdom coming (1 Cor. 10:11; Heb. 1:2), God's people are to begin a new Exodus, already initiated by their Saviour's redemptive death (Luke 9:31). No longer do they go as fugitives, "for the Lord will go before you and the God of Israel will be your rear guard" (Isa. 52:12). "Those who were scattered" will go preaching the Word (Acts 8:4). There will be a new wilderness wandering (Isa. 35:4–9), inaugurated by Jesus in His forty-day trek (Luke 4:1–12), to be mirrored again in Jesus' people. Only,

[65]Johannes Blauw, *The Missionary Nature of the Church* (London: Lutterworth, 1962), 24.

now there will be a highway (Isa. 11:16) along which Egyptians and Assyrians will march together with Israel as God's remnant (Isa. 19:23), a highway of repentance announced by John, heralding the coming of the Kingdom with the coming of the King (Matt. 3:2–3).

This Exodus ministry of the people of God is not theologically or culturally bound to clerical hierarchy. At Pentecost the Spirit baptized for prophetic ministry *all* the house of the Lord (Acts 2:4). In the new theocracy of God, the Spirit's gift for witness touches more than merely judges (Judg. 3:10; 6:34; 15:14) or kings (1 Sam. 16:13) or prophets (1 Sam. 10:6; 2 Peter 1:20–21). In the new day of the Diaspora, all God's sons and daughters will be prophets (Joel 2:28, Acts 2:16–21). Isaiah's promise of the pouring out of the Spirit and the confession of the Lord's name (Isa. 44:3–5) becomes reality as the prophetic office of proclamation becomes the central office of the whole people of God. The people are filled with the Spirit—not alone, but in common with all believers, not occasionally, but again and again. Through the Spirit the church is reconstituted a witnessing body. Thus the Sanhedrin marvels at the word of "uneducated and untrained men" (Acts 4:13). The gospel of the kingdom moves beyond Jerusalem when they are "all scattered throughout the regions of Judea and Samaria, except the apostles" (Acts 8:1). Tentmakers like Paul, merchantwomen like Lydia, jailors, tradespeople like Priscilla and Aquila—these are the people who threaten to "turn the world upside down" (Acts 17:6). The laity's rights are defined in terms of the laity's obligations, and never simply in terms of professional training or salaried employment.

This is not to deny that there is a place for offices or even paid offices in the church.[66] The ardor of the Spirit's gifts is ordered by the Spirit's offices where those gifts, peculiarly heightened, may be exercised. And in those offices, whether it be that of widow

[66]Bergquist and Manickam, *Crisis of Dependency,* 117, miss completely the Pauline correlation between gift and office when they argue that "there are no essential offices, only essential tasks or functions."

(1 Tim. 5:3) or elder who rules, "honor" is more than accolade; it is measured in terms of financial remuneration, with special consideration for "those who work hard at preaching and teaching" (1 Tim. 5:17–18). The contemporary practice of full-time pay for only one office in the church both loses the element of tribute in remuneration and denudes the wholeness of the body in its unbiblical criteria for eligibility for that "honor." In so doing, office becomes a means of dividing laity from laity, those with office from those without office. Sociocultural leadership patterns or the payment or nonpayment of salary, rather than "grace given to us" (Rom. 12:6) "according to the measure of Christ's gift" (Eph. 4:7), become the measure of offices given. The communal service of the one body (1 Cor. 12:4–6; Eph. 4:4) is distorted through a system of financial support for "service," sanctified by custom. The mutual stewardship of calling that is part of every gift is hindered by the prejudicial way in which cultural practice limits the objects of our "honor."

Who are the ministers of the laity? Western acculturated patterns, coupled with Third World indigenous concepts of leadership and group solidarity, tend to reduce ministry from being the work of the whole church, the exercise of the general office of believer, to institutional, ordered ministries or special offices in the body. In the process, "ministry" becomes a Third World synonym for church officials, administration, dignitaries, authorities. The pattern is little different in the Anglo-Saxon world. But "it is not law or power, knowledge or dignity but *service* which is the basis of discipleship."[67] *Charisma,* the giving of Christ's gifts by His Spirit to the church, cannot be severed from *diakonia* as *charisma* actively functioning *in concreto* in the church.[68] *Charisma* leads to *diakonia,* since every *charisma* in the church only finds fulfillment in service.

Acculturating processes also act to create an antithesis be-

---

[67]Hans Küng, *The Church* (New York: Sheed and Ward, 1967), 392.

[68]Herman Ridderbos, *Paul: An Outline of His Theology* (Grand Rapids: Eerdmans, 1975), 441.

tween "charismatic" and "administrative" ministries (between the general and special offices of the believer). Thus leadership is ultimately not defined in terms of the service of gifts but in terms of salaried or nonsalaried, and hence ordained and unordained.[69] In the same way, the "varieties of gifts" in the body (1 Cor. 12:4) that flow into "varieties of ministries" (1 Cor. 12:5) are defined, not in terms of the diversity of spiritual endowments needed for the service of the Word, for governing, for showing mercy, but in terms of economic (paid or unpaid), temporal (full-time or part-time), training (schooled or unschooled) categories. Even the current discussions of "tent-making" ministries do not fully escape the problem. They focus largely on the office of the pastor and, again, not in terms of the exercise of spiritual gifts, but of one's status as full-time or part-time, volunteer or paid.[70] "Ministry" remains a category defined in terms of one office in the church. The corporate conception of the ministry in the church is reduced to one office.

The schooling process of preparation also serves to isolate the ministry from the laity in a way not reflected in the New Testament. The alertness of Illich and Freire to this isolationist dimension may be part of the motivation behind their desire to discard the whole schooling system. But that response appears to be too simplistic for even the more radical evangelical critics of schooling today. Some, like Ted Ward, can point to a long list of schooling characteristics that can hinder learning effectiveness. And many of these characteristics, we add, are at work in theological education to magnify the gulf between preacher and people in a way detrimental to an understanding of the ministry of the people of God. Both preacher and people concur that "all

[69]David M. Paton, ed., *New Forms of Ministry* (London: Edinburgh House, 1965), 31, 84ff.

[70]*A Tent Making Ministry* (New York: Division of World Mission and Evangelism, World Council of Churches, 1962).

learners are assumed to be similar in terms of needs, interests and abilities."[71] Antithetic to the New Testament's appreciation of the diversity of gifts for ministry, this principle of our hidden agenda creates the false expectation that one authoritative figure in the church must possess all the gifts. And concomitant with it is the converse assumption that a nonlearner (theologically unschooled person) must be dissimilar to a learner in terms of needs, interests, and abilities. The effect of this preconception is to emasculate the ministry of all the body (Rom. 12:6–8).

There are also those schooling characteristics the minister has learned in the system and which then become part of the minister's understanding of his or her own calling. "Learners are increasingly made more competitive at the price of cooperation," is transposed into a reinforcement of the minister's self-image as the top of an ecclesiastical hierarchy. This is reinforced again by the schooling assumption, acculturated into the life of the church, that "the teacher is ascribed authority, thus creating a hierarchy based on unearned status."[72] The schooling propensity for abstractionism ("abstractions of experience in the form of language and symbols are substituted for reality") isolates the minister still further from the nontheologically abstracted layperson. And this isolation is underlined by the minister's assumption of the teacher's role and of the schooling preconception that increases the social distance separating teacher from learner by according different sets of rights and expectations to each. Then again the cultural propensity of the minister to the pedagogue ideology is augmented by the school-learned model that "testing is the criterion of success" and "success is the surpassing value."

Ward does not intend these characteristics to support the discarding of the schooling system. They are simply reasons for the continuous necessity of school improvement, inherent charac-

---

[71]Ted Ward, "Schooling as a Defective Approach to Education" (Paper available through the author, Institute for International Studies, Michigan State University, 1978), 2.

[72]Ibid., 3.

teristics in the schooling approach that cannot be escaped even with an extension model. "In other words, if you are going to use a schooling approach, certain problems come along in the bargain. Weaknesses and defects of the sort that we usually focus on during 'school improvement' activities may indeed be normal states, not aberrations!"[73]

The lessons are clear also for establishing standards in theological education. We need to be liberated in the church from seeing schooling at the very center of our concept of theological education, recognizing it (despite its defects) as merely *one* of many valid approaches to education. That liberation must of necessity affect the school-oriented traditions behind ordination requirements, formed in the West and adopted in nonschooling cultures. In the West this tradition has resulted in too many ecclesiastical doors being shut to gifted people who do not meet the schooling requirements. And, in the Third World, it has created the large disparity between the many who perform functionally as ministers (without schooling) and the few whose gifts the church may recognize because they have the necessary academic degrees.

Another focus of change, without resorting to the radical deschooling proposal, might be a new look at curriculum. Discarding the mentality that defines curriculum in terms of courses offered or even as all the experiences the student may have had as a result of his or her relationship to the school, curriculum becomes a search for metaphors by which we seek to define the purpose of the educational experience. Samuel Rowen suggests three of these metaphors that function in the process of theological education. There is the metaphor of *production,* in which the curriculum becomes the means of producing a finished product from the raw material (the theological student). There is the metaphor of *travel,* in which the curriculum is understood as the route the student will travel while under the close supervision of

[73]Ibid., 2.

an experienced guide. Finally is the metaphor of *growth,* in which the curriculum is seen as a greenhouse where each plant (theological student) will grow to its fullest potential under the care of a wise and patient gardener.

> The plants in the greenhouse are of different varieties and each is treated according to its needs. No attempt is made to divert the inherent potential within the individual plant by the whims and desires of the gardener.[74]

Renewal in developing standards of excellence may need to ask which metaphor best describes where we are. Do we want to be there? Are there other metaphors which more accurately describe what we ought to be?

Still another possibility for renewal in this area may lie in a more inclusive understanding of the participants in theological education. In the West, that circle has long been restricted almost exclusively to the ordained minister, the clergy in contrast to the so-called layperson. Can this bifurcation be broken down by programs flexible enough to train both clergy and laypeople in the same classroom? One of the great assets of the theological extension training movement, at least as it has been practiced, for example, in Guatemala, lies precisely here: It has not been restricted either to a clergy training program or to a lay training program.

> Now 250 people representing the whole spectrum of the churches' membership study theology each year in the context of their own homes, congregations and communities—instead of 10 or 15 privileged youth set apart at a seminary campus. Probably 75% of these students have no intention of becoming ordained pastors; but they are eager to study in a system which offers no relief from the demands of daily life and employment, and they expect to serve their congregations voluntarily the rest of their lives. At least 50 students are Indians, second class

[74]Samuel Rowan, "The Future of Theological Education," *Issues for Christian Leaders: Briefs from Westminster Theological Seminary* (Nov./Dec. 1977),3.

> citizens in a country which is striving to obliterate their languages and cultural values through "social integration." Perhaps another 50 are women . . . disenfranchised from the entire ecclesiastical governing structure. The great majority represent the poor, and they could never attend a traditional seminary.[75]

Another exciting model in this area is provided by the Latin American Theological Fraternity. Though not a formal, in-residence program, its goals are worth thinking about in relation to the traditional pattern. It seeks to draw together in an "ethos of study" and biblically-structured praxis the resources of the whole body of Christ. It does this through regularly held consultations on a continent- and nation-wide level; through the requirement that each member of the fraternity submit once a year a written paper reflecting his or her thinking and experience over the previous twelve months; through what amounts to a nonformal learning experience for Christians in the social and behavioral sciences, in the pastorate, in the pulpit, and the pew. Its orientation is deeply contextual. During the next four years it will be promoting research and study papers on such topics as the gospel and culture, structures of power and justice, poverty and wealth.[76] Steering a biblical path throughout its eight-year history between those who "had begun to reinterpret the Christian faith almost wholly in terms of the revolutionary language and principles of political struggle and, on the other hand, the large bulk of Protestant leaders who . . . are decidedly indifferent to the wider, traumatic, political context of their converts and would-be converts,"[77] it has stimulated creative theological thinking by Latin American Christians. Its deliberate effort from the first has been to break down the abstractionism that isolates theology from the life of Latin America and the indifference that isolates the

[75]Kinsler, "Extension," 193–94.

[76]*Theological Fraternity Bulletin* 2–3 (1977): 28.

[77]J. Andrew Kirk, "An Open Forum: Editorial," *Theological Fraternity Bulletin* 3 (1975): 1–2.

church from theologizing. We see this effort as largely successful in its creation of a model for theologizing by all the body of Christ with all of its gifts.

How Do We Teach Theologizing?

Coordinate with the rise of the abstractionist schooling model has grown a focus on theology and more specifically on theology as the academically disciplined, thematic ordering of biblical data, "the scientific presentation of all the facts that are known concerning God and His relations."[78] More often than not, that has been narrowed again to theology as "systematic theology," the results of the process of theory construction from the facts of the Bible.

The result has been a growing incapacity to do theology: our concentration is on theology, not theologizing. Students learn the cumulative cognitive results of the doing of theology. The functional paradigm, reinforced by the technical, professional idioms in which it is couched in the school, minimizes the very thing that every school declares to be its stated purpose in teaching—the process of doing theology.

The schooling model plays a key role in this minimization. Its emphasis on the cognitive aspect of language, abstracted from the realities of human settings and cultures, reduces the context out of which theology as product is formed. The contextual character of all theology, whether good or bad, has been misplaced, buried under the weight of the Western respect for the expert (in this case the theologian). Theology as response to the challenges of history is forgotten in our preoccupation with theology only as the awesome, cumulative history of that response. The pastoral dimensions of theology are befogged by the church's understanding of theology as a schooling science, abstract, done by experts,

[78]B. B. Warfield, *Studies in Theology* (New York: Oxford University Press, 1932), 68.

yielding universal principles applicable in all times and cultures. The concrete relation of theology to the life of the people of God remains obscured.[79] Inevitably, the focus of such theology remains fixed around the traditional loci of anthropology, Christology, soteriology, etc., loci reflecting thematic arrangements for the study of theology as it has, in its past, addressed Western contexts and Western worldviews. The effect of this structural methodology on the Third World church is to leave them further abstracted from their own contexts and its problems. To what part of the historical tradition they identify with "theology" will they go to find answers for such problems as ancestor worship, the power structures of animism, and the Muslim misconstructions of Jesus as the Son of God?

None of this is meant to reject the legitimacy of the office of teacher in the Christian church or the importance of understanding the history of dogma as the history of the Spirit's guiding His church into all the truth. But it must be remembered that Jesus' fulfillment of the office of teacher transformed it as well.

> No longer are "Rabbis" to be adulated and exalted, having chief seats in the synagogue and salutations in the market places. "But be ye not called Rabbi; for one is your teacher, and all ye are brethren" (Matt 23:8). After Christ, Gamaliel can no longer serve as a model teacher for the New Testament church . . . Teaching ministry in Christ's church follows the wisdom ideal as it is realized in the whole counsel of God revealed in Jesus Christ. That wisdom joins knowing, doing and being before God. It would be foolish to suppose that a congeries of teachers in special theories and skills could adequately instruct the people of God in general or candidates for the pastorate in particular. The concept of a Christian faculty requires more than a loose aggregation of specialists distinguished by their contribution to

[79]The booklet *Church and Theology in the Contemporary World,* ed. Paul G. Schrotenboer, (Grand Rapids: Reformed Ecumenical Synod, 1977) illustrates what I mean. The three careful studies of which it consists focus on the nature of theology but remain Western and totally abstracted from the circumstances of the Soweto and Cape Town riots at the time of which they were read.

> the sum of knowledge in a narrow field of intellectual inquiry.[80]

Our argument is simply that the biblical concept of teacher has also been heavily distorted by the Greek cognitive model, a distortion that has been reinforced by the Western ideas of specialization, obscuring the gospel teacher's aim of presenting every man perfect in Christ (Col. 1:28) and the whole church as a pure bride to Christ (2 Cor. 11:2). Karl Rengstorf claims that a radical change took place in the church's conception of teaching under the influence of the early Apologists and the Alexandrian school. The office of teacher in Egypt was in the tradition of Greek and Philonic philosophy. "The Alexandrian school is not a continuation of the work of the first Christian teachers, but the introduction of a Greek institution into the church in Christianized form."[81] Through the impact of that tradition, theology has too often lost its character as the ministry of the body of Christ, serving its own upbuilding in love, the edificatory work of every Christian in sharing with brothers and sisters insights into Scripture. The legitimate place for a teacher as one in whom those gifts of edification are heightened has been transposed into an acculturated model of the professional. And theology has become the professional's job, not the task of the church.

A biblical understanding of contextualization in doing theology can be of service in the restoration of that pastoral dimension to the work of teaching and theologizing. "The teaching goals are to be conformed to the Biblical norms of wisdom rather than to an abstract ideal of knowledge as data storage and retrieval. The teaching community and each teacher must seek to apply to the life of the individual and to the life of the church in the world the truth of God's revelation."[82]

---

[80]Edmund P. Clowney, "Scriptural Considerations on the Calling of a Seminary Teacher" (Mimeographed by the author, n.d.), 2–3.

[81]Gerhard Kittel, ed., *Theological Dictionary of the New Testament* (Grand Rapids: Eerdmans, 1964–76), 2:159.

[82]Clowney, "Scriptural Considerations," 4.

This cannot be accomplished in isolation from the cultural world the theological educator addresses. We need schools without walls and teacher/learners who are at the same time pastors. The International Christian University initiated by Campus Crusade for Christ in California is an effort in this direction. It requires a mixture of academic studies and street experience from all its students. Whether it will fall into the grip of pragmatism (action without correlative reflection), only time will tell. A related experiment is now being initiated by congregations of the Conservative Baptist Church in the northeastern United States. During the time of their studies, students will serve as pastoral interns in settings of their choice—suburban, rural, and urban. The seminary thus becomes a campus-on-wheels, using library resources where they are available: the life of the institution is thus intimately related to the life of the churches in their diverse socio-cultural settings. Seminars are designed to integrate learning with the pastorate. Still another effort in this same direction was tried recently by my own school, Westminster Seminary. During their senior year, students worked in the Miami, Florida area as interns in local churches while stretching their studies over a two-year period. Classes were held two days a week while the student served in the churches. Financial pressures and lack of full support from area churches were the main factors that forced the program to close after only a few years of experimentation.

The efforts, however, must continue in this direction. Peter Davids, Professor of New Testament at Trinity Episcopal School for Ministry, Ambridge, Pennsylvania, tells us why:

> I've taken enough courses and read enough books to realize that a good deal of theology is done without living contact with the Bible, but that even more importantly a good deal of theology and biblical studies is done without contact with life. One suspects such scholars and teachers of having chosen the academy because they were afraid of the pastorate. It is clear that such reflection is not done from a hands-on involvement in human and pastoral life; it is an ivory tower, often effete

> analysis done by people not deeply involved in the church. If Karl Barth was right in citing the need to do theology with the Bible in one hand and the newspaper in the other, such people must have as a motto, "Let not the right hand know what the left hand doeth."[83]

Is there a way out of the impasse? Davids, quoting Richard Rohr, remarks, "the best theology is done not in the academy (although some academics overcome this disadvantage) but in the church and in the world, where the drive for answers to pressing questions is intense and a theological solution to practical issues is a necessity."[84] The shame of such *acontextual* theology is precisely that most of the Western formers of the Western church's thinking and doing were pastors. Calvin worked in the heat of a pastoral charge in Geneva; Augustine did theology in the stress of preserving the church while the Roman Empire was collapsing; Luther, Athanasius, Spurgeon—all were pastors. They theologized, they hammered out theology meaningful to their problems and alive to their day. Our schools have concentrated on the results of their work, often at the expense of learning how they did it. This, adds Davids, "is nothing less than taking a living, vital tradition, drowning it in the embalming fluid of scholastic objectivity and then presenting it to the student as the 'real thing'." If theology is to live today, it must still be done in and by the church on the street.

If it is to work, it also must be done "from the underside" of human cultures. It must be done not only for the white middle-class but also for the poor. It must be done not only with the white middle-class but also with the poor. Orlando Costas emphasizes this in his analysis of the distinctive feature of missiological thought in Latin America, which emerges out of the concrete experience of the oppressed and marginalized. His point is not that Latin America mission and theology studies are less critical than

[83]Peter H. Davids, "So What?" *New College Berkeley Notes* 5 (Fall–Winter 1982–83): 1.

[84]Ibid.

those in the North Atlantic world. Nor that they are more oriented toward praxis. The missiological dimension of theology anywhere bears these characteristics as a critical-reflective task. Rather, the differences are two-fold. In the northern hemisphere, missiological theology is carefully thought out, written reflection. In the South, it is an oral, popular reflection done "on the road" as it were. In the North it is the province of specialized theologians. In the South it is sparked usually by ordinary members of the church, often poor, acting collectively and helped along by a few professional theologians. Further, in Latin America theologizing has overwhelmingly appeared in connection with the issues confronting the church there, in her concrete historical situation—power versus powerlessness, the controllers versus the controlled, "owners" versus "leasers." In Europe and North America, missiology has generally speaking been oriented toward those who are geographically far. And, we add, it remains abstracted from theology oriented toward those who are socially and geographically "visible."

How does one duplicate or try to duplicate the Latin American experience in North America? With boards of trustees, the majority of whom come from disenfranchised minorities—black, Hispanic, Asian. With faculties and student bodies who speak with anger and agony for the same groups. With philosophies of curriculum oriented toward the cities where these voices are loudest.

Encircling all these agenda items, giving them vitality, must be a missiological dimension that embraces the entire spectrum of ways in which the church and Christian persons act and speak redemptively in the world.

In his inaugural address as Professor of World Missions at Emmanuel School of Religion in 1980, Charles Taber includes, among others, the following dimensions of that process.

1. Living in the world as human beings—as neighbors, as citizens of various countries, as workers in various jobs.

We are called as Christians, right in the midst of our so-called secular connections, to be salt and light.

2. Giving testimony to what God has done for us in Jesus Christ. Taber calls this the essence of witness and evangelism.
3. Acts of compassion and concern for human beings in trouble in the name of Jesus Christ. This includes what we do both individually and collectively to ameliorate conditions in the world, to alleviate suffering, and to improve the distribution of the world's goods and the administration of justice in all relationships between persons and nations.
4. Systematic efforts to extend the offer of the gospel to peoples who have not yet heard it, including especially those who are across social and cultural barriers from ourselves (what is traditionally called "foreign missions").
5. Efforts to embody God's ideals for society and the world in the internal life of the church. Notably this will function by exemplifying the ways in which the church is able (ideally) to overcome the hostilities, the hatreds, the fears, the contempts, the misunderstandings between persons and groups alienated from each other.[85]

Embodied in these five points drawn from Taber's list of seven I see an effort to correct what Ed Dayton calls our past "focus on sending missionaries, instead of reaching people." On an institutional level, Taber has joined in an ongoing staff effort to develop at Emmanuel an approach to missions that does not isolate it from the rest of the institution as a separate discipline. Missions and evangelism are not intended to exist *sui generis* and off in a corner. It is a vital dimension of all that is done in the school and it concerns the entire faculty and student body. He comments,

> I know that at Emmanuel, professors of Bible will communicate to students the fact that studying the Bible without seeing mission at its core is like studying the physical

[85]Charles R. Taber, *Graduate Education for World Mission* (Johnson City, Tn.: Emmanuel School of Religion, 1980), 10–18.

> properties of the Statue of Liberty without noticing that it is a statue of a woman holding a torch. . . . The same thing is true of church history, which is deeply concerned, along with its interest in the internal life of the church, with the expansion of the gospel into all the world and with its interaction with the world's societies and cultures. Similarly with Christian doctrine: how one can claim to know anything of the character and activity of God, or of Jesus Christ, or of the Holy Spirit, or of the church; or of the nature of salvation, or the doctrine of last things, without being drawn into their missionary essence? What I am saying is that, far from missions being a distinct discipline demanding its own institutional embodiment, it is an essential perspective which should inform and permeate the entire program of the school.[86]

Given this perspective, missiology's task then becomes that of a gadfly in the house of "theology." In the words of Jerald Gort,

> it must exert itself in and out of season to help theology—especially Western theology—find its way back down from the upper regions of the towers of academia to the ground floor of human reality. . . . By the same token missiology also has a mission to the church. The church, too, must ever be reminded that its *raison d'etre* lies in the gospel of the kingdom. The fellowship of the new covenant must be urgently summoned to obedient covenant response, to live its covenant life. The congregation must be called to become what it is in Pentecost, to reaffirm its being and existence by living in mission.[87]

Theological orthodoxy alone is no guarantee that this world perspective of the Scriptures will receive the attention it is due. Missiology stands by to interrupt the theological conversation at every significant moment with the words, *among the nations*. In this spirit, it seeks to irritate the Herman Ridderboses of the world, who can write a 586-page outline of the theology of Paul and not even include the mission of the church in any of its eighty separate

---

[86]Ibid., 5–7. The quotation is from an earlier draft of the address.

[87]Jerald D. Gort, "The Contours of the Reformed Understanding of Christian Mission: An Attempt at Definition," *Calvin Theological Journal* 15 (1980): 46.

headings. It will aim for unrest in a church history department that divides the history of missions from the history of the church or so concentrates on the history of the Western church as to leave the impression that the world is still flat. It will rebel against a practical theology department that offers only domesticated information for the church "at home" in white suburbia.

What will happen to our educational models and our concern for the two horizons of hermeneutic when one of the horizons is that of a white member of Krishna Consciousness? Does the current discussion of hermeneutic really incorporate those outside of Christ and their thinking about the issues? How will we preserve the cross-cultural, border-crossing nature of the gospel in our educational settings where only three percent of all undergraduate college students are enrolled in any studies dealing with international affairs or foreign peoples and cultures? How can our theological education models function in a country where, according to a UNESCO study of 30,000 children in nine countries, American students ranked next to last in their comprehension of foreign cultures?[88] How can they be changed to remind the church that it is more dangerous to be cautious than to be daring? And what does all this mean for those of us who are asking how we can do theology with and for the poor and hope to accomplish mission out of affluence?

Beyond all this, will our educational agenda of concerns overwhelm us again with a new "Babylonian captivity of the Christian mission"? Will we go on writing our books? And will the 2.8 billion people in the world who do not know Christ continue to die with their noses pressed against the windows of our study?

The impact of the schooling approach to theologizing needs exploration. How deeply has the classroom model of theology by loci affected our inculturation of theology? Can that model be

[88]Gerald H. Anderson, "Facing the Realities of the Contemporary World in Mission," *Educating for Christian Missions,* ed. Arthur L. Walker, Jr. (Nashville: Broadman, 1981), 55–56.

continued, but with significant alteration to minimize the abstractionist qualities learned in the classroom? Could the advantages of the case-study methodology, utilized so effectively in the professional schools of law, business, and medicine, reinforce the pastoral character of theologizing and provide not only a methodology for the teaching of theology but also a model for its doing?[89] Could the approach to the teaching of Old Testament Theology, suggested by the late Dr. Chung-choon Kim, not be a significant attempt to contextualize the Bible? Kim suggests the construction of a class curriculum around those questions the students themselves have, relating the answers to Korean understandings, through team teaching with invited specialists. Thus, a course curriculum would cover not only such topics as the God of the Old Testament and history in the Old Testament, but also nationalism, family, political life, education, etc. Each subject would be dealt with in a three-hour block of time, the first hour led by a specialist introducing, for example, the Korean view of God, the second on the biblical data by the appropriate professor, the third a comparative study, teacher and student seeking an integration and comparison of the previous two hours.[90] Out of this approach, argues Kim, could come a student-oriented creative wrestling with biblical data that was never isolated from each culture's unique understandings. The traditional disciplines in a theological curriculum would not be rejected but restructured, "relating to one another, to the ministry committed to the people

---

[89]For some preliminary exploration into this idea, consult Louis Weeks, "So You're Studying Cases," *The Christian Ministry* (July 1974), 36–38; special issue on "Case Study in Theological Education," *Theological Education* 10 (Spring 1974). A growing number of sample cases in the theological area are now available. See Keith R. Bridston et al., *Casebook on Church and Society* (Nashville: Abingdon, 1974); Marvin K. Mayers, *Christianity Confronts Culture* (Grand Rapids: Zondervan, 1974).

[90]Chung-choon Kim, "Seeking Relevance in Methods of Theological Education," 35–37.

of God, and to the World in which this ministry is to be exercised."[91]

Does this attempt go far enough? Must there be also a restructuring of the entire institution in which the teaching is done? Does the structure of a theological seminary, isolated from community with the body of Christ and from the world which it observes, not teach more about theology than it intends? What would happen in the Systematic Theology class if it were to be attended regularly by members of the Black Muslims or devotees of Krishna Consciousness? Should the same desired impact of that presence not be sought for the institution as a whole? What does the successful ministry of L'Abri as a teaching model say to us about the institutional shaping of theology? Can one isolate the theological formulations of the apologetic work of Francis Schaeffer from the ministry of L'Abri as a Christian community in constant evangelistic dialogue with the world through Christian demonstration of faith and life? Does the teaching work of Farel House, carried on in connection with L'Abri, not ask many valuable questions about the place of an institution in its shaping of the way we do theology?[92]

What is Education?

Contextualization, however, cannot be accomplished if it remains simply a program, a theorizing constructed from the schooling patterns of learning. The development of a pattern of excellence in ministry is not constructed from the model of Greek conceptualizations or Enlightenment speculations. It is formed in "doing the will of God" (Matt. 6:10, 7:21), in "doing the truth" (I John 1:6), in "proving what the will of God is" by the "living and holy sacrifice" of our lives lived out before God and the world, not in conformity to that world, but in being transformed (Rom.

[91]Ibid., 38.

[92]The book by Edith Schaeffer, *L'Abri* (Wheaton: Tyndale, 1969), provides the raw material for this kind of inquiry.

12:1–2). Education, in this connection is, to use the words of Paulo Freire, a form of conscientization, the awakening of the Christian conscience to reflection and action in God's world.

In this process of education, "every command of Christ through the Scripture is *de facto* a command to contextualize. Whether it is a command to love one's neighbor or to disciple the nations, it has not been obeyed until one has struggled with the necessity of utilizing, rejecting, or transforming cultural forms in the process of response and obedience."[93]

This conscientization must be covenant-framed in character. That word "covenant" in Dispensational and Reformed circles alike, too often is limited to intrafraternity differences over the macrocosmic understandings of the nature of revelation history. The debate has significance. But our focus in its usage here is on the demand it places on God's people to live by covenant before the Great King. The word of the covenant given by God forbids us to isolate covenant witness from covenant life, thought from action, truth from practice. Truth is not "in order to goodness" in covenant. Truth is the practice of the will of the covenant God. By our walk "we do not the truth" (1 John 1:6). Education as the pursuit of "sound doctrine" (Titus 1:9) is not the suggestion of an academic exercise but, in terms of our cultural contexts, the expression of covenant faithfulness in a God-centered way of living (Titus 1:6–9, 2:1ff). It is the practice that is truth, a repentance that "leads to the knowledge of truth" (2 Tim. 2:25).

For Paulo Freire, the process of conscience awakening is a pedagogical tool that moves us out of the alphabetization of domination and repression to a critical self-awareness of the possibility and means of liberation. The evangelical world church must confess that, as reflected in ministerial preparation, our response has more frequently defined the process as a call to middle-class upward mobility, a pedagogical apparatus that turns from living under the Lordship of Christ in all of life and culture's

[93]Knapp, "Contextualization," 15.

dimensions to an uncritical self-defense of the status quo. God-centered conscientization cannot be content with either alternative. There must be a critical and growing self-awareness of our restored covenant relationship to the Creator as "men of God" (I Tim. 6:11). And there must be a critical and growing self-awareness of our restored covenant relationship to the context that is the cosmos. We must be "man as he makes his way through the world, not enclosed in himself, not independent and autonomous but as man of God."[94] Our life in the kingdom as sign of liberation and judgment must bring us to a covenant conscientization of our witnessing responsibility to the demands of the life of the kingdom in every situation.

Neither of the two models we have discussed earlier helps us fully in recovering these biblical dimensions to ministerial excellence. The classical model too often fails to see that the gospel we present and live out is a call to reclaim not only souls, but our culture now claimed by Christ as Lord, the development of a whole lifestyle whose center is the kingdom rule of the Messiah come and coming again. The contextualization model of the TEF, molded by the secularization debates of the 1960's, "fails to see that the Gospel first of all calls men out of the darkness of sin, from a world without God and therefore without hope, to the light of Christ."[95] Both pare down the "gospel of the kingdom" (Matt. 24:14) from its theocentric dimensions, the one by a world-dominated praxis of humanization, the other by an evangelical immersion in cultic "churchiness." Both serve ultimately to reinforce a two-realm view of life, one sacred, one secular. Both compromise the character of the Christian ministry, one by accommodating it to the secular dimension, the other to the sacred. One transforms "ministerial preparation" into conformity to the wider demands of the culture and its society, the other into

[94]G. C. Berkouwer, *Man: The Image of God* (Grand Rapids: Eerdmans, 1962), 195–96.

[95]Paul G. Schrotenboer, "Theological Education on the Mission Field in Kingdom Perspective," *International Reformed Bulletin*, 58 (1974): 7–8.

conformity to the narrow walls of the church building. In both the goals of ministry are lost.

There is every reason for hoping that all these signs will change in the future. The volume of literature dealing with questions of "indigenous" theology turns to these questions repeatedly. But one must not be overly optimistic. Theories of contextualization and questions of ministerial preparation still divide, as we have seen, over the key issue of norms of authority behind the models. The acculturation processes, unexamined and uncriticized, wait to amend biblical agendas. And, as important as any of these, the continued impact of Western theorizing and modeling continues to influence and pattern world standards with very little of the self-examination that is going on in the Third World churches.[96] Here, as in so many other places, slivers noted in the eye of the Third World's struggle for the emancipation of theological education may draw larger attention than the two-by-four that continues to plague the eyesight of the Western church.

---

[96]James O. Buswell, "Reply," *Theology and Mission,* ed. David G. Hesselgrave (Grand Rapids: Baker, 1978), 126.

Chapter Eight

Where Do We Go From Here? An Agenda for Consciousness Three

SUMMARY

What issues need to be discussed in this emerging trialogue? Three at least are important.

First, how should we understand the nature of paradigm formation and its relation to worldview? How will this discussion help us in the area of missions and its contemporary dependence on applied anthropology? In what ways can it help theology as that discipline seeks to listen more carefully to the contributions of the churches in Africa, Asia, and Latin America? How should we evaluate the work of Thomas Kuhn and his description of paradigm and model?

Second, myth and symbolism need our attention. Theologians and anthropologists have had a long-standing interest in these areas, but very little bridge-building between the two disciplines has taken place. But even less constructive work in this area has taken place in missiology. The work of Claude Lévi-Strauss and the structuralist school of anthropology may have great usefulness in linking the three disciplines. Mythology flows from the deepest levels of human cultures. Can its study help missions avoid culture change on a more surface level?

Finally, there is the recurring question of relativism. Theologians and missionaries of the evangelical camp have some of their deepest concerns here. But in current discussions, agendas are being addressed to theology by Christian anthropologists like Charles Kraft. What questions should theology address, in turn, to Christian anthropologists? Especially since theologians perceive the theories of anthropologists as constituting the greater open door to syncretism? What hope is there in all of this to achieve a "multiperspectivalism" that will achieve a symphonic balance of models offered by the diverse disciplines?

Chapter Eight

Where Do We Go from Here? An Agenda for Consciousness Three

Many of the signs we have pointed to in this book indicate that we are at a crossroads, at a point where it appears that things might come apart. And that is always a hopeful sign. Donald McGavran keeps whispering in our ear at this time, "There is growth for the church at the point of dislocation." Charles Kraft's work stands as a bridge between three worlds—theology, anthropology, and missions. Even theologian-types are studying contextualization.

What next? My agenda for the coming trialogue includes at least three items. And, like all agendas, it does not supply answers. I only provide my list of questions.

PARADIGM AND WORLDVIEW

Paul Hiebert defines the current revolution in the love/hate relationship between missions and anthropology as a "paradigm shift in epistemology."[1] I concur. But, some readers may ask, what about "the battle for the Bible"? Isn't that crucial? In one sense, it is. But, at the same time, it is not the only crucial issue. Cornelius Van Til, my mentor in many of these things, has pointed out repeatedly that our presuppositions, if left unexamined, more often affect the way we theologize than even a tight view of the Scriptures. A Christian anthropologist, operating from a functionalist paradigm, can do things with even an inerrant Bible that are frightening to me. The issue is not simply "the authority of Scriptures." It is also "the behavioral sciences under the authority of paradigm models." And it is also "the Scriptures under the authority of paradigm models."

I see the need for paradigm discussion in missions. Until now, anthropology's greatest impact on missions has come through the gate of applied anthropology. There is a danger here that we cannot minimize. The virtue of applied anthropology was that it directed anthropology into the practical arena of contemporary human life. But that is also the danger, particularly when it becomes applied missionary anthropology. "The tyranny of the new" can isolate our study from the frameworks or paradigms out of which our models inevitably derive their meanings. We become enamored, for example, with Ruth Benedict's "patterns of culture" in our missionary setting. But the urgency of "application" and our ignorance of the computer-type structure in which Benedict links systems to the biopsychological create quick answers but blur the line between our conclusions and her paradigm framework. I sense this danger deeply as I read the case studies flowing from the "church growth movement." They are not generally conscious of the diversity of models. And this danger becomes more real as theological seminaries, colleges, and Bible institutes increase their curricular attention to questions of applied missionary anthropology. And, in the meantime, our Christian educational institutions reduce and dismantle their anthropology

[1]Paul Hiebert, "Missions and Anthropology: A Love/Hate Relationship," *Missiology* 6 (April 1978): 171.

departments. As theoreticians we can develop models for church growth based on linguistic analogies. But the practitioner is ignorant of the problems in the analogue that call for at least caution in the ways in which the original paradigm is used. Can scholars like Anthony Thiselton help us here?[2]

I see the need for paradigm discussion in theology also. It is important if theology is to open itself to the contributions of Africa and Asia and Latin America. North American theology's inability to deal with questions raised by black theology is not simply or even largely due to the fact that we have neglected issues on the black agenda. That is surely an important admission. Our theology is color-coded to the white and the affluent. But why is this so? Is it enough to say, as one reviewer has done recently in commenting on a documentary history of black theology, that "the world-and-life view resources of an authentic Reformed theology enable one to address the issues raised by these new theologies more biblically"? Is it enough to admit "that much that has been only implicit in such Reformed theology will have to be made very explicit"?[3] Why has it not become explicit after nearly a hundred years or more?

Is part of the answer the pseudo-universalist theoretical paradigm that theology has operated with in the West? Can Thomas Kuhn at least help us in asking new questions? By paradigm he meant something like a constellation of group commitments. A paradigm constitutes a scientist's conceptual world, he argued. It is composed of such things as shared symbolic generalizations, beliefs, and values. It is an ordering belief framework that shapes how a scientist decides what are important

[2]Note his interesting comments on Nida's transformational models in "Semantics and New Testament Interpretation," in *New Testament Interpretation: Essays on Principles and Methods,* ed. I. Howard Marshall (Grand Rapids: Eerdmans, 1977), 97–98.

[3]Fred H. Klooster, "Is Theology Color Blind?" *Reformed Journal* 30 (September 1980): 31. For another approach to the same question, see my review in the *Journal of the Evangelical Theological Society* 25 (June 1982): 238–40.

questions, what things are, and what results signify. Such belief frameworks are not consciously or deliberately developed by the scientists; rather, they are tacitly imposed upon those entering the science. We drew attention to this in noting anthropology's hostility to the missionary, based on the anthropologist's academic methodological preconditioning.

Those who operate in terms of the paradigm, Kuhn continues, perceive their science as rational, self-evident, and universally true. The paradigm, in other words, is inarticulate and metatheoretical.

As the science develops, new information and experimental results are fitted into and interpreted within the prevailing paradigm. Facts that do not fit, or are difficult to fit, are not "seen." Eventually the "puzzle facts" build up to such a pitch that the scientist looks for a new paradigm. He or she undergoes what Kuhn calls a "scientific revolution."

The impact of Kuhn's work in our area should already be apparent. Kraft makes wide use of Kuhn's vision of paradigms and models as "mirrored reality."[4] So, for that matter, have we. But, even in recognizing the value of Kuhn's work, should we not be careful also? Though Kuhn speaks of the paradigm as metatheoretical, he also plays heavily on its conceptual character, its role as a "mental map." Does that do full justice to the metatheoretical character of the paradigm? Is it in danger of compartmentalizing the "religious" character of paradigm to only one felt need among many? Without the faith dimension as central to paradigm, will we inadvertently once more push God to the edge of our "mental maps"?

Wary of this danger, some helpful modifications of the paradigm idea have been suggested by a study group at the Institute for Christian Studies in Toronto. A paradigm, the group suggests, is distinct from a worldview in that it is restricted to a particular field of science, to theology, let us say. Worldview then

---

[4]Charles H. Kraft, *Christianity in Culture* (Maryknoll: Orbis, 1979), 23–33.

becomes the comprehensive belief-framework that colors all of a person's activities. It is a communal direction of the heart, a framework of belief-commitments commonly held by a community of like mind. It includes a person's act of believing, the heart's integrator for all other acts and functions. It includes also the set of beliefs and values flowing from that act of believing.[5]

Out of this worldview structured by the heart flows the paradigm. It is a tool for analysis and therefore conceptual in character. But it also reflects the belief-commitment of the worldview at its source. Its origins in the worldview compel it to the task of integration, of correlation. But that compelling drive is not objectively theoretical in some phenomenological sense. It is never far from what Dooyeweerd might call the pretheoretical commitment of faith. The Sawi worldview of Irian Jaya creates "peace child" paradigms to prevent cultural genocide. The Korean traditional paradigm reinforces the Tan'gun mythology of origins from their worldview to preserve national identity.

This corrected view of paradigm should caution us against a too easy borrowing of anthropological models, constructed with out-of-kilter paradigms. We propose no easy answer, and certainly not a perfect one. Paradigms, by their very limited nature, never are either. They are promoters of patience and humility in the task of any science. That in itself may be their best gift to theology's self-understanding.

Has the prevailing evangelical paradigm of theology and missions been too much a bounded set rather than a centered set? Do Paul Hiebert's warnings about the way we use bounded sets to view conversion have even wider applications?[6] The bounded-set mentality, says Hiebert, creates categories by listing "essential" characteristics. The category is defined by a clear boundary;

[5]Paul Marshall et. al., *The Relation of Paradigm and Worldview, and the Implications of Paradigms for the Social Sciences and Professions* (Toronto: Institute for Christian Studies, 1980), 4.

[6]Paul Hiebert, "Conversion, Culture and Cognitive Categories," *Gospel in Context* 1 (October 1978): 26–28.

objects within the set are standardized by a uniform list of essential characteristics. The bounded set mentality is a static set. There can be no change in its categorical status.

What does this say about the way we do theology? Are our processes of creating theological paradigms too essentialized to deal with the concept of doing theology as praxis? Are our boundaries too rigid to admit missiological newcomers like sociology? Is a bounded-set approach too static to look at the agenda of black theology and raise questions about our models?

Is the solution here to recognize that a paradigm approach functions best when it is a centered-set approach? A centered set

> is created by defining a center, and the relationship of things to that center. Some things may be too far from the center, but they are moving towards the center, therefore, they are part of the centered set. On the other hand, some objects may be near the center, but are moving away from it, so they are not part of the set.[7]

I ask the next question with gentleness and appreciation. Is it possible that we, in our strategies for church growth, operate from a bounded-set paradigm, even while advocating a centered-set paradigm? Does this question lie behind the vocal minority protest in 1980 at the Pattaya Consultation on World Evangelization, when objections were raised to the technical definition of "peoples" and to the "homogeneous unit principle"? The frustration may not have been simply that many did not do their homework. Nor may it have been simply the communications gap between practitioners and strategists. Could it have been also a concern that the "people movement" strategy can become a temptation to establish a new bounded set? Could it have been also a strident request to look at our paradigms again to make sure that there are sufficient safeguards built into them to keep what should be "open" from becoming "closed"?

---

[7]Ibid., 28. Compare also Paul Hiebert, "Sets and Structures: A Study of Church Patterns," in *New Horizons in World Mission,* ed. David J. Hesselgrave (Grand Rapids: Baker, 1979), 223–27.

MYTH AND SYMBOLISM

I also ask for an agenda that includes a large place for the topic of myth and symbolism. Through interaction with Bultmann, Gunkel, and others, these topics have been at least an indirect part of evangelical theology's agenda for some time now. But there are very few bridges in this area of interest between anthropology and theology.[8] And myth and symbolism have become a dominant part of anthropological studies in the last thirty years.

Much of the current emphasis has come from the impact of structuralism and especially from Claude Lévi-Strauss (b. 1909). Following leads of de Saussure and Freud, structural anthropologists have seen human societies as data banks, providing their participants with a ready-made structure in terms of which they must live. These ready-made structures or "models" organize society's experiences, conscious and unconscious, into cultures. Through analysis of a society's symbols or signs, intrinsic to that culture, we seek to understand culture's systems.

With exceptions like Clifford Geertz,[9] the structuralists seem to have little interest in religion as such. But they do pay a great deal of attention to myth and the methodology of symbolism. Lévi-Strauss accepts the notion that the human mind works most characteristically on a subconscious level. The goal of the anthropologist, he contends, is "to grasp, beyond the conscious and always shifting images which men hold, the complete range of unconscious possibilities."[10] The anthropologist may begin by investigating the conscious mind of humanity and the oral and

[8]A very helpful exception is William A. Dyrness, "Symbolism, Modeling and Theology," *The Living and Active Word of God; Studies in Honor of Samuel J. Schultz,* ed. Morris Inch and Ronald Youngblood (Winona Lake, Ind.: Eisenbrauns, 1983), 283–99.

[9]Clifford Geertz, "Religion as a Cultural System," *Reader in Comparative Religion,* ed. W. A. Lessa and E. Z. Vogt (New York: Harper Row, 1972), 167–78.

[10]Claude Lévi-Strauss, *Structural Anthropology* (New York: Basic Books, 1963), 23.

written myths of that mind. But one must gradually move deeper into the unconscious. In doing so, one passes from the particular into the universal. And in the process one will find that the unconscious activity of the mind imposes form upon content.[11]

In this search, the anthropologist seeks to grasp the unconscious structure underlying each institution and each custom, each myth formed. This is done in order to obtain a principle of interpretation valid for other institutions and customs. The study of religion becomes a structural quest for the hermeneutic of the unconscious. And that hermeneutic is displayed in the fundamental characteristic of the human mind, its symbol-forming activity. Through the symbolic, the social and the cultural refer to the unconscious.

Lévi-Strauss's search for the nature of the unconscious mind led him almost inevitably to the study of myth. Of all activities of the human mind, myth making is least ruled by functional necessities and nearest to the unconscious. "Mythology has no obvious practical function." Myths have an internal logic of their own. But they are not "about" the real world. They are symbolic formulae for resolving the value conflicts and the resulting moral quandaries that arise from the structural contradictions in human societies. Thus the typical structure juxtaposes three sets of symbolic elements: those that define a value, desirable object, or course of action; those that define its antithesis; and a third, mediating set that seeks to resolve the conflict between the first two.[12]

For several reasons, we have not dealt with Lévi-Strauss's structuralism earlier in this volume. It is not yet really a part of the trialogue we are describing. The impact of structuralism on theology, and particularly exegesis, is growing in intensity, to be

[11]Claude Lévi-Strauss, *The Raw and the Cooked: Introduction to a Science of Mythology* (New York: Harper & Row, 1969) 1:10.

[12]For his classic treatment of the Oedipus myth as an explication of these elements, consult Claude Lévi-Strauss, "The Structural Study of Myth," *Journal of American Folklore* 67(1955): 428–44.

sure. But it is not doing so in the areas of myth and symbolism we have designated.[13]

In the second place, it remains a storm center of controversy in the discipline of anthropology. To positivist-minded anthropologists, Lévi-Strauss's attention to the unconscious is unverifiable and therefore seems to have no relevance to the empirical world.[14] Others feel that his analysis reflects "fundamental conceptual problems that his position carries to extreme forms, and which have been shared and spread by many of his nominal critics as well as by his defenders."[15] Murray J. Leaf cites four of these problems—a remarkably inconsistent terminological usage, even in the most important of his arguments; his implicit evolutionism; his views of lineage and kinship, in which he is felt to take the characteristics of a part for the characteristic of the whole; and his treatment of conscious native conceptions. To the British neo-structuralists (functionalist school), his concern with establishing facts about "the human mind" are in sharp contrast to their concern with the organization of any particular society or class of societies.

None of this is meant to diminish Lévi-Strauss's impact on the discipline. Reaction to his views, says Adam Kuper, comes closest to that of a "paradigm revolution." "The method," he feels, "is being adapted: but it is more than a method, for Lévi-Strauss has also directed (or redirected) attention to a particular range of problems. This has resulted in a fresh interest among some British social anthropologists in the ways in which people use verbal

[13]For an excellent summary of the impact of structuralism on exegesis, consult Vern S. Poythress, "Structuralism and Biblical Studies," *Journal of the Evangelical Theological Society* 21 (September 1978): 221–37. Compare also Vern S. Poythress, "Philosophical Roots of Phenomenological and Structuralist Literary Criticism," *Westminster Theological Journal* 41 (Fall 1978): 165–71; Daniel Patte, *What is Structural Exegesis?* (Philadelphia: Fortress, 1976).

[14]Annemarie De Waal Malefijt, *Images of Man* (New York: Knopf, 1974), 330–31.

[15]Murray J. Leaf, *Man, Mind and Science. A History of Anthropology* (New York: Columbia University Press, 1979), 257–59.

categories to order their worlds; and the ways in which systems of exchange order social relationships."[16]

It is particularly in the third partner of the trialogue where structuralism seems most silent. It is almost totally absent in applied missionary anthropology of the last twenty years. Leaders in this field have apparently been trained under earlier paradigms. And very few evangelicals would seem to be concentrating their attention on Lévi-Strauss or the needy area we are drawing attention to now.[17] A footnote by Paul Hiebert speaks of Lévi-Strauss and his work on myth as raising "important questions regarding the nature of the human mind and its knowledge."[18] But Hiebert's brief conclusion may be typical of others surveying the situation. Structuralism, he says, "seems on the surface of it to be less useful for missions."[19] Whether that judgment would now be modified by Hiebert I cannot say.

I would suggest that this sort of judgment needs rethinking. Eugene Nida provides us with a model that may help us in attempting a modification of the structuralist themes. Using the concept of transformational generative grammar, Nida sees three kernels of structure in every cultural development—the surface level, the kernel, and the "deep structure" level. At the deep level we face what he calls the "fundamental universal features of religion and their primary characteristics."[20]

---

[16]Adam Kuper, *Anthropologists and Anthropology* (New York: Pica, 1973), 226.

[17]A notable exception, and perhaps a sign of future interest, would seem to be the Ph.D. dissertation of Krikor Haleblian, written for Fuller Theological Seminary in 1982, "Contextualization and French Structuralism: A Method to Delineate the Deep Structure of the Gospel." Unfortunately I had not been able to obtain this dissertation at the time of this writing and can only mention its availability.

[18]Paul Hiebert, "Introduction: Mission and Anthropology," *Readings in Missionary Anthropology II,* ed. William A. Smalley (Pasadena: William Carey Library, 1978), xxiv.

[19]Ibid., xx.

[20]Eugene A. Nida, "New Religions for Old. A Study of Culture Change in Religion," *Church and Culture Change in Africa,* ed. David J. Bosch (Pretoria: N.G. Kerkboekhandel, 1971), 26.

I am aware of the problems in applying such categories as "deep structure" in some metaphorical extension beyond its technical use in linguistics. The metaphor has so much "play" that it can become useless. Further, within linguistics itself the concept of deep structure has its difficulties. The major problem, it would seem, is in the inaccessibility of deep structure to direct observation. Postulates about deep structure cannot prove themselves directly.[21]

At the same time, Nida's point converges with an important one made by the structural anthropologists. It is, in fact, a fundamental axiom of the school. That is to say, the basic structures are to be found "below" the surface of empirical observation. Admitting the strong possibility of arbitrariness that might "read in" the deep structures before "reading them out," admitting that the structuralist search for universals can ultimately become a sort of metaphysics, there are still advantages to our use of the model. It offers the potential for uncovering a greater fullness and depth to the concept of meaning than simply surface or kernel levels.

That is of great value for missions, says Nida. In legalistic religious systems, the focus of attention is always on the surface structures, not the deep structures. People are primarily interested in the forms of religious expression rather than in the "deep structure" significance of such activity. Further, the phenomenon of "loss of faith" can occur with over-attachment to the surface structures. The deep structure is not internalized by the fledgling believer. A gap appears between the surface symbol and its deep structure meaning.

What does all this have to do with my proposal for a new look at symbolism and myth? Missionary anthropology till now has largely concerned itself with cultural practices functioning on the surface and kernel levels of structure. The older "indigenization"

---

[21]Note the strictures on the "deep structure" concept in Vern S. Poythress, "Structural Approaches to Understanding the Theology of the Apostle Paul." (Ph.D. diss., University of Stellenbosch, 1981), 14–18.

discussions are typical of this, with their concerns over indigenous patterns for worship, national leadership, ecclesiastical structure. Often what goes under the more recent rubric of contexualization still clings basically to these old concerns. The only aspect of symbolism in culture that we deal with even in a preliminary way is usually symbolism on the surface level or kernel level.

The danger in all this, if Nida is correct, is externalism, "people movements" that resist the discipling process through their encouraged attachment to the surface level of structures. Externalism asks questions like "How will this movement worship?" "How will prayer be encouraged?" "How will we teach biblical principles on suffering in an animistic culture?" Evangelicalism's questions have not always touched the deep level of structures.

The end of all this can be the collapse of "people movements" and the rise of revitalization movements. Are the African Independent Churches samples of this process? What of the Unification Church of Elder Moon? The gospel has not been internalized on the deep level of culture's structure.

I see one of the values of the study of myth and symbolism exactly here. Myth functions on that deepest level of culture's structure; it is the closest to the heart, the center of change. Yet we do not seem to give it nearly the attention that its culture-forming place would seem to demand. How will we deal with the truth found by Freud that meaning is not always synonymous with consciousness of meaning?

Can structuralism's emphasis on the role of nontheoretical factors in the creation of our "worlds" help us also correlate Kuhn's idea of the paradigm/model with a better understanding of the relationship between myth and reality? Philip Wheelwright has said that "myth . . . is not in the first instance a fiction imposed on one's already given world, but it is a way of apprehending that world. Genuine myth is a matter of perspective first, invention second."[22] Commenting on this statement, William Dyrness adds,

> Theologians also have spoken of fundamental pretheoretical orientations, called variously faith commitments or presuppositions. Perhaps, we will argue, a dialogue at this point with the social sciences may enlarge our understanding of how such positions are formed and how they function in the doing of theology.[23]

Will we find that one of the greatest values of the work of Lévi-Strauss may be at this point? Can a fruitful modification of his insights into mythology and symbolism turn our attention seriously to the most important of structural levels for change? How must those modifications be made? How can they serve us in the evangelization of peoples?

Very recently some preliminary evangelical work has begun to appear in this very area of mythology and symbolism. Don Richardson's gripping study of peace-child mythology from the Sawi culture has initiated discussion in a concrete way as to how myths can be used to present the gospel. Richardson has begun to expand his earlier concept of "redemptive analogies" in his search among world cultures for leftovers of divine revelation. He finds them in the Inca ruler Pachacuti who rejected the capricious, popular god Inti for the little-known, omniscient god Viracocha. Among the African Mbaka and the Burmese Karen are myths which parallel biblical teaching about God, the fall, God's son bringing salvation. What the Calvinist has traditionally called "common grace" Richardson calls "the Melchizedek factor," a general knowledge of God trickling down from an earlier revelation, ready to complement the "Abraham factor," a specific verbal message from God.[24]

---

[22]Philip Wheelwright, *The Burning Fountain: A Study in the Language of Symbolism* (Bloomington: University of Indiana Press, 1954), 150.

[23]Dyrness, "Symbolism, Modeling and Theology," 291.

[24]Don Richardson, *Eternity in Their Hearts* (Ventura, Ca.: Regal, 1981), 14–28, 124–31.

There is much of value here. Richardson has given traditional theological categories like general revelation and common grace missiological contemporaneity and practical life. He has shown us what a study of world mythologies may uncover for missionary use.

Unfortunately, in the process, he has made other choices that to us are not wise. In an extremely flippant style, more sermonic than needed in a book of this sort, he repeatedly sees anthropology as the enemy of missions, "the pursuit of the exotic by the eccentric."[25] He ignores anthropology's own history of development and self-criticism in an extended critique of naive cultural evolutionism. And he opts strongly for Wilhelm Schmidt's diffusionist paradigm, with its strong support of a nearly universal concept of a high god in human cultures. In doing so he weds the evangelical to a long discarded anthropological model, rejected for good reasons. Miriam Adeney's excellent review of Richardson's book comments on this point:

> One is uneasy with Richardson's wedding of our faith to one theoretical perspective, namely diffusionism. Although there are many nearly universal phenomena in folk religion, such as beliefs in witchcraft, magic, mana, taboos and divining, most anthropologists find diffusionist explanations for these untenable. More emphasis is given to the psychological unity of persons as they encounter the same physical universe and common human problems. Surely God can "set eternity in [human] hearts"—program revelation about himself—through uniformities in the human mind, human situations and nature, as well as through diffusion of a sky god narrative.[26]

Unless deeper and more careful research than this now begins, we may well fail in several areas. Our lack of sophistication in the history of cultural anthropology will drive us to models that have surface attractions to the evangelical but mesmerize us into missing

[25]Ibid., 40.

[26]Miriam Adeney, "Review of 'Eternity in Their Hearts'," *Missiology* 10 (January 1982): 123–27.

their empirical defects. Further, our Western pragmatism, undisciplined by anthropological insight, can make common cause with functionalist leftovers that may also be lurking in our missionary anthropology paradigms. And we will create one more "spiritual laws booklet" that will allow us to substitute in any culture the right "redemptive analogy" for the appropriate blank page in our books from which we have previously extracted the national myth. In doing so, we will be in danger of abstracting the existing "redemptive analogy" from its deep level structure and use it as a strategical ploy on the surface level of function. We need help in resisting the possibility of that temptation. That must come with a richer and more careful study of the meaning of myth and symbolism in human cultures.

RELATIVISM

Cultural anthropology is deeply aware of the affective reality of relativism. And it understands that relativism primarily in terms of accepting "the validity of [a given] culture (or individual), whether or not one's own set of values predisposes one to *approve* of the behavior of that culture (or individual). A belief in the validity of other cultures does not obligate one to approve of such customs as cannibalism, widow burning, infanticide, premarital sex, polygamy and the like. But it does insist that *one take such customs seriously within the cultural context in which they occur* and attempt to appreciate the importance of their function within that context."[27] To speak, then, of a cultural value or practice as "relative" is to understand that each item derives its culturally adequate meaning from something else, the larger frame, to which it is related and in which it appears to fit.[28]

Theologians and missionaries of the evangelical school have some of their deepest concerns precisely at this point. They suspect

[27]Kraft, *Christianity in Culture*, 50.

[28]Bruce J. Malina, *The New Testament World. Insights From Cultural Anthropology* (Atlanta: John Knox, 1981), 13.

that more is at stake than simply a recognition of multi-cultural validity. And too often they are quite right. They cannot ignore the naturalism and humanistic worldview that anthropologists too often affirm. Lurking behind the legitimacy of "cultural validity" they also see that worldview's suspicions about ultimate truth. They "have felt it important that their theologies be firmly based upon and give strong witness to theological absolutes. Evangelical theologians have, therefore, tended to regard divinely endorsed absolutes as the proper major focus of their study. Anthropologists, in reaction, have made the culturally relative aspects of human existence their focus."[29]

I see relativism as a continuing agenda item for the future. Debate, in one sense, has already begun. The major work of Charles Kraft, to which we have continuously referred in this book, has returned to this area over and over again. The bulk of his attention is devoted to opening up insights for the evangelical into missiological and theological topics provided by such disciplines as anthropology, linguistics, and communications. Hopefully the reader will by now be aware of just how rich the author of this work considers these insights to be.

Unfortunately, however, discussion at this stage is very one-way. Christian anthropologists like Kraft, with full backgrounds in theology, are a rarity. And when discussion is heard, it is largely monologue: anthropologists speaking to theologians and missionaries. Theologians in the West, coming to the arena with educational backgrounds largely drawn from the area of liberal arts, find themselves ill-equipped to respond to anthropological or linguistic insights. No one has yet appeared with the qualifications to write essays asking questions like, "Can theological insights assist anthropological studies?" Anthropological questions for the theological learner, even coming from the Christian, sound so new that they are perceived as threatening to the faith "once for all delivered." The place given to caution and humility about

[29]Charles Kraft, "Can Anthropological Insight Assist Evangelical Theology?" *Christian Scholar's Review* 7 (1977): 171–72.

theory/models, developed as a functional methodology by cultural anthropology, is minimized by the evangelical in theology and missions.

The need for theological input is acute, not simply for its own sake, but for the sake of missionary anthropology. As an anthropological outsider and recognizing the need for self-criticism on the part of theologians (even better, missiologists with theological hobbies), I venture to offer several areas where discussions of relativism by evangelical anthropologists need study. I seek to parallel, in doing so, the valuable suggestions of Kraft aimed at the theologians.[30]

1. I ask for a fuller discussion of the models with which anthropologists have worked and out of which they have developed their view of human cultures. If Christian theology seems to be unaware of its culture-boundness within Western culture, Christian anthropology has often suffered a similar lack of awareness of its data-boundness within an academic paradigm. We have drawn some of the effects of those paradigms in earlier chapters, the twisting effect they have had on understandings of the Bible and human cultures. It is quite true, as Kraft has indicated, that our Western values have led us to expect both a single right answer to every question and the superiority of answers developed by Western academicians to the answers developed by the members of any other culture (or by nonacademicians within our own culture).

This is abundantly evident in the theological realm, and our cautious, at-arm's-length approach to Third World theologizing, or to black theology closer to home. Is there not a similar danger for the Christian anthropologists who are often equally ill-prepared to accept the possibility that there might be more than one valid approach to our understanding of many issues, depending on one's paradigm perspective? I am aware of those in the discipline of cultural anthropology who call for the use of many paradigms. I

[30]Ibid., 173–79.

am not aware that these suggestions are being communicated effectively to the missionaries who seem generally to be ignorant of the limitations of the paradigms being used by their anthropology teachers. Kraft and Hiebert wisely warn us that evangelical theologians in their attitude toward innovation and change stand on a continuum that ranges from "open" to "closed" with respect to innovation and diversity.[31] Attitudes toward relativism are different depending on where the theologian stands on that axis. Must we not also warn against the possibility of there being "closed" and "open" evangelical anthropologists? Of scholarship so closed-minded to other anthropological and theological paradigms that the dynamic of alternatives is not functionally real?

2. I repeat the wise warning of Kraft against our theological over-attachment to those parts of the Scripture that are couched in thought-forms culturally closest to Western culture. Different portions of Scripture do speak more effectively to people of different cultures. But again, this may be a two-edged sword. May it not be possible that our anthropological insights also show a similar over-attachment, a limitation in method, that ends up picking and choosing among biblical themes those convenient to our paradigm? Ramseyer, whom we quoted earlier, accuses Kraft of minimizing the redemptive-historical significance of the shift from Old Testament to New Testament in favor of his own agenda. We have cautioned similarly against the way in which his methodology can crowd into a theoretical corner clear biblical perspectives embodied in the nature of revelation, and traditional theological understandings of "illumination." The effect of this can be to enforce evangelical fears about relativism, rather than to minimize them.

3. Traditional theology has been so thoroughly academic that it has branded itself as an elitist activity, done by specialists. The Bible, under such a perspective, has been seen more as a textbook than a down-to-earth guidebook for Christian lifestyle in the

[31]Charles Kraft, *Christianity in Culture,* 39–41.

world's cultures. What can be done to reduce that image and liberate theology to function on the streets of Philadelphia or Tokyo?

But similarly, does anthropology escape the charges any more easily because of its fieldwork and its orientation to human societies? The discipline continues to debate the role of the anthropologist in directed social and cultural change. In cultures of abject poverty and oppression, where does the academician stop and the humanitarian take over? Admittedly, that sort of question is easier for the evangelical, making use of anthropology in such a setting, to answer. But the danger remains as real for anthropology as for theology. What concrete fruits can we now see produced by the missionary better equipped with at least a preliminary understanding of anthropology? The missionary commitment of the theologian frequently is what keeps him or her rooted in the reality of people with needs that must be met. Is this same commitment also what keeps the budding missionary anthropologist from floating out of cultures in some sort of pre-advent secret rapture? The lack of fit between the concerns of seminaries and the needs of cultures and their peoples is not only characteristic of theology—it can also infect the missionary anthropologist. Strategy planning for church growth can hinder both theologian and anthropologist from participation in evangelism. The drawing board looks better than the street.

4. Theology's past attachment to traditional metaphysical philosophy has produced much of value. It has also reinforced a static conceptualization of reality, where we ask, "How do I think about truth?" not "How do I live truth?" It is a limitation we have commented on frequently in this book. Relativism, out of this background, becomes largely a propositional danger, a fear over the loss of packaged conceptions.

Is the same danger not equally apparent for anthropology? Its ninteenth-century agenda for study was created by the Enlightenment set of questions that arose in the eighteenth century. It has moved a long way from that agenda. But many of the original questions still remain. What is the role of the cognitive and the rational in the creation of cultural worldviews? in myth making? in the ethnopsychology of cultures? What metatheoretical precommitments affect the secular anthropological models? Is the cognitive the only or even the largest of barriers to revolutions in "paradigm change"?

We have seen also the static nature of the functionalist model and its contribution to the shaping of Consciousness Two. We have expressed our concerns that that static picture of cultures has left its impact in missionary anthropology. Have we really come any closer to asking, through these models, "How can I live truth?" Or have we simply substituted a word and now ask, "How do I think about cultures?" Is it possible that some new understanding of the nature of doing theology can help both cripples to walk? Can a dynamic concept of "covenant living" challenge the static heritage of both theology and anthropology?

5. Kraft warns against the shadows of theology's dark past: the virtual exclusion of interest in human beings and a tendency to major in God and His ideals. It is a criticism he levels in other places more particularly at the Reformed perspective. He sees it as "too constraining to deal adequately with the very important human side of missionary involvement."[32] Out of this has come, he continues, an evangelical way of thinking that has tended to be more God-centered than interaction-centered. People and their part in the interaction are often slighted.

There is force to Kraft's argument that needs acknowledgment. Are we as evangelicals afraid that if we regard people highly we will only be able to do so by lowering our concept of God? Do we minimize the range of acceptable variation allowed by God in humanity's response to the Creator? Can anthropology help us in achieving a better balance?

---

[32]Charles Kraft, "Review of 'A World to Win'," *Christian Scholar's Review* 7 (1977): 226. His criticism of J. H. Bavinck's idea of *possessio* may flow out of this same concern for an overemphasis on divine intrusion. Cf. Kraft, *Christianity in Culture,* 345–46.

At the same time, what will keep anthropology from the reverse side of the imbalance? Has not anthropology's dark side been a virtual exclusion of interest in God and a tendency to major in people? It has certainly been that in the Arminian theological tradition. What of an anthropology formed in alliance with that tradition? Will it maximize the range of acceptable variation allowed by God in His dealings with humanity? And which "imbalance" will drive us closer to relativism? A God-centered perspective or one that is more oriented to people?

Are there any indications on the horizon that we may find some paradigm shifts that will help us in our doing theology? Help us in the emerging trialogue of the future? Help in avoiding the curse of relativism and find its blessing? Some hints are beginning to appear in what Dr. Vern S. Poythress, following (as yet) unpublished leads from John Frame, calls "multiperspectivalism."

Borrowing from his study of linguistics and modifications of structuralism, Poythress has recently looked at the efforts to find the "core" of Pauline theology. Is there, he asks, a single objectively "best" way to understand Paul's theology? He answers that there are many ways of conceiving of the "structure" of that theology. There are indeed some erroneous ways. But there is more than one "right" way as well. A countless number of approaches may reveal fruitful patterns for helping us in that quest for understanding.

Using the concept of "holiness," he seeks to demonstrate that it can be used as a "governing" motif to unlock the total scope of Paul's theology. To quote him:

> Themes within Paul's theology can be likened to mountain tops within the territory. The traditional way of doing biblical theology is to seek for the one "highest" mountain, the one most important theme. Only from this one highest mountain can the whole territory be surveyed. My approach still acknowledges that some mountains are higher than others: some themes are more important than others. But it also says that the whole territory can be surveyed from *any* of the mountain tops.

> Paul's epistles unveil multidimensional "territory", so that any theme can be used as a starting point.[33]

Poythress is not out to defend "holiness" as the macrostructure of Paul's theology. He only seeks to show that the ability of a motif, a perspective, to unlock the whole does not belong only to one supposed "governing" perspective, or "angle."

This does not mean, however, that all approaches to Paul are "equal." Nor does it mean that there is no possible distinction between an erroneous and a correct interpretation of Paul. Poythress is not advocating a pluralism that always hesitates at the words, "heresy," or "mistake." The existence of stable language patterns in the Pauline writings, the regular connections that they bear to one another, and the relative prominence of the use of each pattern, all provide controls on interpretation and the hermeneutical process. Two approaches from different starting points or different centers will, if both are correct, prove to be complementary rather than contradictory to one another.

What does all of this mean for hermeneutic? It seeks to explain biblical phenomena in terms of a system of relations. That principle can be used in a reductionist way, as Poythress points out elsewhere.[34] Structural relations even within the text are relative to the genre, the language, the style, and the circumstances of the author. And there is therefore a danger that the increasing perception of these multiple relations may lead to relativizing the Bible. The Bible then yields to a latent historicism.

But this perception potentially yields great benefits as well. There is potential here to correct an insensitivity on the part of Biblical scholars toward the complex textures of language and literature. The emphasis on relations between different parts of the biblical text can help us better appreciate the unity and coherence of more than one book.

Beyond this area, there are the questions it raises for the doing

---

[33]Poythress, "Structural Approaches to Understanding," 201-2.

[34]Poythress, "Structuralism and Biblical Studies," 231–35.

of theology. Theologizing becomes symphonic (an image used by Lévi-Strauss), each of the parts contributing to the whole, the whole becoming in the process of harmonization more than simply the sum of the parts. Multiperspectivalism as a theological methodology becomes a style of life, a hermeneutic, a way of thinking in which one takes a limited number of starting perspectives and uses them to see the whole. Poythress has begun to explore these very implications.

Often, one pattern of studying the Scripture can block out other possible patterns. As a result, our cultural worldviews, our paradigms both help us and hinder us. But in this symphonic theology the contributions of the non-Western world easily fit. Theologizing becomes like studying a diamond. Using more than one perspective, looking at more than one facet of the diamond, helps us see the whole all the better. What is missed by one, another may see. What is seen incorrectly by one, another may correct.

Does heresy become unrecognizable in this symphony of perspectives? Will one person's "heresy" become another person's "perspective"? Will we find with Kraft that "it is likely that most of the 'heresies' can validly be classed as cultural adaptations rather than as theological aberrations"?[35]

I think not. Each perspective, to be sure, has a distinct focus of interest. But each perspective, Poythress reminds us, is in the end dependent on the others. It is intelligible only in the context of the others. This insight parallels one of the criteria suggested by Peter Toon for deciding whether any given doctrine is a valid development within the paradigm tradition. Says Toon, "a doctrine based on one of these major interpretations [Lucan, Pauline, and so forth] is acceptable as long as it is presented in such a way so as not to deny but rather to complement the teaching of other major interpretations."[36]

---

[35]Kraft, *Christianity in Culture,* 296.

[36]Peter Toon, *The Development of Doctrine in the Church* (Grand Rapids: Eerdmans, 1979), 117.

Further, each perspective is in principle harmonizable with the others. Any one perspective, when expanded far enough, is found to involve the others and, in fact to encompass the others. Each can be viewed as an aspect of the others. Again, this parallels another criteria of Toon: "The new doctrine must positively cohere with (that is, be entailed by, not merely consistent with) what is already believed at other points."

Because of the tendency to human oversight or one-sided emphasis, each perspective is useful in helping us to notice facts and relationships that tend to be further in the background in the other perspectives. Or to borrow Toon's language again, "A developed doctrine should clarify the unity of God's revealed will, as it is portrayed in one of the 'theologies of the Bible' or as it is portrayed in the total Bible."[37]

For the missionary this can be a liberating exercise. Theologizing becomes more of a dynamic process rather than one virtually completed in the West. More than simple indoctrination, it is transformed into a dynamic discovery engaged in by human beings in all human cultures. It is hemmed in and bombarded from three perspectives (to use the formulae of John Frame)—the normative perspective of the Bible, the situational perspective of cultural, social time and place, and the existential perspective of our humanity as images of God. It does not fear relativism. The normative perspective is always there to provide balance. Rather, it embraces relativism in a creative sense. For interacting with the normative and balancing it are the situational and the existential angles to be considered and savored.

What will such an approach do to our traditional Western theology? To our traditional conflicts? The Lord may still have a few surprises for us. But for that, we wait for the end of His book. Mine is finished. I only intended to set the agenda, not to solve it.

[37]Ibid., 119.

Bibliography

Adeney, Miriam. "Review of 'Eternity in Their Hearts'." *Missiology* 10

______. "Review of 'Christianity in Culture'." *Radix* 2 (Jan./Feb. 1980): 25–26.

Albright, William Foxwell. *From the Stone Age to Christianity*. Garden City, NY: Doubleday Anchor, 1957.

Alt, Albrecht. "The God of the Fathers." In *Essays on Old Testament History and Religion*. London: Oxford University Press, 1966.

Altizer, Thomas. *Mircea Eliade and the Dialectic of the Sacred*. Philadelphia: Westminster Press, c. 1963.

Anderson, Charles C. *Critical Quests of Jesus*. Grand Rapids: William B. Eerdmans Publishing Company, 1969.

Anderson, Gerald H., ed. *Asian Voices in Christian Theology*. Maryknoll: Orbis, 1976.

______. "Facing the Realities of the Contemporary World in Mission." In *Educating for Christian Missions,* edited by Arthur L. Walker, Jr. (Nashville: Broadman Press, 1981), 49–58.

Baal, J. van. *Symbols for Communication. An Introduction to the Anthropological Study of Religion*. Assen: Van Gorcum, 1971.

Baird, Robert D. *Category Formation and the History of Religions*. The Hague and Paris: Mouton and Company, N.V., 1971.

Balz, Heinrich. *Theologische Modelle der Kommunikation. Bastian-Kraemer-Nida*. Gütersloh: Gütersloher Verlaugshaus, 1978.

Barbour, Ian G. *Issues in Science and Religion*. New York: Harper Torchbooks, 1971.

______. *Myths, Models and Paradigms*. New York: Harper and Row, 1974.

Barnes, Harry Elmer. *An Intellectual and Cultural History of the Western World. Volume II*. New York: Dover Publications, Inc., 1965.

Barnett, Homer. *Anthropology in Administration*. New York: Harper and Row, 1956.

Barr, James. *The Semantics of Biblical Language*. London: Oxford University Press, 1961.

Barth, Karl. *The Epistle to the Romans*. London: Oxford University Press, 1953.

Battles, Ford Lewis. "God Was Accommodating Himself to Human Capacity." *Interpretation* 31 (1977): 19–38.

Bavinck, Herman. "The Future of Calvinism." *The Presbyterian and Reformed Review* 5 (1894): 1–24.

Bavinck, J. H. *The Impact of Christianity on the Non-Christian World*. Grand Rapids: William B. Eerdmans Publishing Company, 1949.

Berg, Johannes van den. *Constrained By Jesus' Love*. Kampen: J. H. Kok, 1956.

Bergquist, James A. "The TEF and the Uncertain Future of Third World Theological Education." *Theological Education* 9 (Summer 1973): 244–53.

_____, and P. K. Manickam. *The Crisis of Dependency in Third World Ministries*. Madras: Christian Literature Society, 1974.

Berger, Peter L., and Richard J. Neuhaus, eds. *Against the World for the World*. New York: Seabury Press, 1976.

Berkhof, Louis. *Systematic Theology*. Grand Rapids: William B. Eerdmans Publishing Company, 1949.

Berkouwer, G. C. *Man: the Image of God*. Grand Rapids: William B. Eerdmans Publishing Company, 1962.

Berndt, Manfred. Chairman, *Commission on Non-Traditional Study of the Association of Theological Schools, Southeast Asia Triennium April, 1974–March, 1977. Reports and Recommendations*. Hong Kong: Association of Theological Schools, Southeast Asia, n.d.

Bianchi, Ugo. *The History of Religions*. Leiden: E. J. Brill, 1975.

The Bible and Theology in Asia Today. Asian Perspectives No. 30. Taichung, Taiwan: Asia Theological Association, 1982.

Black, Matthew, and William A. Smalley, eds. *On Language, Culture and Religion: In Honor of Eugene A. Nida*. The Hague: Mouton, 1974.

Blauw, Johannes. *The Missionary Nature of the Church*. London: Lutterworth Press, 1962.

Bleeker, C. J. *The Sacred Bridge*. Leiden: E. J. Brill, 1963.

Boas, Franz. *Race, Language and Culture*. New York: The Macmillan Company, 1940.

Bosch, David J. "Theological Education in Missionary Perspective." *Missiology* 10 (January 1982): 13–34.

_____. *Witness to the World*. Atlanta: John Knox Press.

Bowers, Paul. "Accreditation as a Catalyst for Renewal in Theological Education." *East Africa Journal of Evangelical Theology* 1 (1982): 11–21.

Brainerd, Edward. "The 'Myth' of Programmed Texts." *Evangelical Missions Quarterly* 10 (July 1974): 219–23.

Braun, Neal. *Laity Mobilized*. Grand Rapids: William B. Eerdmans Publishing Company, 1971.

Brend, Ruth M., ed. *Advances in Tagmemics*. Amsterdam: North-Holland, 1974.

_____, and Kenneth L. Pike, eds. *The Summer Institute of Linguistics: Its Work and Contributions*. The Hague: Mouton, 1977.

Brew, J. O., ed. *One Hundred Years of Anthropology*. Cambridge, Mass.: Harvard University Press, 1968.

Bridston, Keith R., Fred Foulkes, Ann Myers, and Louis Weeks. *Casebook on Church and Society*. Nashville: Abingdon Press, 1974.

Brislick, Richard W., and Paul Pedersen. *Cross-Cultural Orientation Programs*. New York: Gardner Press, 1976.

Burridge, Kenelm O. "Introduction: Missionary Occasions." *Mission, Church and Sect in Oceania,* James A. Boutilier, Daniel T. Hughes, and Sharon Tiffany, eds. (Ann Arbor: University of Michigan Press, 1978), 1–30.

Burwell, Ronald J. "Comments." *Current Anthropology* 21 (April 1980): 169.

Buswell, James O., III. "Contextualization: Theory, Tradition, and Method." *Theology and Mission,* edited by David J. Hesselgrave. (Grand Rapids: Baker Book House, 1978), 87–111.

Campbell, Joseph. *Creative Mythology*. New York: Viking Press, 1968.

_____. "Case Study in Theological Education." Special issue of *Theological Education* 10 (Spring 1974).

Chaney, Charles L. *The Birth of Missions in America*. Pasadena: William Carey Library, 1976.

Childs, Brevard. *Biblical Theology in Crisis*. Philadelphia: Westminster Press, 1970.

Clowney, Edmund P. "Scriptural Considerations on the Calling of a Seminary Teacher." Mimeographed privately by the author, n.d.

Coe, Shoki. "In Search of Renewal in Theological Education." *Theological Education* 9 (1973): 233–43.

———. "Reflections." *Northeast Asia Journal of Theology* nos. 18/19 (March/Sept. 1977): 70–78.

Collingwood, R. G. *An Autobiography*. London: Oxford University Press, 1939.

Conn, Harvie M. "The Concept of the Reason in the Theology of John Calvin." Unpublished Th.M. thesis submitted to Westminster Theological Seminary, Philadelphia, 1958.

———. "Training the Layman for Witness." *Training for Missions,* edited by Paul G. Schrotenboer. (Grand Rapids: Reformed Ecumenical Synod, 1977), 74–103.

———. "Contextualization: Where Do We Begin?" *Evangelicals and Liberation,* edited by Carl E. Armerding. (Phillipsburg, NJ: Presbyterian and Reformed Publishing Company, 1977), 90–119.

———. "Contextualization: A New Dimension for Cross-Cultural Hermeneutic." *Evangelical Missions Quarterly* 14 (January 1978): 39–46.

———. "Theologies of Liberation." *Tensions in Contemporary Theology. 3rd Rev. Ed.,* Stanley Gundry and Alan Johnson, eds. (Chicago: Moody Press, 1979), 327–434.

———. "Review of 'Black Theology: A Documentary History, 1966–1979'." *Journal of the Evangelical Theological Society* 25 (June 1982): 238–40.

———. *Evangelism: Doing Justice and Preaching Grace*. Grand Rapids: Zondervan Publishing House, 1982.

Coote, Robert, ed. *Missions From the West in a New Key*. Abington, Pa.: Partnership in Mission, n.d.

———. "The Gospel and Culture." *Gospel in Context* 1 (January 1978): 19–21.

Costas, Orlando. *Theology of the Crossroads in Contemporary Latin America*. Amsterdam: Rodopi, 1976.

_____. *Christ Outside the Gate. Mission Beyond Christendom.* Maryknoll: Orbis Books, 1982.

Davids, Peter H. "So What?" *New College Berkeley Notes* 5 (Fall–Winter 1982–83): 1.

DeJong, J. A. *As the Waters Cover the Sea. Millennial Expectations in the Rise of Anglo-American Missions, 1640–1810.* Kampen: J. H. Kok, 1970.

DeMoor, J. C. *Towards a Biblically Theo-logical Method.* Kampen: J. H. Kok, 1980.

DeRidder, Richard R. *The Dispersion of the People of God.* Kampen: J. H. Kok, 1971.

DeVries, Jan. *Perspectives in the History of Religions.* Berkeley: University of California Press, 1977.

Dillenberger, John. *Protestant Thought and Natural Science. A Historical Study.* Nashville: Abingdon Press, 1960.

Dooyeweerd, Herman. *A New Critique of Theoretical Thought. Volume II.* Philadelphia: Presbyterian and Reformed Publishing Company, 1955.

_____. *In the Twilight of Western Thought.* Philadelphia: Presbyterian and Reformed Publishing Company, 1960.

_____. *Roots of Western Culture. Pagan, Secular and Christian Options.* Toronto: Wedge Publishing Foundation, 1979.

. Douglas, J. D, ed. *Let the Earth Hear His Voice.* Minneapolis: World Wide Publishers, 1975.

Durkheim, Emile. *The Elementary Forms of the Religious Life: A Study in Religious Sociology.* New York: The Macmillan Company, 1915.

Dryness, William A. "Putting the Truth in Human Terms." *Christianity Today* 24 (April 18, 1980): 515–16.

_____. "Symbolism, Modeling and Theology." *The Living and Active Word of God. Studies in Honor of Samuel J. Schultz,* Morris Inch and Ronald Youngblood, eds. (Winona Lake, Ind.: Eisenbrauns, 1983), 283–99.

Eliade, Mircea. *Cosmos and History: The Myth of the Eternal Return.* New York: Harper and Row, 1959.

_____. *The Quest. History and Meaning in Religion.* Chicago: University of Chicago Press, 1975.

Elias, John L. *Conscientization and Schooling.* Philadelphia: Westminster Press, 1976.

Engle, Richard W. "Contextualization in Missions: A Biblical and Theological Appraisal." *Grace Theological Journal* 4 (1983): 85–107.

Escobar, Samuel. "The Social Responsibility of the Church in Latin America." *Evangelical Missions Quarterly* 6 (Spring 1970): 129–52.

Evans, G. R. *Old Arts and New Theology: The Beginnings of Theology as an Academic Discipline*. New York: Oxford University Press, 1980.

Evans-Pritchard, E. E. *Theories of Primitive Religion*. London: Oxford University Press, 1965.

———. "Religion and the Anthropologists." *Practical Anthropology* 19 (1972): 193–206.

"Faculty Development in Third World Theological Education." *WCC Education Newsletter,* no. 3 (June 1972): 2.

Festinger, Leon. *A Theory of Cognitive Dissonance*. London: Tavistock Publications, 1959.

Fleming, Bruce C. E. *Contextualization of Theology*. Pasadena: William Carey Library, 1980.

Frame, John M. *Van Til: The Theologian*. Phillipsburg, NJ: Pilgrim, 1976.

———. "Doctrine of the Knowledge of God." Mimeographed lecture notes, Westminster Theological Seminary, 1980.

Franklin, Karl J., and Kenneth A. McElhanon. "Bible Translation and Linguistics." *Journal of the American Scientific Affiliation* 31 (March 1979): 13–19.

Frase, Ronald G. "A Sociological Analysis of Brazilian Protestantism: A Study of Social Change." Unpublished Ph.D. dissertation submitted to Princeton Theological Seminary, Princeton, NJ, 1975.

Freire, Paulo. *Pedagogy of the Oppressed*. New York: The Seabury Press, 1968.

Gaffin, Richard B., Jr. "Contemporary Hermeneutics and the Study of the New Testament." *Studying the New Testament Today,* edited by John H. Skilton. (Nutley, NJ: Presbyterian and Reformed Publishing Company, 1974), 3–18.

———. "Systematic Theology and Biblical Theology." *The New Testament Student and Theology,* edited by John H. Skilton. (Presbyterian and Reformed Publishing Company, 1976), 32–50.

———. "Comments on: 'Is There More Than One Way to Do Theology?' " *Gospel in Context* 1 (January 1978): 22.

_____. "Old Amsterdam and Inerrancy?" *Westminster Theological Journal* 44 (Fall 1982): 250–89.

Geertz, Clifford. "Religion as a Cultural System." *Reader in Comparative Religion,* W. A. Lessa and E. Z. Vogt, eds. (New York: Harper and Row, 1972), 167–78.

Gilliland, Dean. "Phenomenology as Mission Method." *Missiology* 7 (October 1979): 451–59.

Glasser, Arthur, et al, eds. *Crucial Dimensions in World Evangelization.* South Pasadena: William Carey Library, 1976.

Goldenweiser, A. A. *Early Civilization: An Introduction to Anthropology.* New York: Alfred A. Knopf, 1922.

Gort, Jerald D. "The Contours of the Reformed Understanding of Christian Mission: An Attempt at Definition." *Calvin Theological Journal* 15 (1980): 47–60.

Gundry, Robert H. *Matthew. A Commentary on His Literary and Theological Art.* Grand Rapids: William B. Eerdmans Publishing Company, 1982.

Gundry, Stanley. "Evangelical Theology: Where *Should* We Be Going?" *Journal of the Evangelical Theological Society* 22 (March 1979): 3–13.

Hahn, Herbert F. *The Old Testament in Modern Research.* Philadelphia; Fortress Press, 1966.

Haleblian, Krikor. "Contextualization and French Structuralism: A Method to Delineate the Deep Structure of the Gospel." Unpublished Ph.D. dissertation submitted to Fuller Theological Seminary, Pasadena, Ca., 1982.

_____. "The Problem of Contextualization." *Missiology* 11 (January 1983): 95–111.

Hashimoto, Ryuzo. "Reformulating the Historic Creed." *International Reformed Bulletin,* no. 60 (1975): 2–8.

Hatch, Elvin. *Theories of Man and Culture.* New York: Columbia University Press, 1973.

Hazard, Paul. *European Thought in the Eighteenth Century.* Middlesex: Penguin Books, 1965.

Heidel, Alexander. *The Babylonian Genesis.* Chicago: University of Chicago Press, 1942.

_____. *The Gilgamesh Epic and Old Testament Parallels.* Chicago: University of Chicago Press, 1946.

Helberg, J. L. "The Place of the Creeds in a Young Christian Church." *International Reformed Bulletin,* no. 42 (Summer 1970): 18–21.

Henry, Carl F. H. "The Cultural Reletivizing of Revelation." *Trinity Journal* 1 (Fall 1980): 153–64.

Hesselgrave, David J., ed. *Theology and Mission.* Grand Rapids: Baker Book House, 1978.

———, ed. *New Horizons in World Mission.* Grand Rapids: Baker Book House, 1979.

Hiebert, Paul. "Introduction: Mission and Anthropology." *Readings in Missionary Anthropology II,* edited by William A. Smalley. (South Pasadena: William Carey Library, 1978), xv–xxv.

———. "Missions and Anthropology: A Love/Hate Relationship." *Missiology* 4 (April 1978): 165–80.

———. "Conversion, Culture and Cognitive Categories." *Gospel in Context* 1 (October 1978): 24–29.

———. "Sets and Structures: A Study of Church Patterns." *New Horizons in World Mission,* edited by David J. Hesselgrave. (Grand Rapids: Baker Book House, 1979), 217–27.

Hinchliff, Peter. "The Selection and Training of Missionaries in the Early Nineteenth Century." *The Mission of the Church and the Propagation of the Faith,* edited by G. J. Cuming. (London: Cambridge University Press, 1970), 131–35.

Hoekema, Anthony. "The Missionary Focus of the Canons of Dort." *Calvin Theological Journal* 7 (November 1972): 209–20.

Hoffman, Paul E., ed. *Theological Education in Today's Africa.* Geneva: Lutheran World Federation, 1969.

Holtrop, Philip. "A Strange Language." *Reformed Journal* 27 (February 1977): 9–13.

Hooykaas, R. *Religion and the Rise of Modern Science.* Grand Rapids: William B. Eerdmans Publishing Company, 1972.

Horton, Robin. "African Conversion." *Africa* 41 (1971): 85–108.

Illich, Ivan. *Deschooling Society.* New York: Harper and Row, 1970.

"Is Asian Evangelical Theology Possible?" Special issue of *Asia Theological News* 9 (January–March 1983).

Johnson, A. R. "Divine Kingship and the Old Testament." *Expository Times* 62 (1950–1951): 36–42.

_____. *The One and the Many in the Israelite Conception of God.* Cardiff: University of Wales, 1961.

Kaiser, Walter, Jr. "Meanings from God's Message: Matters for Interpretation." *Christianity Today* 22 (October 5, 1979): 30–33.

_____. *Toward an Exegetical Theology*. Grand Rapids: Baker Book House, 1981.

Kasdorf, Hans. "The Legacy of Gustav Warneck." *Occasional Bulletin of Missionary Research* 4 (July 1980): 102–7.

Kim, Chung-choon. "Seeking Relevance in Methods of Theological Education." *Northeast Asia Journal of Theology,* no. 7 (September 1971): 29–41.

_____. "The Contextualization of Theological Education." *Northeast Asia Journal of Theology,* no. 12 (March 1974): 1–9.

Kinsler, F. Ross. "Extension: An Alternative Model for Theological Education." *Learning in Context* (Bromley, Kent: Theological Education Fund, 1973), 27–49.

_____. "Theological Education by Extension: Service or Subversion?" *Missiology* 6 (April 1978): 183–94.

Kirk, J. Andrew. "An Open Forum: Editorial." *Theological Fraternity Bulletin,* no. 3 (1975): 1–4.

Kittel, Gerhard, ed. *Theological Dictionary of the New Testament, Volume II.* Grand Rapids: William B. Eerdmans Publishing Company, 1964.

Klooster, Fred H. "Missions—the Heidelbert Catechism and Calvin." *Calvin Theological Journal* 7 (November 1972): 181–208.

_____. "The Uniqueness of Reformed Theology." *Calvin Theological Journal* 14 (April 1979): 32–54.

_____. "Is Theology Color Blind?" *Reformed Journal* 30 (September 1980): 30–31.

Knapp, Stephen C. "Contextualization and Its Implications for Evangelical Churches and Missions." Unpublished paper available through Partnership in Mission, Abington, Pa., n.d.

_____. "Introducing 'Gospel in Context'." *Gospel in Context* 1 (January 1978): 1.

Kornfield, William J. "The Challenge to Make Extension Education Culturally Relevant." *Evangelical Missions Quarterly* 12 (January 1976): 13–22.

Kraemer, Hendrik. *A Theology of the Laity*. Philadelphia: Westminster Press, 1958.

Kraft, Charles. "Can Anthropological Insight Assist Evangelical Theology?" *Christian Scholar's Review* 7 (1977): 165–202.

———. "Review of 'A World to Win'." *Christian Scholar's Review* 7 (1977): 225–27.

———. "The Contextualization of Theology." *Evangelical Missions Quarterly* 14 (January, 1978): 31–36.

———. *Christianity in Culture*. Maryknoll: Orbis Books, 1979.

———, and Tom N. Wisley, eds. *Readings in Dynamic Indigeneity*. Pasadena: William Carey Library, 1979.

———. "Conservative Christians and Anthropologists: A Clash of Worldviews." *Journal of the American Scientific Affiliation* 32 (September 1980): 140–45.

Krass, Alfred. "Contextualization for Today." *Gospel in Context* 2 (July 1979): 27–30.

———. *Evangelizing Neopagan North America*. Scottdale, Pa.: Herald Press, 1982.

Kromminga, John H. "The Shape of a New Confession." *Calvin Theological Journal* 7 (November 1982): 146–57.

Kuhn, Thomas. *The Structure of Scientific Revolutions*. Chicago: University of Chicago Press, 1962.

Kuper, Adam. *Anthropologists and Anthropology*. New York: Pica Press, 1974.

Lawrence, Peter. *Road Below Cargo: A Study of the Cargo Movement in the Southern Madang District of New Guinea*. Manchester: University of Manchester Press, 1964.

Leaf, Murray J. *Man, Mind and Science. A History of Anthropology*. New York: Columbia University Press, 1979.

Leenhardt, Maurice, ed. *Note Books on Primitive Mentality*. London: Oxford University Press, 1976.

Leeuw, Gerardus van der. *Religion in Essence and Manifestation*. London: Allen and Unwin, 1938.

———. "Confession Scientifique." *Numen* 1 (1954): 8–15.

Lévi-Strauss, Claude. "The Structural Study of Myth." *Journal of American Folklore* 67 (1955): 428–44.

_____. *Structural Anthropology*. New York: Basic Books, 1963.

_____. *The Raw and the Cooked: Introduction to a Science of Mythology. Volume I*. New York: Harper and Row, 1969.

Lévy-Bruhl, Lucien. *Primitive Mentality*. New York: The Macmillan Company, 1923.

Loewen, Jacob A. *Culture and Human Values: Christian Intervention in Anthropological Perspective*. South Pasadena: William Carey Library, 1975.

Lowie, Robert. *Primitive Religion*. New York: Boni and Liveright, 1924.

Luzbetak, Louis. *The Church and Cultures*. South Pasadena: William Carey Library, 1970.

_____. "Two Centuries of Cultural Adaptation in American Church Action: Praise, Censure or Challenge?" *Missiology* 5 (January 1977): 51–72.

Machen, J. Gresham. *The Origin of Paul's Religion*. Grand Rapids: William B. Eerdmans Publishing Company, 1947.

Mackie, Steven G. "Functionalism in Ministerial Training." *Study Encounter* 3 (1967): 180–85.

_____. *Patterns of Ministry*. London: Collins, 1969.

Malefijt, Annemarie De Waal. *Images of Man. A History of Anthropological Thought*. New York: Alfred A. Knopf, 1974.

Malina, Bruce J. *The New Testament World. Insights From Cultural Anthropology*. Atlanta: John Knox Press, 1981.

Malinowski, Bronislaw. *Magic, Science and Religion*. New York: Doubleday Anchor Books, 1948.

Manuel, Frank E. *The Eighteenth Century Confronts the Gods*. New York: Atheneum, 1967.

Marshall, Paul, et al. *The Relation of Paradigm and Worldview, and the Implications of Paradigms for the Social Sciences and Professions*. Toronto: Institute for Christian Studies, 1980.

Mayers, Marvin K. *Christianity Confronts Culture*. Grand Rapids: Zondervan Publishing House, 1974.

_____, and Stephen Grunlan. *Cultural Anthropology*. Grand Rapids: Zondervan Publishing House, 1979.

McConnachie, John. *The Significance of Karl Barth*. London: Hodder and Stoughton, 1931.

McCurry, Don, ed. *The Gospel and Islam. A 1978 Compendium*. Monrovia, Ca.: MARC, 1979.

McGavran, Donald A. "A Missionary Confession of Faith." *Calvin Theological Journal* 7 (November 1972): 133–45.

———. *The Clash Between Christianity and Cultures*. Washington, DC: Canon Press, 1974.

McQuilkin, J. Robertson. "The Behavioural Sciences Under the Authority of Scripture." *Journal of the Evangelical Theological Society* 20 (March 1977): 31–43.

———. "Limits of Cultural Interpretation." *Journal of the Evangelical Theological Society* 23 (June 1980): 113–24.

Mead, Margaret. *Coming of Age in Samoa*. New York: Morrow, 1928.

Ministry in Context. Bromley, Kent: Theological Education Fund, 1972.

Mobley, Harris W. *The Ghanaian's Image of the Missionary*. Leiden: E. J. Brill, 1970.

Moore, James R. *The Post-Darwinian Controversies*. Cambridge: Cambridge University Press, 1979.

Moorehouse, Geoffrey. *The Missionaries*. Philadelphia: J. B. Lippincott, 1973.

Murray, John. "Systematic Theology." *The New Testament Student and Theology*, edited by John H. Skilton, ed. (Presbyterian and Reformed Publishing Company, 1976), 18–31.

Nacpil, Emerito. "The Question of Excellence in Theological Education." *Missions Trends No. 3. Third World Theologies*, Gerald H. Anderson and Thomas F. Stransky, eds. (Grand Rapids: William B. Eerdmans Publishing Company and New York: Paulist Press, 1976), 25–28.

Neill, Stephen. *The Church and Christian Union*. London: Oxford University Press, 1968.

Newbigin, Lesslie. "Theological Education in a World Perspective." *Ministerial Formation*, no. 4 (1978): 3–10.

Nicholls, Bruce J., ed. *Defending and Confirming the Gospel. The Report of the 1975 Consultation of the Theological Commission of the World Evangelical Fellowship*. New Delhi: WEF Theological Commission, n.d.

———. *Contextualization: A Theology of Gospel and Culture*. Downers Grove, Ill.: Inter Varsity Press, 1979.

Nicholls, William. *Systematic and Philosophical Theology*. Baltimore: Penguin Books, 1969.

Nida, Eugene A. *Message and Mission*. New York: Harper and Row, 1960.

______. *Customs, Culture and Christianity*. London: Tyndale House, 1963

______. "Missionaries and Anthropologists." *Practical Anthropology* 13 (Nov./Dec. 1966): 273–77, 287–88.

______. "New Religions for Old: A Study of Culture Change in Religion." *Church and Culture Change in Africa,* edited by David J. Bosch. (Pretoria: N.C. Kerkboekhandel, 1971), 9–44.

______. *Language, Structure and Translation*. Stanford: Stanford University Press, 1975.

Niebuhr, H. Richard, and Daniel D. Williams, eds. *The Ministry in Historical Perspectives*. New York: Harper and Brothers, 1956.

Noth, Martin. *History of Israel*. London: A. and C. Black, 1960.

Nuñez, Emilio Antonio. "Contextualization—Latin American Theology." *Latin American Pulse* 11 (February 1976): 1–6.

O'Brien, Jim. "Ford Lewis Battles: 1915–1979, Calvin Scholar and Church Historian Extraordinary." *Calvin Theological Journal* 15 (November 1980): 166–89.

Olthuis, James H. "Must the Church Become Secular?" *Out of Concern for the Church* (Toronto: Wedge Publishing Foundation, 1970), 105–25.

Orr, James, ed. *International Standard Bible Encyclopedia. Volume III*. Grand Rapids: William B. Eerdmans Publishing Company, 1955.

Osborne, Grant R. "The Evangelical and Redaction Criticism: Critique and Methodology." *Journal of the Evangelical Theological Society* 22 (December 1979): 305–22.

"Our Hope for Theological Education in the Future." *South East Asia Journal of Theology* 13 (1971): 25–29.

Packer, James I. "The Gospel: Its Content and Communication." In *Down to Earth. Studies in Christianity and Culture,* John R. W. Stott and Robert Coote, eds. (Grand Rapids: William B. Eerdmans Publishing Company, 1980), 97–114.

Padilla, René. "Hermeneutics and Culture—A Theological Perspective." In *Down to Earth. Studies in Christianity and Culture,* John R. W. Stott and Robert Coote, eds. (Grand Rapids: William B. Eerdmans Publishing Company, 1980), 63–78.

Pailin, David A. "Some Eighteenth-Century Attitudes to 'Other Religions'." *Religion, Journal of Religion and Religions* 1, part 2 (1971): 83–108.

Partridge, William L., and Elizabeth M. Eddy. "The Development of Applied Anthropology in America." *Applied Anthropology in America,* E. M. Eddy and W. L. Partridge, eds. (New York: Columbia University Press, 1978), 3–45.

Paton, David M., ed. *New Forms of Ministry*. London: Edinburgh House Press, 1965.

Patte, Daniel. *What is Structural Exegesis?* Philadelphia: Fortress Press, 1976.

Phillips, Clifton L. *Protestant America and the Pagan World. The First Half Century of the American Board of Commissioners for Foreign Missions, 1810–1860.* Cambridge, Mass.: East Asian Research Center, Harvard University Press, 1969.

Piet, John H. *The Road Ahead.* Grand Rapids: William B. Eerdmans Publishing Company, 1970.

Pike, Kenneth. *Language in Relation to a Unified Theory of the Structure of Behavior*. The Hague: Mouton, 1977.

Plog, Fred, and Daniel Bates. *Cultural Anthropology*. New York: Alfred A. Knopf, 1976.

Poerwowidagdo, R. J. "Reformulating the Historic Creed." *International Reformed Bulletin,* no. 60 (1975): 9–17.

Polman, A.D.R. "The Confession in Crisis." *International Reformed Bulletin,* no. 60 (1975): 25–32.

Poythress, Vern S. "Structuralism and Biblical Studies." *Journal of the Evangelical Theological Society* 21 (September 1978): 221–37.

———. "Philosophical Roots of Phenomenological and Structuralist Literary Criticism." *Westminster Theological Journal* 41 (Fall 1978): 165–71.

———. "Structural Approaches to Understanding the Theology of the Apostle Paul." Unpublished Th.D. dissertation submitted to the University of Stellenbosch, South Africa, 1981.

"Programme on Theological Education: An On-Going Concern of the Churches Now an Integral Part of the WCC." *Ministerial Formation,* no. 1 (January 1978): 3–5.

Ramm, Bernard. *Special Revelation and the Word of God*. Grand Rapids: William B. Eerdmans Publishing Company, 1961.

_____. *The Christian College in the Twentieth Century*. Grand Rapids: William B. Eerdmans Publishing Company, 1963.

_____. *Varieties of Christian Apologetics*. Grand Rapids: Baker Book House, 1965.

Ramseyer, Robert L. "Christian Mission and Cultural Anthropology." *Exploring Church Growth,* edited by Wilbert Shenk. (Grand Rapids: William B. Eerdmans Publishing Company, 1983), 108–16

Ream, W.G.B. "The Support of the Clergy in the First Five Centuries A.D." *International Review of Missions* 45 (October 1956): 420–28.

Recker, Robert. "An Analysis of the Belgic Confession As To Its Mission Focus." *Calvin Theological Journal* 7 (November 1972): 158–80.

Reid, W. Stanford. "Calvin and the Founding of the Academy of Geneva." *Westminster Theological Journal* 18 (November 1955): 1–33.

Reist, Benjamin A. *Toward a Theology of Involvement. The Thought of Ernst Troeltsch*. Philadelphia: Westminster Press, 1966.

Richardson, Don. *Eternity in Their Hearts*. Ventura, Ca.: Regal Books, 1981.

Ridderbos, Herman. *Paul: An Outline of His Theology*. Grand Rapids: William B. Eerdmans Publishing Company, 1975.

_____. "Evaluation." *RES Theological Forum* 9 (January 1982): 51–56.

Ro, Bong-rin. "TAP Administrator Reports on Visit to Africa." *Theological News* 4 (October 1972): 5–6.

Robinson, H. Wheeler. *The Christian Doctrine of Man*. Edinburgh: T. and T. Clark, 1911.

Rogers, Jack, and Donald McKim. *The Authority and Interpretation of the Bible: An Historical Approach*. New York: Harper and Row, 1979.

Rogerson, John. *Anthropology and the Old Testament*. Atlanta: John Knox Press, 1979.

Rowen, Samuel. "The Future of Theological Education." *Issues for Christian Leaders: Briefs from Westminster Theological Seminary* (November/December 1977), 1–3.

Rowley, H. H. *The Unity of the Bible*. New York: Meridian Books, Inc., 1957.

Samuel, Vinay, and Chris Sugden. "Comments on 'The Contextualization Continuum'." *Gospel in Context* 2 (July 1979): 17–19.

Sapir, Edward. "The Status of Linguistics as a Science." *Language* 5 (1929): 207–14.

Savage, Peter. "Four Crises in Third World Theological Education." *Evangelical Missions Quarterly* 9 (Fall 1972): 28–34.

Schaeffer, Edith. *L'Abri*. Wheaton: Tyndale House, 1969.

Schrotenboer, Paul G. "On Creeds and Making New Ones." *International Reformed Bulletin,* no. 42 (Summer 1976): 9–17.

———. "Theological Education on the Mission Field in Kingdom Perspective." *International Reformed Bulletin,* no. 58 (1974): 2–9.

———, ed. *Church and Theology in the Contemporary World.* Grand Rapids: Reformed Ecumenical Synod, 1977.

Segundo, Juan Luis. *The Liberation of Theology*. Maryknoll: Orbis Books, 1976.

The Seoul Declaration. Toward an Evangelical Theology for the Third World. Taichung, Taiwan: Asia Theological Association, 1982.

Sharpe, Eric. *Comparative Religion. A History*. London: Duckworth, 1975.

Smalley, Stephen S. "Redaction Criticism." *New Testament Interpretation. Essays on Principles and Methods,* edited by I. Howard Marshall. (Grand Rapids: William B. Eerdmans Publishing Company, 1977), 181–95.

Smalley, William A. "Ten Years of 'Practical Anthropology'." *Practical Anthropology* 10 (Jan./Feb. 1963): 1–5.

———, ed. *Readings in Missionary Anthropology II.* South Pasadena: William Carey Library, 1978.

Smit, Harvey. "An Approach to Practical Apologetics: with Specific Reference to the Japanese Scene." *The Christian Faith in the Modern World,* edited by Paul G. Schrotenboer. (Grand Rapids: Reformed Ecumenical Synod, 1970), 1–12.

Smith, W. Robertson. *The Religion of the Semites. 3rd Ed.* London: A. and C. Black, 1927.

Soedarmo, Raden. "The Place of the Creed in a Young Church." *International Reformed Bulletin,* no. 42 (Summer 1970): 22–27.

Sommers, John G. *Beyond Charity: US Voluntary Aid for a Changing Third World.* Washington, DC. Overseas Development Council, 1977.

Sontag, Frederick. "A Plea for Common Sense." *Missiology* 7 (July 1979): 365–68.

Stipe, Claude. "Anthropologists Versus Missionaries: The Influence of Presuppositions." *Current Anthropology* 21 (April 1980): 165–68.

Stott, John R. W., and Robert Coote, eds. *Down to Earth. Studies in Christianity and Culture*. Grand Rapids: William B. Eerdmans Publishing Company, 1980.

Sumithra, Sunand. "Third World Theologians Consultation, Seoul, 1982—An Evaluation." *Aim* 13 (November 1982): 9–16, 21.

Sweet, William Warren. "The Rise of Theological Schools in America." *Church History* 6 (1937): 260–73.

Taber, Charles R. " 'Practical Anthropology'—A Look Ahead." *Practical Anthropology* 15 (Nov./Dec. 1968): 241–44

_____. "Change and Continuity." *Missiology* 1 (January 1973): 7–13.

_____. "Is There More Than One Way to do Theology?" *Gospel in Context* 1 (January 1978): 4–10

_____. "The Limits of Indigenization in Theology." *Missiology* 6 (January 1978): 53–79.

_____. "Contextualization: Whose Ox is Being Gored?" *Gospel in Context* 1 (October 1978): 2–3.

_____. "Contextualization: Indigenization and/or Transformation." In *The Gospel and Islam: A 1978 Compendium*, edited by Don McCurry. (Monrovia: MARC, 1979), 143–54.

_____. *Graduate Education for World Mission*. Johnson City, Tn.: Emmanuel School of Religion, 1980.

_____. "Hermeneutics and Culture—An Anthropological Perspective." In *Down to Earth. Studies in Christianity and Culture*, John R. 3pW. Stott and Robert Coote, eds. (Grand Rapids: William B. Eerdmans Publishing Company, 1980), 79–94.

_____. "Missiology and the Bible." *Missiology* 11 (April 1983): 229–44.

_____. "Contextualization." *Exploring Church Growth*, edited by Wilbert Shenk. (Grand Rapids: William B. Eerdmans Publishing Company, 1983): 117–31.

A Tent Making Ministry. New York: Division of World Mission and Evangelism, World Council of Churches, 1962.

Theological Education and Ministry. Reports from the North East Asia Theological Education Consultation. Seoul, Korea. Tainan, Taiwan: The Presbyterian Bookroom, 1967.

"Theology from the Third World." *JSAC Grapevine* 1 (February 1977): 1–7.

Thiselton, Anthony. "Semantics and New Testament Interpretation." In *New Testament Interpretation. Essays on Principles and Methods,* edited by I. Howard Marshall. (Grand Rapids: William B. Eerdmans Publishing Company, 1977), 75–104.

———. *The Two Horizons: New Testament Hermeneutics and Philosophical Description*. Grand Rapids: William B. Eerdmans Publishing Company, 1980.

Tillich, Paul. *The Religious Situation*. New York: Henry Holt and Company, 1932.

———. *Systematic Theology, Volume I*. Chicago: University of Chicago Press, 1951.

Timmer, John. "G. C. Berkouwer: Theologian of Confrontation and Co-Relation." *Reformed Journal* 19 (December 1969): 17–22.

Tippett, Alan. *Solomon Islands Christianity*. New York: Friendship Press, 1967.

———. *Church Growth and the Word of God*. Grand Rapids: William B. Eerdmans Publishing Company, 1970.

———. *People Movements in Southern Polynesia*. Chicago: Moody Press, 1971.

———. "Anthropology and Post-Colonial Mission Through a China Filter." *Missiology* 1 (October 1973): 465–96.

Toon, Peter. *The Development of Doctrine in the Church*. Grand Rapids: William B. Eerdmans Publishing Company, 1979.

Training in Context. Bromley, Kent: Theological Education Fund, 1973.

Van Oss, Adriaan C. "A Response to Claude Stipe." *Current Anthropology* 21 (April 1980): 176.

Van Til, Cornelius. *The Defense of the Faith*. Philadelphia: Presbyterian and Reformed Publishing Company, 1955.

———. *A Christian Theory of Knowledge*. Presbyterian and Reformed Publishing Company, 1969.

Vander Stelt, John. *Philosophy and Scripture: A Study in Old Princeton and Westminster Theology*. Marlton, NJ: Mack Publishing Company, 1978.

Verkuyl, Johannes. *Contemporary Missiology. An Introduction.* Grand Rapids: William B. Eerdmans Publishing Company, 1978.

Voget, Fred A. *A History of Ethnology*. New York: Holt, Rinehart and Winston, 1975.

Volf, Miroslav. "Doing and Interpreting: an Examination of the Relationship Between Theory and Practice in Latin American Liberation Theology." *Themelios* 8 (April 1983): 11–19.

Vos, Geerhardus. *Biblical Theology*. Grand Rapids: William B. Eerdmans Publishing Company, 1948.

Waardenburg, Jacques. *Classical Approaches to the Study of Religion. Aims, Methods and Theories of Research. Volume I: Introduction and Anthology*. The Hague and Paris: Mouton and Co., N.V., 1973.

Ward, Ted. "Schooling as a Defective Approach to Education." Unpublished paper available through the author, Institute for International Studies, Michigan State University, 1978.

Warfield, B. B. *Studies in Theology*. New York: Oxford University Press, 1932.

Warren, Max. *The Missionary Movement From Britain in Modern History*. London: SCM Press, 1965.

_____. *Social History and Christian Missions*. London: SCM Press, 1967.

Webster, Douglas. *Survey of the Training of the Ministry in the Middle East.* Geneva: Commission on World Mission and Evangelism, World Council of Churches, 1962.

Weeks, Louis. "So You're Studying Cases." *The Christian Ministry* (July 1974), 36–38.

Wheelwright, Philip. *The Burning Fountain: A Study in the Language of Symbolism*. Bloomington: University of Indiana Press, 1954.

Widjaja, Albert. "Beggarly Theology: A Search for a Perspective Toward Indigenous Theology." *South East Asia Journal of Theology* 14 (1973): 39–45.

Wolf, Eric. *Anthropology*. New York: Norton, 1974.

Wolters, Al. "Truth as Relational." *RES Theological Forum* 9 (January 1982): 7–11.

Woodbridge, John D. *Biblical Authority: A Critique of the Rogers/McKim Proposal*. Grand Rapids: Zondervan Publishing House, 1982.

Yamamori, Tetsunao, and Charles R. Taber, eds. *Christopaganism or Indigenous Christianity?* South Pasadena: William Carey Library, 1975.

Zahrnt, Heinz. *The Question of God*. New York: Harcourt, Brace and Javonovich, 1966.

Zorilla, Hugo. "Crucial Issues in Theological Education in Latin America." *Mission–Focus* 5 (March 1977 Supplement).

Index of Biblical References

Genesis
1:26 232
28:13 73
31:42 73
49:24 73

Exodus
5:1 291
6:7 233
19:6 233, 291
34: 6–8 230

Numbers
23:19 230

Deuteronomy
4:10 291
32:4 230

Judges
3:10 292
6:34 292
15:14 292

1 Samuel
10:6 292
16:13 292
21:1–6 170n

Psalms
25:5 230
26:3 230
31:6 230
66:16 241
86:11 230
87 291
119:89–90 230

Isaiah
2:2–4 291
11:16 292
19:23 292
35:4–9 291
40:8 230
44:3–5 292
52:12 291
55:11 230
56:6–8 291

Daniel
8:12 230
9:13 230
10:21 230

Hosea
2:20 230
4:1 230

Joel
2:28 292

Malachi
3:6 230

Matthew
3:2–3 292
5:17 199
5:29–30 237
5:38–42 188
6:10 231, 309
7:21 232, 309
11:2–6 255
16:3 234
18:5 237
22:29 234
23:8 300
24:14 311
28:18–20 291

Mark
1:2–3 170n
2:26 170n
4:11 243
4:17 237

Luke
4:1–12 291
4:18–21 255
9:31 291
24:25 234
24:47 291

John
3:20–21 235
8:31–36 231
15:10–11 231
17:6–8 235
20:31 234

Acts
1:8 291
2:4 292
2:16–21 292
4:13 292
7:44–47 291
8:1 292
8:4 291
15 240
15:14 290
15:21 240
16:37 188
17:6 292

Romans
1:18 235
8:21 198
9:33 239
12:1–2 309
12:6 293
12:6–8 295
14:1–15:7 237
14:15 238
14:20, 23 238
15:1 238
15:2 273
16:25–26 226

1 Corinthians
1:17 237
1:27–28 255
3:22–23 239
5:10 236
6:1–5 243
8:1 273
8:1ff. 237
8:10–11 237
8:12 238
8:13 237
9:19–23 158
10:11 226, 291
10:22 239
10:23ff. 237
11:18 291
12:3 241
12:4 294
12:4–6 293
12:5 294
14:23–24 244
14:26–28 291

2 Corinthians
5:17 236
11:2 301

Galatians
1:4 236
2:1–10 240
2:20 236
3:23–24 198

Ephesians
2:20 246
3:8–10 226
4:4 293
4:7 293
4:16 290

Colossians
1:13 236
1:25–27 226
1:28 301
2:18–23 238
3:15 290
4:5 244

1 Thessalonians
4:12 244

2 Thessalonians
2:1 291

1 Timothy
1:8–11 231 I1 3:15 246
4:1ff. 238
4:6ff. 231
5:3 293
5:17–18 293
6:3–5 231
6:11 311

2 Timothy
1:13 231
2:1 231
2:25 310
4:1ff. 231

Titus
1:6–9 229, 310
1:9 229, 231, 310
2:1ff. 229, 310
2:1–5 231
2:11, 12 244

Hebrews
1:1–2 226
1:2 291
11 170n
11:31 231
12:18–24 291

James
1:1 291

1 Peter
1:1 291
2:4–5 291
2:9 233
2:9–10 290

2 Peter
1:20–21 292
1:21 173, 215

1 John
1:6 232, 309, 310
2:19 226
4:8 235

Index of Persons

Adeney, Miriam, 154n, 328
Albright, William Foxwell, 70
Allen, E. L., 24n
Allen, Rolland, 11, 281
Alt, Albrecht, 73, 105
Altizer, Thomas, 100
Anderson, Charles C., 65
Anderson, Gerald H., 212, 307
Anderson, Rufus, 79, 281
Aquinas, Thomas, 133, 198, 200–201, 273–74
Aristotle, 30, 217
Astruc, Jean, 28
Athanasius, 303
Augustine, 30, 156, 303

Baal, J. van, 58, 95
Baird, Robert, 102
Balz, Heinrich, 148
Barbour, Ian, 19, 20, 34, 165
Barnes, Harry Elmer, 29
Barnett, Homer, 141, 152
Barr, James, 71–72, 113–14
Barth, Karl, 110, 154, 217, 303
Bates, Daniel, 112, 141n
Battles, Ford Lewis, 219
Bavinck, Herman, 221–22
Bavinck, J. H., 119, 334n
Baxter, Richard, 275
Bayle, Pierre, 28–29, 31
Becker, Carl, 42
Benedict, Ruth 96, 99, 316
Berg, Johannes van den, 34–36
Bergquist, James A., 266, 282, 284, 292n
Berkhof, Louis, 219, 222
Berkouwer, G. C., 219–20, 311
Berndt, Manfred, 273
Bianchi, Ugo, 41
Blauw, Johannes, 291
Bleeker, C. J., 109
Boas, Franz, 94, 96–97, 98
Boccaccio, Giovanni, 27
Bonaparte, Napoleon, 23
Bosch, David J., 221–22, 245n
Bousset, Wilhelm, 65
Bowers, Paul, 271n
Brainerd, Edward, 270n
Brandon, S. G. F., 107
Braun, Neal, 281
Bridston, Keith R., et. al., 308n
Brislick, Richard W., 74
Brosses, Charles de, 37, 40–41
Brown, Driver, Briggs, 72
Bultmann, Rudolf, 110–11, 192, 215–16, 321
Burridge, Kenelm O., 17
Burwell, Ronald J., 134, 135
Buswell, James O., III, 181, 312
Butler, Bishop Joseph, 34

Calvin, John, 156, 186, 216–19, 274, 279, 303
Campbell, Joseph, 99
Carey, William, 35
Chaney, Charles L., 83
Childs, Brevard, 104, 233
Chomsky, Noam, 147
Clement of Alexandria 273, 301
Clowney, Edmund P. 300–301
Codrington, R. H., 138
Coe, Shoki, 177-79, 265, 284–85
Collingwood, R. G., 15
Comte, Auguste, 31, 38
Confucius, 23, 131
Conn, Harvie M., 177n, 185, 253n, 258–59, 265n, 274, 280, 285n
Coote, Robert, 182
Costas, Orlando, 233, 256–57, 303–4
Couch, Beatriz Melano, 259
Cudworth, Ralph, 32

Darwin, Charles, 52, 61
Davids, Peter, 302–3

Dayton, Ed, 305
DeJong, J. A., 82
Delitzsch, Friedrich, 64
DeMoor, J. C., 220n
DeRidder, Richard R., 245n
DeVries, Jan, 27, 59
De Waal Malefijt, Annemarie, 30, 37, 41, 96, 323
Dillenberger, John, 24–25
Dodd, C. H., 104
Dooyeweerd, Herman, 20n, 49n, 137, 165n, 319
Duchrow, Ulrich, 118
Durkheim, Emile, 16, 31, 56–58, 62, 68, 70–71, 82, 84, 90, 94, 103–104
Dye, T. Wayne, 150
Dyrness, William, 154n, 321n, 327

Eddy, Elizabeth M., 91, 139, 140
Eliade, Mircea, 63, 90, 95–96, 99, 107, 118, 118n
Elias, John L., 277n
Eliot, John, 83
Ellegard, Alvar, 52
Engle, Richard W., 234n
Escobar, Samuel, 216, 285
Euhemerus, 27
Evans, G. R., 217–218
Evans-Pritchard, E. E., 16–17, 63, 107

Festinger, Leon, 53–54
Fleming, Bruce C. E., 180n, 184
Fontenelle, Bernard, 30–31
Frame, John, 15, 17–18, 220, 234, 335, 338
Franklin, Karl J., 147n
Frase, Ronald G., 277
Frazer, Sir James, 16, 31, 41, 51, 55, 65–68, 97, 106
Freire, Paulo, 247, 277, 294, 310
Freud, Sigmund 29, 31, 41, 90, 95, 97–99, 100, 106, 118, 321, 326
Friedrich, Gerhard, 71

Gaffin, Richard B., Jr., 172, 203, 214n, 227, 228
Gatu, John, 123
Geertz, Clifford, 321
Gilliland, Dean, 109
Goldenweiser, A. A., 57–58, 96
Gort, Jerald D., 224, 306
Graham, Billy, 137
Grandmaison, Millin de, 22
Grunlan, Stephen, 120
Gundry, Robert H., 236n
Gundry, Stanley, 129–30
Gunkel, Herman, 65, 70, 321
Gutiérrez, Gustavo, 11, 216, 232
Gutmann, Bruno, 281

Hahn, Herbert F., 67n, 104–5
Haleblian, Krikor, 181n, 184, 192–94, 324n
Hashimoto, Ryuzo, 251
Hatch, Elvin, 101
Hazard, Paul, 25
Heidegger, Martin, 110, 215
Heidel, Alexander, 64n
Helberg,J. L., 248
Helvétius, Claude Adrien, 22
Henry, Carl F. H., 154–56, 168
Herbert, Lord of Cherbury, 32
Herskovits, Melville Jean, 96
Hiebert, Paul, 13, 78, 80, 120, 132, 138–39, 145, 316, 319, 324, 332
Hinchliff, Peter, 55, 77
Hobbes, Thomas, 28
Hoekema, Anthony, 244
Holtrop, Philip, 230–31
Hooke, S. H., 60, 67–68, 70
Hooykaas, R., 20n
Horton, Robin, 52
Hume, David, 29, 34, 37, 38–40, 41, 42, 49
Husserl, Edmund, 107, 110

Illich, Ivan, 277, 294

Johnson, A. R., 67–68, 70
Jung, Carl Gustav, 90, 95, 99
Junod, H., 138

Kaiser, Walter, Jr., 215n
Kant, Immanuel, 24–25, 49
Kasdorf, Hans, 76
Kato, Byang, 176, 181
Kim, Chung-choon, 286, 308–9
Kinsler, F. Ross, 266–67, 270, 277, 282, 298
Kirk, J. Andrew, 298

Kittel, Gerhard, 71–72, 112–13
Klooster, Fred, 223, 245, 317
Knapp, Stephen, C., 183, 277n, 289, 310
Kornfield, William J., 270
Kraemer, Hendrik, 280
Kraft, Charles, 19, 20, 79n, 113, 120, 121, 128, 144, 149–50, 154–58, 162, 164, 167–75, 181, 189, 198, 200, 203–4, 214, 215, 227, 235, 314, 315, 318, 329–31, 332, 334, 337
Krass, Al, 117, 119n, 120, 218, 226
Kristenson, William Brede, 107
Kroeber, A. L., 96
Kromminga, John H., 242–43
Kuhn, Thomas, 15, 50, 54, 134, 164, 314, 317–18, 326
Küng, Hans, 293
Kuper, Adam, 101, 103, 323–24
Kuyper, Abraham, 115-116, 165

Lang, Andrew, 31, 59
Lawrence, Peter, 52
Leaf, Murray J., 323
Leenhardt, Maurice, 69, 139
Leeuw, Gerardus van der, 95, 107–08
Legters, L. L., 142
Lévi-Strauss, Claude, 11, 21, 314, 321–24, 327, 337
Lévy-Bruhl, Lucien, 31, 41, 68–70, 78
Lightfoot, J. B., 186
Livingstone, David, 11, 78
Locke, John, 24
Loewen, Jacob, 146, 151, 183
Lowie, Robert, 58n, 96
Luther, Martin, 279, 303
Luzbetak, Louis, 119, 144, 198–201

McConnachie, John, 110
McElhanon, Kenneth A., 147n
McGavran, Donald, 153, 194–96, 244, 315
Machen, J. Gresham, 240
Mackie, Steven G., 286n
McKim, Donald, 213
McQuilkin, J. Robertson, 121, 122, 175
Malina, Bruce J., 329
Malinowski, Bronislaw, 16, 17, 29, 91, 98, 101–2, 106, 107, 118–19, 120, 123
Manickam, P. K., 282, 292n
Manuel, Frank E., 22–23, 27–28, 39n
Marshall, Paul, et. al., 319
Marx, Karl, 232
Mayers, Marvin K., 120, 308n
Mbiti, John, 11, 253
Mead, Margaret, 96, 98–99
Melanchthon, Philip, 274
Merrifield, William R., 151
Michaelson, Wesley, 256
Mobley, Harris W., 83
Moffat, Robert, 55
Moore, James, R., 48, 52, 53n
Moorhouse, Geoffrey, 79
Morrison, Robert, 11
Mowinckel, Sigmund, 66–67
Müller, Max, 21, 31, 59, 71–72
Murray, John, 222, 225

Nacpil, Emerito P., 268
Nazario, Victor, 288n
Neill, Stephen, 222
Newbigin, Lesslie, 222n
Newton, Isaac, 27
Nicholls, Bruce, 181
Nichols, William, 110
Nida, Eugene, 113, 119, 128, 143, 143n, 144, 146, 147, 148, 152, 154, 155, 156, 157, 162, 166–67, 317n, 324–26
Niebuhr, H. Richard, 156, 199, 200
North, Eric, M., 148
Noth, Martin, 105
Nuñez, Emilio Antonio, 182

O'Brien, Jim, 217n
Olthuis, James H., 202
Origen, 273
Osborne, Grant R., 235n
Otto, Rudolf, 90, 94–96, 100, 108
Packer, J. I., 193
Padilla, René, 124, 216, 247
Pailin, David A., 25–26, 32–33, 35
Partridge, William, 91, 139, 140
Patte, Daniel, 323n
Pedersen, Paul, 74
Phillips, Clifton L., 83

Piet, John H., 245n
Pike, Kenneth L., 128, 142–43, 149–51, 157
Pinnock, Clark, 168
Plato, 30, 108, 193
Plog, Fred, 112, 141n
Poerwowidagdo, R. J., 251
Polman, A. D. R., 246
Poythress, Vern S., 323n, 325n, 335–37
Price, David, 151n

Radcliffe-Brown, A. R., 91, 101–3, 104
Radin, Paul, 41
Rameau, Jean-Philippe, 22
Ramm, Bernard, 34n, 169, 171–72, 274
Ramseyer, Robert, 174, 176, 332
Ream, W. G. B., 279
Recker, Robert, 245
Redfield, Robert, 91
Reid, W. Stanford, 274
Renan, Ernst, 192
Rengstorf, Karl, 301
Reist, Benjamin A., 75n
Reyburn, William, 146
Richardson, Don, 48, 327–329
Ridderbos, Herman N., 214, 236, 238, 293, 306–7
Ritschl, Albrecht, 109
Ro, Bong-rin, 268–69
Robbins, Frank, 142
Robinson, H. Wheeler, 69
Rogers, Jack, 213
Rogerson, John, 60, 66, 69, 106
Rohr, Richard, 303
Rousseau, Jean-Jacques, 23, 39
Rowen, Samuel, 278n, 296–97
Rowley, H. H., 104

Sapir, Edward, 96, 99, 111, 112, 142
Saussure, Ferdinand de, 93–94, 111, 113, 321
Savage, Peter, 267n, 276
Schaeffer, Edith, 309n
Schaeffer, Francis, 168, 309
Schleiermacher, Friedrich, 234
Schmidt, Wilhelm, 36, 58, 63–64, 138, 328
Schrotenboer, Paul G., 241, 311
Segundo, Juan Luis, 258–59
Sergeant, John, 35
Sharpe, Eric, 23n, 59n, 76, 90, 108
Shuckford, Samuel, 28
Simon, Richard, 28
Smalley, Stephen S., 235
Smalley, William, 144, 146
Smit, Harvey, 237, 239
Smith, E., 138
Smith, W. Robertson, 62, 74, 97
Soedarmo, Raden, 249
Sommers, John G., 213
Sontag, Frederick 191
Spurgeon, Charles H., 303
Stipe, Claude, 51–52, 133–34, 136, 137–38, 165
Strauss, D. F., 192
Sugden, Chris, 193
Sumithra, Sunand, 191–92, 205
Sundkler, Bengt, 282
Sweet, William Warren, 275

Taber, Charles, 115, 117, 122, 145–47, 183, 190, 193, 196–97, 205, 224, 241, 247, 250, 255, 284, 304–6
Taylor, J. Hudson, 131
Taylor, Robert B., 146
Thiselton, Anthony, 71, 113, 215, 317
Tillich, Paul, 100, 110
Timmer, John, 218, 220
Tindal, Matthew, 32
Tippett, Alan, 48, 131, 138, 152–53, 183
Toffler, Alvin, 13
Toland, John, 32
Toon, Peter, 204, 337–38
Townsend, W. Cameron, 142, 143
Trench, Richard, 72
Troeltsch, Ernst, 75–76, 109
Tylor, E. B., 16, 21, 41, 51, 56, 61, 62, 65, 101

Underhill, Ruth, 96

Van Oss, Adriaan C., 51
Van Til Cornelius, 15, 18, 34n, 255, 316
VanderStelt, John, 213
Venn, Henry, 79, 85, 280
Verkuyl, Johannes, 76n
Vico, Giambattista, 37–38
Vinay, Samuel, 193

Voget, Fred, 42–43, 141
Volf, Miroslav, 232
Voltaire, Francois, 22, 23–24
Vos, Geerhardus, 171, 225, 227

Waardenburg, Jacques, 96
Ward, Ted, 294–296
Warfield, B. B., 299
Warneck, Gustav, 75–76, 79
Warner, Lloyd, 91
Warren, Max, 35–36, 77
Weber, Max, 104–5
Webster, Douglas, 264
Weeks, Louis, 308n
Wellhausen, Julius, 61–62, 64, 73, 106
Westcott, B. F., 186
Wheelwright, Philip, 326–27
Whorf, Benjamin, 111–12
Widengren, George, 107
Widjaja, Albert, 287
Winckler, Hugo, 64
Wisley, Tom N., 79n, 181
Wolf, Eric, 135, 137–38
Wolters, Al, 214
Wonderly, William, 113, 144
Woodbridge, John, 214n
Wrede, Wilhelm, 65

Yoder, John Howard, 278, 281

Zahrnt, Heinz, 95
Ziegenbalg, Bartholomew, 77
Zorilla, Hugo, 269

Subject Index

Accomodation, 198–202
Adiaphora, 195, 236–40
Acculturation, 11, 133, 135, 312
Africa, 78, 122, 203, 212, 221, 266, 284, 317
  African churches, 281, 282
  African Independent Churches, 11, 326
  African religions, 41, 76, 253, 327
  African theology, 247, 253, 254, 269
Agnosticism, 51
Akan, 83–84
Aletheia, 230, 231
Allegorism, 26–27, 28–29
American Bible Society, 143, 145
American Board of Commissioners for Foreign Missions, 79
American Indians, 35, 41, 51, 58, 83, 92
Amphictyony, 105–6
Analogy, 34, 169–70, 317
Analytic philosophy, 144
Animism, 41, 56, 61, 152, 300, 326
Anthropological Society of London, 78
Anthropomorphism, 30–31, 48, 215
Applied anthropology, 91–92, 103, 114, 136, 139–42, 146, 316
Applied missionary anthropolgy, 12, 53, 131, 138–47, 150–51, 152, 153, 199, 316, 324, 325, 329, 331, 333
Architecture, 84, 117
Arminianism, 84, 335
Art, 120
Asia, 122, 177, 212, 221, 246, 247, 251, 254, 266, 267, 268, 281, 284, 304, 317
Asia Theological Association, 163, 177269
Association of Theological Schools in South East Asia, 268, 272–73
Assyriology, 60
Athanasian Creed, 252
Atheism, 51
Atonement, 62, 131
Augsburg Confession, 223
Australia, 58, 80, 135
Babylon, 67, 70
Base Ecclesial Communities, 256
Belgic Confession, 245
Bible, 202, 216, 223, 228, 229, 235, 236, 298, 303, 331, 332–33, 338
  application of, 122, 186, 220, 234–35
  authority of, 121, 154, 168, 190, 191, 214, 316
  inerrancy of, 168, 169, 170, 184, 227, 316
  inspiration of, 154, 168–75, 192, 194, 202, 214, 227
  translation, *Note 142–45, 147–49, 157
Biblical theology, 174–75, 224–29, 233, 332-33
Black theology, 122, 129, 132, 187, 247, 253, 256–57, 317, 320, 331
Bounded sets, 117, 320
Brazil, 132, 191, 276–77
Britain, 34–36, 221, 222, 275
Buddhism, 75, 131, 239
Burma, 327
Calvinism, 84, 115, 195, 216, 219–20, 221, 222, 223, 224, 242, 251, 310, 317, 327, 334–35
Campus Crusade for Christ, 302
Canons of Dordt, 244
Capitalism, 132
Change, 37, 91, 92, 103, 111, 116, 119, 123, 133, 136, 140–41, 178, 202, 235, 241, 243, 259, 265, 267, 283, 287, 326, 327, 333
China, 23, 83, 131–32, 133, 187, 212
Christology, 65, 300, 305
Christopaganism, 177
"Church Growth" movement, 124, 153, 196, 316–17, 320–21, 333

Church-mission relations, 123–24
Church Missionary Society, 79
Civilizing as a mission motive, 34–35, 36, 76, 78–80
Clan, 57, 58, 62, 104–06 I3 Clergy, 257, 266, 272–82, 292–94, 295, 297, 311–12
Colonialism, 35–36, 55, 76, 78–80, 82, 84, 113, 123, 131, 247-48, 272, 284, 285
Common grace, 132, 328
Common Sense Realism, 213–14
Communication, 94, 117, 123, 147, 148, 149, 152, 154, 155, 158, 166–67, 174, 181–82, 183, 184, 188–90, 228–29, 231, 250, 284, 320, 330
Communion, 62, 239
Community, Christain, 246–57, 293–94, 309
Comparative religions, 12, 77
Confucianism, 131, 187, 281
Conservative Baptist Church, 302
Conscientization, 290, 310, 311
Consciousness One, 47–86, 89, 90, 91, 92, 94, 96, 97, 100, 112, 113, 114, 116, 122, 123, 164, 171, 181, 185
Consciousness Two, 49, 51, 54, 89–124, 174, 191, 195, 202, 241, 334
Consciousness Three, 138, 147
Contextualization, 11, 12, 116, 117, 122, 129–30, 157, 163–64, 176, 177–79, 181, 183, 189, 196, 218, 221, 223, 226, 227, 231, 234, 240, 242, 243, 253, 256–57, 258, 265–72, 277, 283–86, 287, 288, 299, 301, 302–3, 309, 310, 311, 312, 326
Conversion, 218, 276, 320
"Corporate personality," 69–70
Corpus Christianum, *Note 114, 221, 246
Covenant, 105, 167, 195, 217, 218, 219, 220, 224, 229–35, 290, 310, 311, 334
Creation, 67
Creeds, 221, 222, 223, 229, 242–46, 250, 252, 253
Culture, 56–57, 58, 70–71, 78, 82–84, 89, 97, 98, 99, 102–6, 111–12, 115–16, 121–22, 133, 135–36, 152, 156–57, 169, 182, 195–96, 198–99, 235–41, 283–84, 286–87, 298, 316, 326, 329, 331, 334
Curriculum, 269, 271, 276, 296–97, 304, 308
Dance, 84
Darwinism, 12, 41, 47–49, 52–53, 61, 63, 74, 102–3, 328
Dead Sea Scrolls, 192–93
Declaration of the Sixth Theological Consultation of the Asia Theological Association, 177, 185
Decontextualization, 180, 257, 258–60
Deism, 26, 31–33, 36, 81
Demons, 30, 116, 239, 258
Demythologization, 132, 215
Developmentalism, 36, 37–38, 38–40, 43, 56, 58, 59, 61–62, 63, 66–68, 70, 74, 75, 82, 84, 90, 96, 323
Diachornic approach, 20, 48, 93
Dialogue, 167, 218, 241, 242
Didache, didaskalia, 234
Diffusionism, 36, 51, 62–65, 82, 90, 328
Dispensationalism, 310
Doctrine, progress of, 204, 223, 300, 338
Documentary hypothesis, 28, 61–62
Dreams, 39
Drumming, 84
Dynamic equivalence, 124, 147–49, 152, 155, 157, 166, 167, 168, 170, 171, 173, 174, 181, 214, 229
Dynamic indigeneity, 164, 181
East India Company, 36
Ecclesiology, 252
Economics, 92, 104, 105, 123, 135, 141, 178, 180, 241, 244, 253, 254, 258, 259, 271, 283, 285, 294
Education, 290, 294–99, 302, 303, 307–08, 309–12, 316–17
Egypt, 23, 27, 40, 70, 233, 292, 301
Egyptologists, 60
Eidetic vision, 108
Emet, 230–32
Emmanuel School of Religion, 304, 305–6
Enculturation, 11, 308

Enlightment, 17, 21, 24, 25–33, 35, 37, 42–43, 48, 201, 309, 333
Epoché, 108–9
Eschatology, 226, 227, 229, 233, 236, 238, 253, 259, 289
Ethnography, 37, 40, 42, 144
Ethnopsychology, 21, 334
Ethnotheology, 141, 144, 151–59, 163, 165, 176, 181
Etic-emic standpoints, 151–52, 157–59, 190, 191, 203–4, 205, 228, 252
Etymology, 59, 72, 112, 113–14, 186
Euhermerism, 26, 27–28
Europe, 22, 77, 114, 183, 215, 249, 284, 304
Evangelical Foreign Missions Association, 182
Evangelical Theological Society, 129
Evangelization, 14, 18, 124, 148–49, 241–246, 305, 327
Exegesis, 185–87, 203, 205, 225, 233–36, 259, 323
Existentialism, 110, 192
Faith 50, 60, 110, 119, 201, 231, 237–39, 241–42, 318–19, 327
Feminism, 129
Fetishism, 40–41
Forms, 102, 150, 239
France, 22–23, 28
Freudianism, 29, 326
Fuller Theological Seminary, 5, 144
Functionalism, 70, 90–92, 94, 96, 98, 101–6, 109, 116–21, 123, 135, 316, 323, 329, 334
Fundamentalism, 115
"Future Shock," 13
das Ganz Andere, 94
Ghana, 83–84
Gospel "core," 81, 118, 192–96, 203
Gospel in Context, 183–84
Grammemics, 149
Greece, 22–23, 26–29, 193, 239, 309
Guatemala, 297
Heart, 13, 15, 49, 50, 319, 326
Heidelberg Catechism, 242, 245
Hellenism, 65, 70
Heresy, 170, 243, 336, 337
Hermeneutic, 110, 111, 121, 122, 143, 165, 178, 179, 183, 184–92, 203, 205, 215, 216, 223, 227, 231, 232, 254, 258, 259, 260, 267, 268, 284–85, 289, 307, 322, 336, 337
Hermeneutical spiral, 183, 188, 233, 235, 241, 242
High-god concept, 63
Hinduism, 76, 77, 246, 309
History of Religions school, 99
Holiness, 62, 238, 335–36
Holland, 221, 249
Holy Spirit, 65, 168, 170, 172, 173, 221, 224, 231, 292, 300, 306
Homogeneous units, 11, 124, 220, 320
Homologein, 246
Hope, 259, 260
Hopi, 111–12
Human, 55, 65–70, 89–90, 97–102, 111, 334–35
Humanism, 50, 136, 141, 164, 180, 274, 289, 311, 330
Ideology, 135, 226, 229, 244, 254, 259, 265, 285, 287, 295
Idolatry, 39, 81, 100, 197, 237, 239
Illumination, 170, 172, 173, 332
Image of God, 78, 80–81, 232
India, 36, 76, 77, 248, 282
Indigenization, 11, 114–15, 117, 122, 150, 177, 181–82, 191, 221, 249, 271, 283–86, 326
Indigenous church formula, 79–80, 85, 115, 280–81
Individualism, 84, 85, 102, 290
Indonesia, 249, 250, 251, 267, 286–87
International Christian University, 302
International Missionary Council, 263
Irrationalism, 90, 95, 118
Islam, 26, 33, 131, 187, 190, 246, 252, 254, 300, 309
Israel, 61–62, 64, 67, 104–6, 169, 259, 291
Japan, 221, 251, 282, 333
Judaism, 33, 197, 218, 240
Justice, 105, 178, 180, 187, 197, 253, 254, 256, 259, 271, 284, 288, 305
Kingdom of God, 35, 109, 132, 195, 202, 203, 224, 229, 231, 236, 242, 255, 258, 292, 311
Kinship, 11, 58, 71, 102–6, 323
Koran, 190
Korea, 81, 191, 212, 248, 250, 257, 282, 286, 308–9, 319

Krishna Consciousness, 309
Kulturkreise, 63
Kurios, 65
L'Abri, 309
Laity, 257, 279, 280, 290–99
Language, 31, 48, 58–60, 69, 71–73, 92–93, 100, 110, 111–14, 122, 164, 167, 169, 171, 202
origins of, 92–93
Langue, 93, 94
Latin America, 212, 221, 247, 254, 256, 258, 266, 269–270, 277, 282, 284, 298, 304, 317
Latin American Theological Fraternity, 298–99
Lausanne Committee for World Evangelization, 5, 163, 176
Lexicography, 112–13, 186
Liberal theology, 60, 73, 109, 110, 115, 131, 186
Liberation theology, 129, 216, 232–233, 253, 258–59
Liberty, Christian, 236–40
Lineage, 84, 323
Linguistics, 11–12, 20–21, 59, 71–73, 92–94, 113–14, 142–45, 146, 149–51, 155, 173, 183, 185, 285, 317, 325, 330, 335
Liturgy, 181, 182, 193, 283, 326
London Missionary Society, 77
Luther's Catechism, 223
Magic, 51, 63, 66, 67, 68, 101, 107, 328
Mana belief, 63, 108, 328
Marxism, 16, 131, 192, 232, 298
Meaning, 187, 234–35, 239
Melanesia, 152
Mesopotamia, 64
Metaphors, 47–50, 53, 148
Metaphysics, 40, 43, 82, 130, 211, 213–14, 217–18, 325, 334
Mexico, 91, 221
Millennialism, 82
Miracles, 28, 29, 39, 201, 256
Missio Dei, 178, 180, 285, 288
Models, 47, 49–50, 53, 156–57, 164–76, 223, 225, 312, 318, 321, 327, 331–32
Modernization, 136
Monolatry, 61
Monotheism, 33, 36, 39, 56, 61, 63, 70
Moratorium, 11, 123, 284
Multiperspectivalism, 335–39
Music, 84, 117, 120
Mysterium, 90, 94, 95
Myth, 16, 17, 21, 22, 27, 37, 58, 64, 71, 99–100, 110, 321–29, 334,
origins of, 26–31, 37–38, 56, 58–59, 73
"Myth and Ritual" school, 67
Nationalism, 90, 308
"Natural law," 200, 201
"Natural religion," 26, 31–33, 34, 39, 56
Natural revelation, 116
Neoorthodoxy, 110, 154–55, 168
Neutrality, 50, 136, 141–42, 201, 226, 238, 239
New Testament, 60, 104, 110, 174, 189, 215, 237, 290
Numinous, 95
Oedipus complex, 98
Old Testament, 60, 62, 64, 66–67, 74, 104, 106, 169, 174, 198, 308
Ontology, 100, 115, 130, 211, 217–18, 219–20, 231, 242–43
Oppression, 187, 188, 212, 253, 254, 259, 283, 286, 304, 333
Ordination, 279, 281, 282
Panbabylonianism, 64, 67
Pantheism, 32
Paradigm, 14, 16, 20, 47, 49–50, 53, 54, 65, 73, 97, 118, 134–36, 141, 164–65, 166, 167, 168, 171, 172, 173, 174, 175, 199, 213, 215, 249, 257, 299, 316–20, 327, 326, 331, 332, 334, 335, 337
Parole, 93, 94
Passivity, 84–86, 122–24, 158, 269
Pattaya Consultation on World Evangelization, 320
Paul, 65, 104, 154, 158, 188, 217, 227, 228, 229, 231, 233, 236–41, 244, 292, 306, 335–36
Pentateuchal criticism, 28, 64, 73
Phenomenology, 18, 95, 107–9, 110, 117, 118, 319
Philippines, 212, 268
Pietism, 84, 141, 253
Polemics, 218–19

Politics, 92, 115, 132, 135, 141, 178, 241, 253, 254, 258, 260, 271, 283, 285, 289
Polygamy, 269, 329
Polytheism, 39, 40, 56, 61, 63, 70
Population statistics, 213
Positivism, 31, 38
Poverty, 105, 210, 178, 187, 212–13, 253, 254, 255, 256, 257, 259, 277, 283, 285, 286, 298, 303–4, 307, 333
Power, 124, 253, 257, 283, 298
"Power encounter," 48
Practical Anthropolgy, 117, 145–47
Pragmatism, 140, 302, 329
Praxis, 11, 229, 232-235, 298, 304, 311, 320
"Prelogical mind," 31, 68–70, 78
Presbyterian Church of India, 248
Presuppositions, 15–16, 17, 18, 47, 49, 90, 109, 117, 133, 134–35, 167, 185, 187, 213–14, 226, 229, 255, 258, 316, 327
Primal religion, 81
"Primitive mentality," 25, 30–31, 40–41, 66, 68, 69, 78, 97, 101, 114
"Primitive religion," 16, 17, 23, 56, 61
Professionalization, 278–83, 287, 288, 299, 301
Prophetic witness, 257–60, 267, 285
Prophets, 104, 105, 259
Provincialism, 191–97, 203
Psalms, 66, 227
Psychology, 91, 95, 97–100, 111, 135, 148, 149
Racism, 188, 191, 247, 250, 255–56, 259
Rationalism, 37–41, 47, 52, 53, 63, 66, 90, 193
Realism, 19–20, 50
Reason, 17, 18, 21, 24–25, 26, 30, 32, 33, 34, 36, 39, 42, 56, 80–81, 101–2, 199, 200, 201, 273, 274, 318
Redaction criticism, 235–36
Redemption, 187, 202, 239, 260, 289, 291
Redemptive analogy, 48, 132, 327–29
Reformation, 221, 222, 223, 242, 244, 274, 279–80
Relativism, 12, 18, 51, 75–76, 138, 154–55, 329–38
Religion, 16, 17, 19, 21, 25–26, 28, 31–33, 36, 38, 50, 56, 57, 61–65, 66–68, 90–91, 95–96, 106–11, 118–20, 166, 241, 318, 321, 322, 325
  "essence" of, 105, 107
  origin of, 40–41, 53, 56–58, 59, 62, 70
  pluralism of, 116
Religionsgeschichte school, 64, 75
Renaissance, 27
Revelation, 24, 32–34, 36, 37, 100, 110, 154, 155, 156, 166, 167–75, 214–215, 225, 228, 320, 333
  divine origin of, 166, 172, 173, 174
  general revelation, 132, 170, 327–29
  receptor-oriented, 155, 167–75, 230–32, 236
Ritual, 102, 120
Roles, social, 135, 187–88
Rome, 22, 38
Rosetta stone, 23
Sacred/profane, 57, 90
Sacrifice, 62, 98, 239
Salaried ministry, 278–82, 293, 294
Samoa, 98–99
Sawi, 132, 189, 240, 319, 327
scholasticism, 217–19, 274
Secularism, 134, 137, 180, 283, 286, 288, 311
Seoul Declaration of the Third World Theologies Consultation, 163, 175–76, 191–92, 254, 271
Shinto, 251
Siberian religions, 41
Sin, 180, 258, 288, 311
Skandalon, 237, 239
Social gospel, 109, 254
Social psychology, 53–54, 68–69, 91
Social systems and groups, 92, 93, 103, 132, 135, 139, 241, 253, 255, 258, 271, 285, 305, 321, 324
Society of Applied Anthropology, 92
Sociology, 57, 68, 90, 91, 101, 104, 105, 124, 149, 254
Son of God, 131, 300
Son of Man, 65
South Africa, 55, 77, 300
Sphere sovereignty, 165

Structuralism, 21, 94, 147, 321–24, 325, 327, 335
Summer Institute of Linguistics, 113, 142–45, 148
Supernaturalism, 81, 119, 120, 166, 198–202, 274
Supracultural, 156, 197–205, 223
Symbols, 57, 58, 99–100, 111–12, 113, 120, 148, 317, 321–29
Synchronic approach, 20, 21, 93, 94, 114
Syncretism, 12, 65, 117, 131, 176–84, 188–90, 194–96, 205, 223, 247, 272, 288
Tagmemics, 149–51
Teacher, 300–2
Technology, 254, 283, 288, 299
Theism, 52, 137
Theography, 158, 204
Theological education, 14, 114, 132–33, 213, 263–312, 333
Theological Education by Extension, 266–67, 269–71, 297–98
Theological Education Fund, 177–80, 253, 264–65, 283, 311
Theologizing, 158, 164, 184, 203, 211, 217, 219, 221, 223, 224–60, 290, 299–309, 331, 337, 338
Theology, systematic, 225, 227–28, 299, 309
Third world, 14, 124, 178, 265, 277, 280, 283, 284, 288, 293, 296
Third world churches and theologies, 14, 115, 123, 191, 192, 204, 205, 212, 221, 222, 223, 224, 225, 244, 246, 247, 248, 249, 250, 251, 252, 253, 256–57, 264, 266, 271, 281, 300, 312, 331
Tribalism, 82, 98, 104–5, 106
Totem, 57, 58, 62, 98
Transcultural, 202, 243
Translation, 113, 142–45, 147–49, 155–56, 157, 181, 217, 234, 241
Trinity Episcopal School for Ministry, 302
Trinity Evangelical Divinity School, 6, 176
Tübingen school, 185–86
Uganda, 85, 191, 250
Unification Church, 326
Urbanism, 254, 256, 302
Westminster Standards, 223, 242, 248, 250
Westminster Theological Seminary, 243, 302
Willowbank Consultation on the Gospel and Culture, 5, 163, 182–83
Words, 71–72, 112, 113, 114, 121, 164, 169, 187
World Council of Churches, 11, 177–80
World Evangelical Fellowship, 271
Worldview, 13, 15, 47, 49, 106, 120, 192, 220, 254, 300, 315–20, 330, 334, 337
Wycliffe Bible Translators, 113, 142